1
2
9
10
18

Principles of Golf Architecture

By Richard Mandell

Author's Note

All golf courses identified with bold letters within the captions of this book are Richard Mandell Golf Architecture projects. Other courses, identified in regular letters within captions, are not.

T. Eliot Press
2208 Midland Road
Pinehurst, North Carolina 28374

This book was set in Adobe Garamond (11 point)
Printed and bound in the United States of America

10 9 8 7 6 5 4 3 2 1

Library of Congress Control Number: 2021946816
ISBN: 978-0-9794836-4-6

"Although golf architecture may be a curious and irregular form of architecture, it is architecture none the less. It has to do with building, planning, constructing in as true sense as the most ambitious works of genius with which the art is usually associated. Cathedrals, bungalows, gardens, and golf courses may appear to be conflicting examples of constructive ability, yet the principles governing them follow precisely on the same lines."

- Herbert Newton Wethered and Tom Simpson

Dedicated to all those who demand great golf architecture

The Elements of Golf Architecture

The Elements of Design are the building blocks that architects, designers, artists, sculptors, and inventors utilize to create a composition of two or three dimensions.

The Principles of Golf Architecture

The Principles of Design are the methods that architects, designers, artists, sculptors, and inventors apply to the Elements of Design to create a composition of two or three dimensions.

IN

Introduction

The Elements of Design vs. the Principles of Design

Throughout the creative process, whether it's in art, architecture, or the creation of a golf course, designers utilize certain building blocks in the structure of their work. These building blocks are known as the Elements of Design. One definition of the word "element" is *"a component or constituent of a whole or one of the parts into which a whole may be constructed."* For instance, bricks and mortar are elements of every masonry wall.

The Elements of Design are Line, Space, Shape, Form, Texture, Color, and Scale. They can be thought of as the details that make up a painting, drawing, piece of pottery, interior space, golf hole, etc. Elements of Design are the tools used to organize a composition that's both aesthetically pleasing and functional at the same time. The design possibilities are almost endless. Everything that's created includes smaller components that make up the whole. Well done or poorly executed, all designed objects will contain most, if not all, of the Elements of Design.

Hole #12, Lake Forest Country Club in Hudson, Ohio. Elements of Design such as line, form, and shape are individual components working together to make up a greater whole. (Courtesy: Richard Mandell Golf Architecture)

Art may always be aesthetically pleasing yet rarely does it serve a specific function beyond enjoyment through observation. A physical piece of art may function to fill a blank space on a wall but the art itself does not serve a function, like a piece of furniture or a golf course bunker does.

One of my favorite phrases, "Form Follows Function," illustrates the point that the shape of an object, whether it's a building, a seven-iron, a chair, or a putting green, should be primarily based upon its intended function or purpose. Form Follows Function is the short and sweet version of building architect Louis Sullivan's original commentary on the concept:

> *"Whether it be the sweeping eagle in his flight, or the open apple-blossom, the toiling work-horse, the blithe swan, the branching oak, the winding stream at its base, the drifting clouds, over all the coursing sun, form ever follows function, and this is the law. Where function does not change, form does not change.*
>
> *The granite rocks, the ever-brooding hills, remain for ages; the lightning lives, comes into shape, and dies, in a twinkling. It is the pervading law of all things organic and inorganic, Of all things physical and metaphysical, Of all things human and all things super-human, Of all true manifestations of the head, of the heart, of the soul, That the life is recognizable in its expression, That form ever follows function. This is the law."*

So what does all that Sullivan waxed poetically actually mean? Sullivan's most famous apprentice, Frank Lloyd Wright, smoothed the rhetoric out for everyone else when he soon thereafter declared *"Form and function should be one, joined in a spiritual union,"* simply meaning that the purpose for why an object is being designed should be the starting point for its ultimate appearance.

In other words, the intended function of the object shall determine the *form* that object shall take. For example, it makes no sense for a wheel to take the form of a square, rectangle, or triangle if the purpose of the wheel is to help move things from one point to another in an efficient manner. The circular form of the wheel allows for a smooth rolling system to transport objects, people, animals, etc. from point A to point B. A square wheel would not roll. Its function would be neither effective nor efficient. The round form of the wheel directly serves the function of transporting objects or people. Hence, form follows function.

"This one 'feels' better, but it seems the other one has more going for it." (Courtesy: Patrick Gainer)

A common golf course design element whose form follows its function is the flat form of the surface of a teeing ground. It allows golfers to begin play on a golf hole without having a variable lie. The form (flat surface) serves the function (starting a golf hole from a level lie): Form follows function (any debate whether a flat starting point is a requisite for beginning a golf hole is a separate discussion for a later date).

The origin of the teeing ground was a logical spot immediately adjacent to the previous hole, originally it was one club-length away, then expanded to two club-lengths. No one knows for sure, but I'm guessing the game's forefathers gravitated to a flat spot to start the next hole through pure instinct. Again, the form (flat spot) served the function (the start of the next hole).

The maxim of form following function can never be achieved without the Elements of Design to help create the form necessary to achieve the function. Every designed, evolved, or discovered object includes Line, Space, Shape, Form, Texture, Color, and Scale; the Elements of Design.

The most applicable definition of the word principle is "*An accepted or professed guideline of action or conduct.*" There are no rules to follow in the application of the Principles of Design. The fact there are no hard rules - only principles - is what separates the design philosophy of one person from that of another. One is free to interpret the Principles of Design any way one prefers. Nowhere is that more true than in golf course design.

Typically, the Elements of Design - the building blocks - are the components of a designed feature. How those elements are composed is usually determined through the use of the Principles of Design: Balance, Rhythm, Contrast, Emphasis, Movement, Proportion, Unity, and Variety. Designers apply the Principles of Design (e.g. the verbs) to the Elements of Design (e.g. the nouns) to create something. The way one applies those Principles of Design to the Elements of Design is the differentiation between successful design and poor design, function and uselessness, attractive art and disagreeable art.

The manner that the Principles of Design are applied to the Elements of Design produces the final expression of the work being produced, and also how it's interpreted by the user of the work (either through simple visual means or through interaction). If the user interprets what the designer sought to express, then the Principles of Design were successfully applied to the Elements of Design. The result is a form which leads to a function that's properly utilized in a satisfying way. Those who consider function in applying the Principles of Design typically end up producing objects that are more useful on a day-to-day basis.

The overuse or underuse of specific principles can often make or break a design. As one or more principles are not used, a design can often become visually disturbing. Yet if all the Principles of Design are incorporated into a form, the resulting design will most likely be considered - at a minimum - aesthetically pleasing. A design exceeds aesthetics and approaches true function when multiple principles of design work to achieve a singular goal.

The difference between classical design and more abstract thinking lies in the application of specific Principles of Design as they are meant to be understood, versus one who may turn a principle on its head just to see what the results may yield. Pablo Picasso most likely decided to utilize "non-proportion," so to speak, as a primary principle of his works of art in contrast to Auguste Renoir, whose impressionist approach made sure the elements of his work were in more realistic proportion. Someone like Rembrandt utilized the principles of design to stay even closer to a realistic vision than Renoir did.

Picasso's relative peer in the golf course design world may very likely be Desmond Muirhead, who thumbed his nose at the conventional approach to course design. He ignored the functional needs for the game of golf. Rather, he re-purposed art into golf architecture from other fields, such as eastern religions and Greek mythology (as he did for the holes at the former Stone Harbor Golf Club in Cape May, New Jersey).

L to R: Picasso's *Portrait of Dora Maar*, Renoir's *Jeanne Samary in a Low Necked Dress*, and Rembrandt's *The Kitchen Maid.* (Courtesy: Richard Mandell Golf Architecture)

Along the way, he often ignored the Principles of Proportion or Balance (among others) to make a statement, such as replicating a prominent physical feature of actress Marilyn Monroe as mounds to turn the dogleg sixth hole at Aberdeen Golf & Country Club in Boynton Beach, Florida. He besmirched the Element of Scale in much of his work in order to "shock and awe." Not surprisingly, Muirhead's use of the Elements and Principles of Design in unconventional ways often turned golfers and critics away from his golf courses.

A contemporary of Muirhead's, Pete Dye, turned the world of golf architecture upside down as well, but with a much more successful result. Although he may have taken the less classical (maybe, say, predictable) approach to the Elements of Design, he inherently understood the Principles of Design and embraced them in the features he and his shapers (machine operators) created in the field.

Muirhead's Marilyn Monroe Hole at Aberdeen Golf & Country Club in Boynton Beach, Florida.
(Courtesy: Richard Mandell Golf Architecture)

Dye, however, didn't intend to shock and awe like Muirhead. Rather, he had a different perspective. Dye focused on nature being more stark and contrasting, rather than seeing it as a smooth erosive process like earlier designers Harry Colt and Alister MacKenzie. In fact, in this sense, when bringing such an abstract designer like Muirhead into the fray, Dye seems to fall more in the center, with Colt, MacKenzie, and other Golden Age designers on one end of the spectrum and Muirhead on the other.

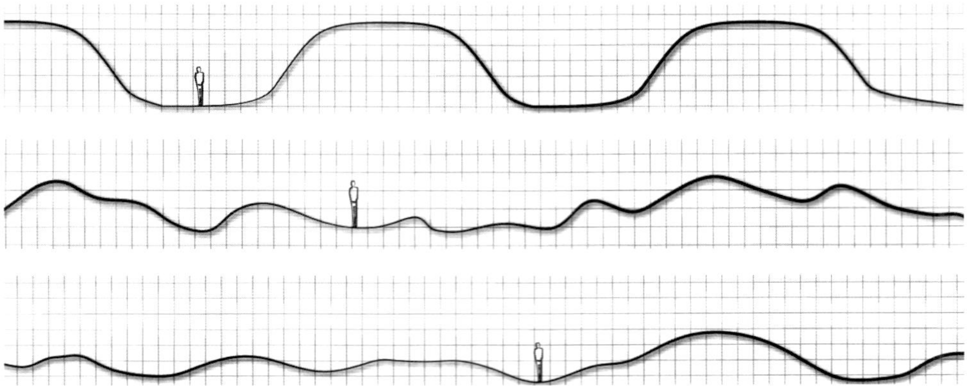

From Muirhead's geometric shaping and extreme scale (top) to MacKenzie's replication of ocean waves as inspiration (bottom), Pete Dye's interpretation of nature (middle), while still quite dramatic, is sandwiched between both Muirhead and MacKenzie on the design spectrum. (Courtesy: Patrick Gainer)

Some golf architects rely on specific Elements of Design more often than others, creating a distinction to the approach and appearance of their work. For instance, Dye leans heavily on the Principle of Emphasis with his use of singular mounds to challenge golfers strategically, whereas an older contemporary of his, Robert Bruce Harris, focused (maybe too much) on the Principle of Balance by consistently flanking greens with a single bunker on each side.

Trained as a landscape architect in Chicago in the mid-twentieth century, Harris' work was primarily to serve municipalities that typically were too underfunded to even be in the golf business. As a result, his work was primarily focused on maintenance-friendly layouts with features that were simple in shapes and simple to maintain when time and manpower were at a premium.

His philosophy moved toward the needs category as opposed to wants and desires categories. For example, course superintendents in his day needed, at minimum, to rake bunkers and mow greens but did not need to worry about perfect roll or even bunker sand consistency. His response was to design a limited number of bunkers, almost all exclusively round, and far enough away from putting surfaces to accommodate large-scale mowing equipment to get the job done in a swift, machine-like fashion.

Harris's use of the Element of Line in his work was minimal because circles were easier to rake than intricately-shaped bunkers with capes and bays, fingers, etc. When it came to scale, each bunker was similar standardize maintenance efficiencies. As a result, scale was not a principle Harris emphasized beyond the most basic of functions.

A contrasting approach to Scale is the work of early designer Charles Blair Macdonald, coupled with the exact opposite use of the Element of Line as well. Macdonald was known for creating large, deep bunkers on many of his courses, which typically had a geometric square or rectangular shape to them - the opposite end of the spectrum to Harris's circular features.

Granted, Macdonald had better pieces of land to work with than Harris usually did. Yet his success far exceeded that of Harris through his application of specific Principles of Design, specifically his grand use of Scale to make a statement that stands out as memorable. His frequent use of line as a straight form, contrasting with the roll of the topography, also contributed to his memorable work. This was achieved through his use of the Principles of Contrast, Emphasis, and Movement. In a nutshell, Macdonald's use of the Elements of Design (Line, Scale) as well as theapplication of those elements through the *Principles of Design* resulted in much greater success than Harris's interpretation of line (through round shapes) applied through the Principles of Repetition and Balance.

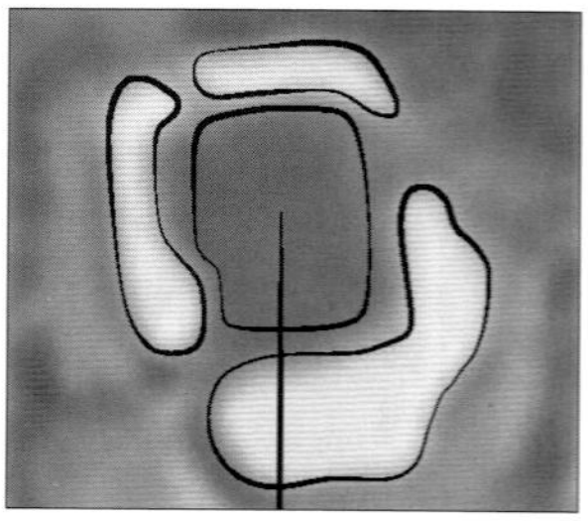

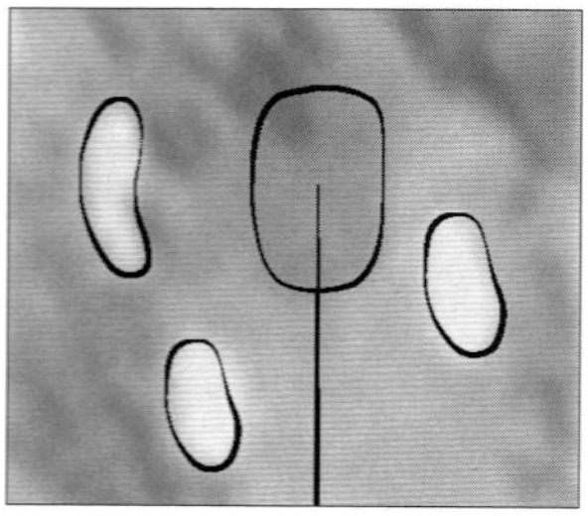

L: 1937 Charles Blair Macdonald bunkers (4th hole at Yale Golf Course in New Haven, Connecticut).
R: 1957 Robert Bruce Harris bunkers (5th hole at Azalea City Golf Course in Mobile, Alabama).
(Courtesy: Patrick Gainer)

Golf architecture is such a specialized art form that depends not only on existing conditions of the ground but also tradition, physical ability (the swing), strategy, and the mind. As a result, there are many other principles specific to the art of golf architecture. They may not be thought of in such a way as balance or rhythm, per se, but they make the art form unique and the game of golf so fascinating for so many. Principles of Design such as Mystery, Quirk, and Randomness, contribute greatly to the fascination one has with the art form known as golf architecture. Throughout each of the following chapters are examples of how the elements and principles of design are applied to the process of golf architecture, particularly how they shape design in terms of strategy and aesthetics.

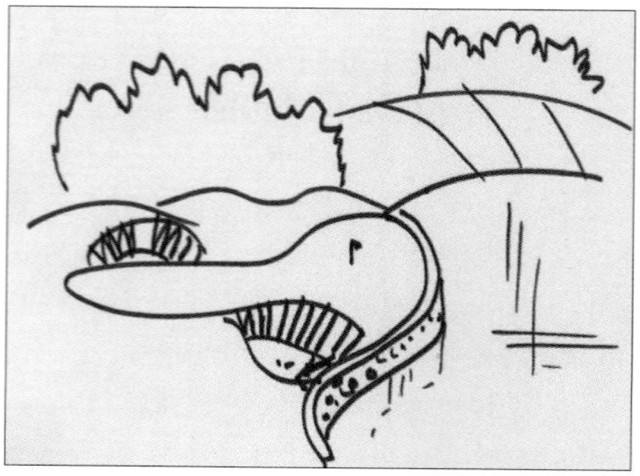

Original Desmond Muirhead Sketch
(Courtesy: Richard Mandell Golf Architecture)

01 The Element of Line

Line - The continuous path of a point.

Line is the continuous movement of a point along a surface. It's the most basic Element of Design, whether in nature or on paper. Line is the Element used to create an infinite variety of shapes and forms that define spaces and create patterns. Its ultimate form controls movement through the user's eye leading to a specific function. In nature, Line is expressed as the edge or border between two components.

Lines come in two forms - straight and curved. Each exudes different emotions in a person, most likely in a sub-conscious way. The straight line is direct and forceful, emoting certain stability to the observer. It leads the eye directly to a focal point. There is no leisurely path to that focal point. Rather, there is an intentional, dominant route to be taken with little or no alternative. In addition, a straight line portrays a more formal aspect of design, one that's decidedly cut and dried, right or wrong, black or white. Simply put, a straight line starts here and ends there.

The three elemental variations on the straight line used throughout nature and design are the horizontal, the vertical, and the diagonal. The best way to express a horizontal line is one which is parallel to the earth's plane. The connection between the earth and a horizontal line reflects stability, calm, and relaxation. Frank Lloyd Wright's dominant use of the horizontal is the working definition of his "Organic Architecture:" a strong connection to the ground. His dominant use of the horizontal line can be seen in his most recognizable works, such as Fallingwater in Bear Run, Pennsylvania, or the Robie House in Chicago.

Frank Lloyd Wright's Robie House in Chicago, Illinois boasts strong horizontal lines throughout that visually attach it to the ground. (Courtesy: Richard Mandell Golf Architecture)

The opposite of horizontal is vertical, a line running perpendicular to the earth and stretching toward the sky. A vertical line directs the observer upward, into the unknown. It exudes a feeling of high expectations and lofty goals. Its contrast to the base plane of the earth can be nerve wracking and exciting at the same time.

Diagonal is the third variation of a straight line. As one end of a diagonal line moves in a specific direction, there ceases to be a clear relationship to the ground. The result is movement away from comfort with a suggestion of intentional direction.

A curved line is much more informal. Firstly, it's not so direct. A curve takes its time to get from point A to point B. Along the way, it allows for a leisurely pace and brings in different viewpoints, distracting the observer from the final destination. There is a lack of rigidity in its form that allows the observer to relax a bit, get comfortable in his or her surroundings, and feel safe and assured. Yet the magnitude of a curved line can bring out a variety of emotions in the observer that results in a certain tension. Sharp curves may suggest conflict, instability, or confusion rather than the smooth grace a softer curve expresses. Some may see an acute shape as more interesting and complex; a free-flowing, slow curve may be seen as a tad boring.

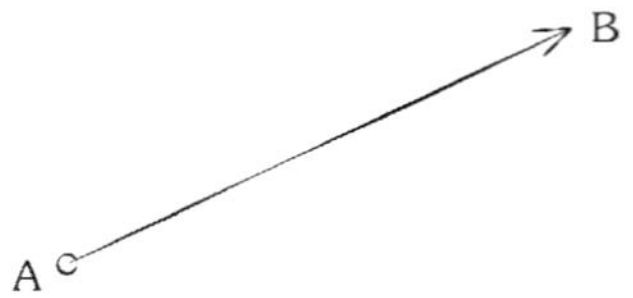

Direct and Forceful

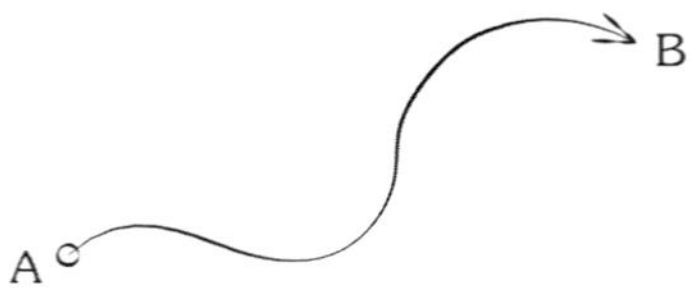

Graceful; Leisurely Pace

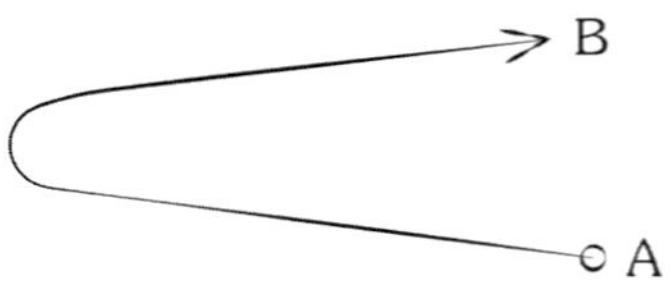

Conflict or Confusion

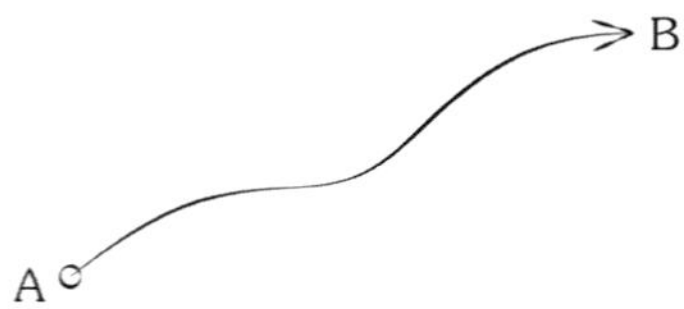

Boring; Lacking Commitment

In golf architecture, oddly enough, the strongest expression of the Element of Line is the one the player cannot actually see: the centerline of a golf hole. A horizontal line would best communicate the way to play a hole, expressing a direct approach. This is because the game's strategy begins with the idea that the shortest distance between two points is a straight line, often represented by the horizontal "centerline" of a golf hole. The diagonal line in golf architecture, however, represents a strong suggestion of intentional direction as an alternative path to the more direct one.

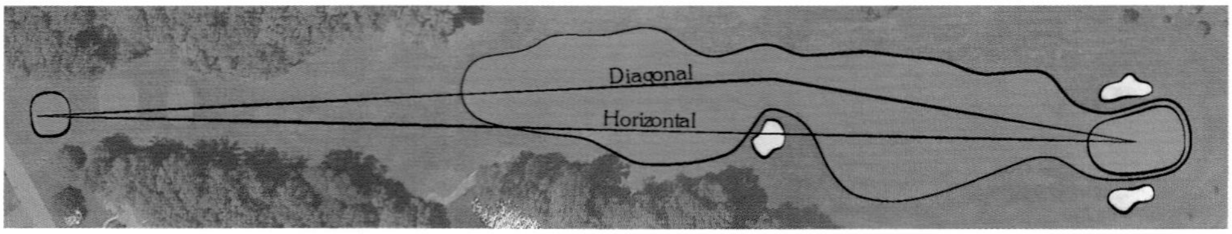

Hole #6, The Water's Edge Country Club in Penhook, Virginia. The horizontal line is represented by a hole's centerline. The diagonal line suggests an alternative path. (Courtesy: Richard Mandell Golf Architecture)

Strategy is created when a diagonal line forms varying angles of play off a horizontal centerline. Width is the primary component necessary to create such angles. The wider the golf hole the larger the angles are between the horizontal centerline and the diagonal alternative lines, providing golfers with multiple routes beyond the direct line of play. But the narrower a golf hole is the smaller the angles are, limiting the number of options.

Hole #10, Keller Golf Course in Maplewood, Minnesota. Fairway cross bunkers come into play on the second shot yet more green is available for the approach from that angle. Avoiding them by playing to the right side makes the green entry narrower and brings sand into play on the approach to this par five. (Courtesy: Richard Mandell Golf Architecture)

My favorite quote in golf architecture comes from Max Behr, best known for his role in promoting strategic design through his writings, and as Editor of Golf Illustrated from 1914 to 1918. His writings notwithstanding, Behr's design work in the 1920's along the West Coast of the United States epitomized strategic design, grounded in his approach to the horizontal and the diagonal:

> *"The direct line to the hole is called the line of instinct, and to make a great hole you must break up that line in order to create a line of charm. The line of charm is the provocative path that shaves off distance and provides an ideal line into the green, usually by skirting bunkers and other hazards. The golfer wants the most direct line he can find to the hole, while the architect uses bunkers and other hazards to create risk and reward options that suggest the ideal line for the player, or the line of charm."*

To clarify, the line of instinct is represented as the horizontal line and the line of charm is the diagonal, avoiding whatever hazards that may be laid out along that line of instinct. The diagonal line signifies multiple options to negotiate the line of instinct, provided there is enough width to allow for those options.

My favorite example of Behr's thinking is A. W. Tillinghast's dogleg left, par-five 4th hole on the Black Course at Bethpage State Park in Farmingdale, New York. Not only is the line of instinct so clearly interrupted by fairway bunkers (encouraging Tillinghast to create an alternate line of charm), those hazards fit beautifully into the landscape without requiring much change, if any, to the existing ground.

A. W. Tillinghast's fourth hole on the Black Course at Bethpage State Park in New York, restored by Rees Jones, is the epitome of Max Behr's line of charm. (Courtesy: Larry Lambrecht)

There are traditionally three schools of thought when it comes to defining strategy on a golf course. They are known as the Penal School, Strategic School, and Heroic School, with each reliant on the Element of Line. A golf hole defined by a single, horizontal line of instinct without diagonal alternatives is the basis for the Penal School. Simply put, a penal golf hole has no line of charm at all. The only choice is to play straight along the line of instinct from point A (tee) to point B (hole). If golfers stray off line, they will be penalized with a less than desirable lie (undulating ground, sand, rough, water, etc.) or an awkward angle or view to the target.

Another way to describe the Penal School is to picture an airport runway. An incoming plane must land on the runway or disaster will strike from which recovery is bleak. This runway strategy has become so prevalent in the latter half of the twentieth century that the game of golf has gone from fun and enjoyable to a painful slog for most. Of course, that runway strategy - hit it straight down the middle or be penalized - is the epitome of a straight line (the horizontal).

Conversely, the Strategic School of Design is exactly what Behr had in mind when describing the line of charm. The Strategic School places hazards along the line of instinct to create the diagonal line of charm. It's best epitomized by challenging the golfer to gain a reward rather than to penalize the golfer for failure. The idea of gaining an advantage such as more distance, a better angle into the target, or a better view of the target through the interaction of a hazard is counter intuitive to the more generally accepted idea of avoiding hazards to avoid penalty. The concept puts a more positive spin on the game of golf by promoting success rather than avoiding failure.

A hole with a single bunker located in the middle of a fairway illustrates the idea of a hazard challenging the golfer rather than penalizing the golfer. Here the golfer chooses one of four different options off the tee that best matches the golfer's ability or appetite for risk on a given day: short, long, left, or right. However, a hole with a pair of bunkers within reach along both the left and right sides will force the golfer to attempt to hit a tee shot down the middle of the fairway. Failing to do so will find sand or rough. The golfer is penalized for not hitting the required shot even though they had no other choice. In this example, four sand bunkers are used to offer just one choice off the tee (straight down the middle). Those hazards have more potential to penalize rather than reward the golfer.

Hole #9 Blue, Army Navy Country Club in Arlington, Virginia (above) and Hole #2 Keller Golf Course in Maplewood, Minnesota (following page). Contrasting strategic approaches with bunkers promoting one option down the middle off the tee (above) and a single bunker challenging the golfer to consider four options off the tee (below).
(Courtesy: Richard Mandell Golf Architecture)

The final school, the Heroic, is a blend of the Penal and Strategic. Heavily promoted by Robert Trent Jones, Sr. in his heyday, it's strategic in the sense that the golfer has choices to make based on their ability. However, it's penal as well because the golfer has some element of forced carry to negotiate to gain an advantage.

A heroic golf hole is characterized by a prominent hazard (typically water) set at a diagonal to the line of instinct off the tee. The riskiest route is along the line of instinct but will result in the most reward (usually a decrease in length for the next shot). The safer route along the line of charm will avoid the most risk but results in the least reward (usually a longer shot to the target).

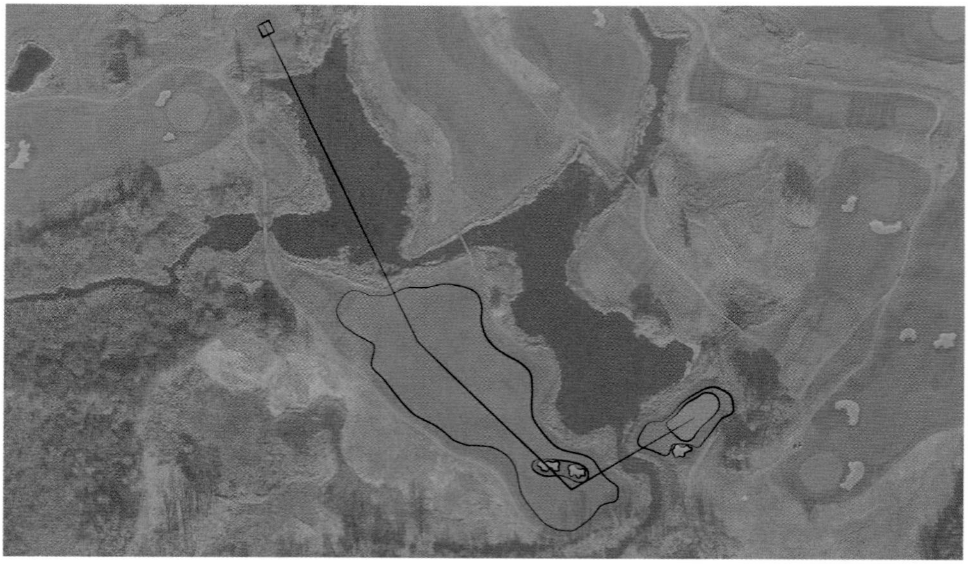

Hole #16, Braemar Golf Course in Edina, Minnesota. Although the width of the hole affords numerous strategic routes, water down the left side is the heroic hazard that draws golfers to consider how much risk to take from both the tee and the second shot to gain a shorter, equally risky route with subsequent shots. (Courtesy: Richard Mandell Golf Architecture)

Whereas horizontal and diagonal lines are best illustrated in the discussion of golf course strategy, the vertical line is best expressed in the trajectory of the golf ball's flight. Trajectory is the upward and subsequent downward path of the ball made from the moment a golf club makes contact to the point the ball returns to the ground. This vertical line in golf course design comes into play when designing specific targets for various shot types.

For example, the depth of a green may be based upon the expected trajectory of a successful second shot coming into the hole. A long par four or five will usually mean a low trajectory (such as a 3- or 4-iron, for instance) and may have a deep target to compensate for the amount of bounce and roll as a result of the ball's initial trajectory. A shorter hole, on the other hand, typically has an approach shot with a club that's designed to create a much higher ball flight. A successful shot with a nine-iron or wedge will enable the ball to come off its steep trajectory with very little bounce and roll. Therefore, the green can be more shallow.

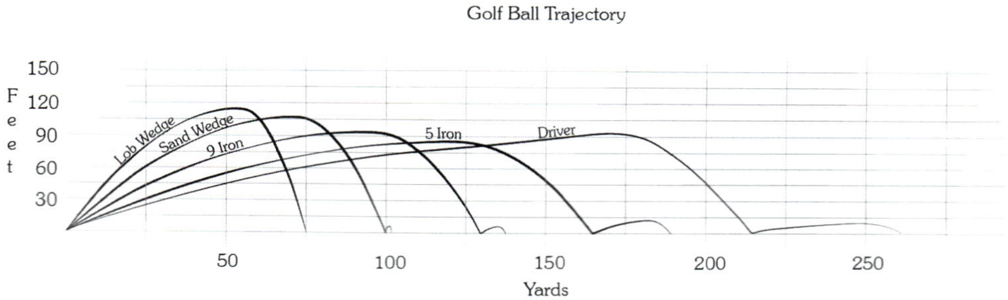

Recently, another element of design as it relates to the vertical line (trajectory) has gained ground in my mind as a means of strategic design. Truth be told, I happen to dislike trees on golf courses if they create a narrow target, eliminate strategic choices, or inhibit grass growth. The removal of trees from a golf course is such a hot-button issue that I'm tempted to remind the well-intended admirers of our tall, wooded friends that golf is played on grass, not on trees.

Nonetheless, while undertaking the renovation of Keller Golf Course in Maplewood, Minnesota, I encountered a one-hundred foot oak tree directly along the line of instinct (between the tee and green) at the 150-yard fourth hole. With absolutely no chance of removal while getting out of the state alive, I was forced to make do with this vertical hazard that is clearly in the golfer's way. The solution to improve playability was to move the one bunker on the hole from directly in front to the left of the green so those who could not play over the tree had an unobstructed path beneath its canopy to the putting surface.

Hole #4, Keller Golf Course in Maplewood, Minnesota.
(Courtesy: Richard Mandell Golf Architecture)

Over the years, I came to the realization that the challenge for the better player on a hole like this was the ability not only to control distance and direction, but to control the vertical as well. One can hit an eight-iron the correct distance on target regardless of trajectory pretty consistently. But when forced to hit the ball a specific height as well, the challenge of a short-iron shot is ramped up even more.

The fourth hole at Keller is much more challenging as a result of the need to control trajectory with the tee shot. But despite its iconic status and this added strategic element, I will refrain from replicating this concept elsewhere because a tree between a tee and green just doesn't have any precedence in the origins of golf.

Another way architects introduce the vertical line in golf course design is through the utilization of mounds. When creating mounds as part of a greens complex, varying the height of adjacent mounds, as well as greenside mounds from hole to hole, can subtly keep the golfer on their toes when trying to get up and down.

Hole #2, Isla Del Sol Yacht & Country Club in St. Petersburg, Florida. Mounds of varying heights increases short game challenge and visual interest. (Courtesy: Richard Mandell Golf Architecture)

A variation in heights of these obstacles will require adjusting the angle of one's club at address to pitch the ball higher or lower, based on the mound's height as well as the distance from ball to hole. As much as I am intrigued by the influence a tree can have on trajectory, I'd rather stick to varying the heights of mounds on a golf course as a means of trajectory challenge instead.

Hole #11, Royal Portrush in Northern Ireland circa 1897 (Courtesy: R. Welch, Belfast)

The Element of Line in golf course design is what creates the shapes of all golf course features, from tee boxes to fairways to sand bunkers to putting surfaces. Linear edges are continuously expressed between grass and sand, fairway and rough, in play and out of bounds. In certain eras of golf course design, that juncture was clearly and intentionally defined, and in others the line was blurred to create a seamless transition from feature to feature.

Going back to the earliest days of golf, architecture was more about uncovering golf holes already inhabiting nature rather than delineating the lines of play. Defined lines rarely exist in nature, so when man's hand is not active, it makes sense that lines tend to cloud. Over the next few centuries, though, that line slowly came in and out of focus as people altered nature in the design of golf holes and maintenance practices were able to accommodate such variation.

Just as the intensity of line in defining borders has varied over the history of golf architecture, the dominance of both straight and curved lines has varied over time as well. Considering William Kent's famous line that "*nature abhors a straight line,*" links courses were dominated by curved features because they were found in nature. The Renaissance architect and garden designer knew that a straight line just didn't naturally exist in the world.

But in Tom Simpson's era of the dark ages of golf course design (toward the latter part of the nineteenth century), straight lines absolutely defined square greens and rectangular, coffin-shaped sand bunkers, curiously moving away from nature. I call this era the "Utilitarian Period" of golf design when the goal was to create as many courses to play as quickly as possible. Design was secondary to feeding the need for playing fields.

Hole #4, Royal Dornoch in Scotland circa 1896 (Courtesy: Ewing & Co.)

At the turn of the twentieth century architects like Donald Ross and Tom Bendelow tended toward the more formal (i.e. unnatural) shapes of the previous era even as strategic principles began to take shape. This transitional period I call the "Functional Period" of golf design. Swinging toward the Golden Age of golf course design, Ross and his contemporaries (George Thomas, Tillinghast, MacKenzie) began utilizing curved lines in an attempt to replicate nature more and more, advancing both the strategic and aesthetic.

Hole #12, Beverly Country Club, Chicago, Illinois circa 1920's (Courtesy: Beverly Country Club)

As the game moved toward the mid-twentieth century and design moved toward conditioning and efficient maintenance, engineered curves delineated round bunkers and kidney-shaped teeing grounds. This "Early Earthmoving Period" evolved into the "Age of Excess" by the eighties. By the onset of the nineties and into the 21st century, in response to the more formalized design and artificial work of the previous decades, golf architects returned to a more natural appearance, blurring the line between features once again.

Hole #18, Sand Hills Golf Club in Mullen, Nebraska (Courtesy: Dick Youngscap)

The feature that most contributes to the character of a golf course is the sand bunker. Line is the element that contributes most to such variety. Square or rectangular bunkers like those Charles Blair Macdonald and his associates introduced are a strong contrast to the natural appearance of the rest of his golf courses. Pete Dye utilized the straight line in many of his bunkers as well, while contrasting those with circular bunker shapes at the same time. Dye's simple circular bunkers were balanced by the intricate shaping of the rest of his features, constantly creating visual movement. Yet other architects who used circular-shaped bunkers weren't aware enough to balance their circles with contouring of the ground, often leaving them lying helplessly on flat ground or propped up on a dirt pimple rising abruptly upward.

Hole #17, Pete Dye's PGA West Resort Course circa 1980's
(Courtesy: Richard Mandell Golf Architecture)

The visual impact of a circular bunker is not as effective as the visual impact of a bunker composed of lines forming a more random shape, simply because the eye is engaged more when following a more intricate shape. The Element of Line is a series of points along a path and the human eye subconsciously connects those points to create the line. When the golfer's eye views a circular bunker, the connection is almost instantaneous, eliminating any long-term visual interest in the mind. A random shape mixed of curves and straight segments demands more time and attention from the eye. The result is more visual interest and a better experience for the golfer.

Hole #2 White, Army Navy Country Club in Arlington, Virginia. The pot bunker in the foreground has fewer points for the eye to follow than the cape-and-bay bunker near the green.
(Courtesy: Richard Mandell Golf Architecture)

Line is the most literal Element of Design. All the other elements (Space, Shape, Form, Texture, Color, and Scale) depend on lines (drawn or visualized) for their own existence. Space would never cease without the Element of Line. Color would lose its individuality, muddying the edges, if not for line separating it from another. Line forms all shapes and defines the form of each shape. The tiniest lines (as well as the largest) work together to create the texture of an object. Finally, the scale of an object depends on lines to help define how one portion of the object relates to another portion of the object. On a golf course, lines are everywhere. Line defines not just strategy; it also characterizes just about every feature seen and encountered, from the shape of trees to the shape of tees and everything in between.

Hole #7, The Water's Edge Country Club in Penhook, Virginia. The strong curvilinear sand lines form an equally strong bunker shape. (Courtesy: Richard Mandell Golf Architecture)

02 The Element of Space

Space - A three-dimensional area within which objects exist.

The three-dimensional area where objects exist, Space, can be divided into the area within which objects exist (positive space) and the area *beyond* which objects exist (negative space). Positive space specifically refers to the area represented inside the line, which defines its specific form. Negative space is the area outside that same line, encompassing its own contrasting shape. Both positive and negative spaces are the embodiment of the dualistic yin and yang, complementing each other while at the same time acting as interdependent forms.

Positive space can be one's urn just as easily as negative space can be two faces. (Courtesy: Patrick Gainer)

I was first exposed to the concept of positive versus negative space in one of my early design studios in college. That lesson first opened my eyes to view a particular object in multiple ways. Some humans are pre-conditioned to look at things only one way, but when considering positive and negative space, a whole other perspective is exposed to the viewer.

Site planning is the creation of adjacent spaces. A disjointed plan is evident when one focuses on creating individual areas without exploring how those spaces relate to each other at the same time. One must consider the form of the negative space that surrounds each of those positive spaces, how that negative space helps connect those spaces, and its function within the overall design.

Site planning in golf architecture is when a golf architect lays out holes on the property (routing the golf course) and proceeds when they begin to lay out the space of each golf hole. The spaces that make up a hole are tees, fairways, hazards, and greens. Each can be viewed upon as positive spaces. The extent of rough on a given golf hole can be considered the negative space. The aesthetic impact of a particular golf feature is strengthened by the negative space imparted on that feature's positive space. Without the existence of the outside (negative) space of a cape-and-bay bunker,

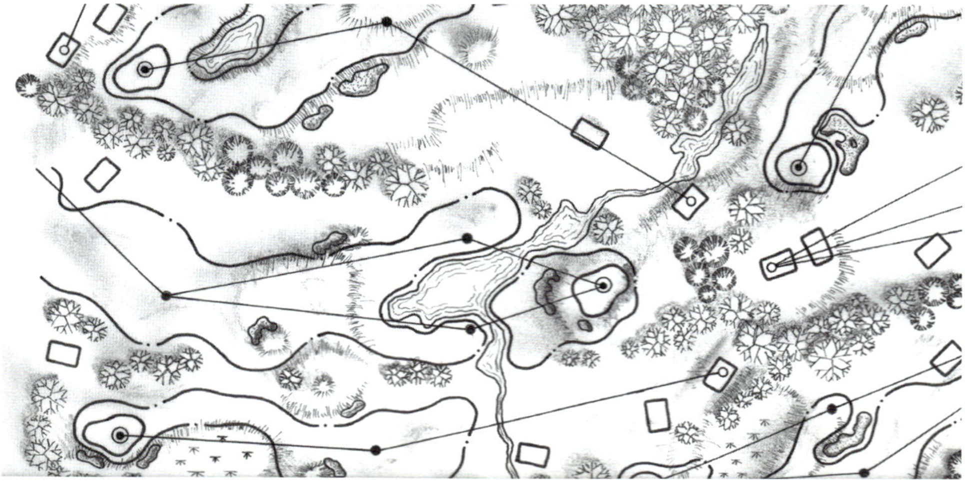

Adjacent golf holes (positive space) relate to one another through the negative space between them.
(Courtesy: Richard Mandell Golf Architecture)

for instance, the line created by the space and the visual impact on the surrounds is not as effective. When properly designed, the negative space of a fairway line developed by the bunker may be just as visually captivating as the sand bunker itself.

Positive space and negative space change based on different perspectives. For instance, fairway is the negative space when it relates to the positive space of a bunker edge. Yet fairway becomes the positive space when contrasted with adjacent rough, which then becomes the negative space.

In golf architecture, the relationship between adjacent spaces is strong when they are linked through strategy. For instance, placement of fairway bunkers that influence a golfer's decision is directly related to the part of the fairway which is adjacent to those bunkers. Whereas the hazard is the positive space that defines a strategic choice, the adjacent fairway is the negative space the golfer sees as the target.

Hole #14, Braemar Golf Course in Edina, Minnesota. Fairway bunkers are the positive space that strategically shapes the fairway as negative space.
(Courtesy: Richard Mandell Golf Architecture)

Penal hazards are spaces that don't strategically relate to the intended target. For example, there is no strategic relationship between a fairway and sand bunkers located along its sides that strictly catch shots that miss the fairway. Neither the bunkers nor the fairway are strategically dependent upon each other. The fairway stands alone as its own space to be negotiated by the golfer. The bunkers only exist to catch missed shots and don't impact a strategic choice by the golfer other than simple survival. In penal situations like this, the relationship between adjacent spaces is weak.

The positive space of the fairway bunkers on this hole don't strategically relate to the negative space of the fairway on this penal hole. (Courtesy: Richard Mandell Golf Architecture)

The location and shape of the spaces surrounding a putting surface influence how a golfer strategically considers the target (the green). For instance, the best approach to play a Redan hole is to bounce the tee shot onto the front right portion (highest point) of the putting surface and allow the ball to track along the slope to the green's lowest point at the back left corner when the flagstick is set there. The ill-advised, yet most instinctual approach, is to play the tee shot left of the two front left bunkers. Because of the length and necessary trajectory of the tee shot, it's virtually impossible to keep a ball on the putting surface when taking that route. Strategically, the space created by the two front left bunkers relates to the space created by the putting surface because those bunkers guard the front left portion of the green and force a risky tee shot. In this instance, the Redan's surrounding bunkers relate to the green because of the inherent strategy in choosing that line of flight to the hole.

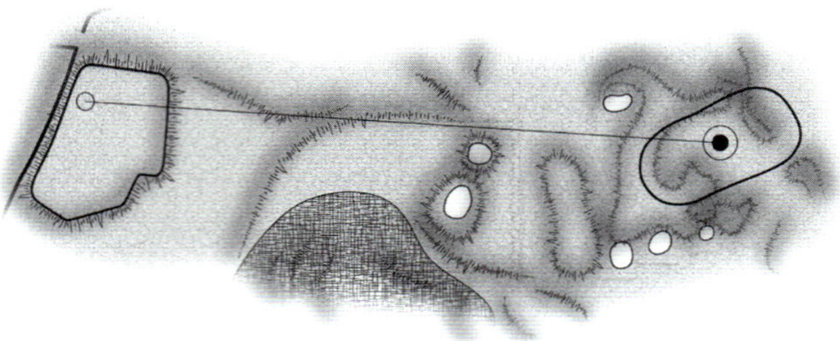

The first example of a "Redan" is the 190-yard par-three 15th at North Berwick Golf Club West Links, East Lothian, Scotland (Courtesy: Patrick Gainer)

Redan Hole at North Berwick Golf Club West Links in Scotland Circa 1906 (Courtesy: M. Sutton)

Three additional bunkers protect the front right portion of the Redan's putting surface and are also crucial to the strategy of the hole. Golfers who understand where the tee shot should land to take advantage of the green's predominant slope must attempt to play as close to those bunkers as possible in order to use the backside of their faces to kick balls towards the back left corner of the putting surface. Tee shots that miss this slope will usually end up in one of those bunkers. The negative space than makes up the kick-slope on the far side and the bunker face on the tee side is crucial to the strategy of the hole. This negative space also forms a visual bridge between the sand and the green.

Many Redan holes designed by Charles Blair Macdonald and his disciples (Seth Raynor, Charles Banks, and Ralph Barton) are excellent examples of how the negative space created between the back side of a bunker and the putting surface creates a pleasing, naturally-appearing composition. For example, the sixth hole at Yeamans Hall Club, a Redan designed by Raynor in Hanahan, South Carolina, now has a trio of sand bunkers aligned along the back side of the green extending the

In both strategic and aesthetic terms, the back face of the bunkers bleeding into the putting surface on the sixth green at Yeamans Hall Club in South Carolina creates a strong relationship between adjacent spaces. (Courtesy: Richard Mandell Golf Architecture)

length of the putting surface. The ridge connecting these bunkers to the putting surface seamlessly flows into both the edge of the green and the edge of each bunker because the negative space connecting the bunkers and the green was designed and shaped with consideration of the positive spaces it connects.

The Element of Space is neglected when designers couple odd-shaped features such as greens and surrounding hazards with little relationship to each other. Without addressing the element of Space, a green complex can become disjointed and evoke a poor reaction from the golfer. A strong visual relationship between a putting surface and adjacent hazards is one where both the negative and positive spaces are intentionally considered in the design process.

Hole #7, Tanglewood Championship Course in Clemmons, North Carolina: Before (L and below) and after (R and bottom of page). Intentionally designed negative space between surrounding features can be the difference between a design that's pleasing to the eye and one that's not. (Courtesy: Richard Mandell Golf Architecture)

One of the strongest visual relationships on a golf course is between the positive space of fairway lines and the negative space of surrounding rough. The negative space created by fairways is a void that leads the eye to a line defining the edge of the playing area, typically in the form of trees, rough, sandy waste, or native areas.

The advent of rough in golf course design evolved through the desire to penalize poorly hit shots, eventually transitioning into a strong visual design component as well. The deeper the rough, the stronger the line between it and the fairway became, strengthening aesthetic impact but inadvertently increasing difficulty also.

Although "contour mowing" originally followed the contours of the ground, this 1960's approach to mowing fairways became more and more curvilinear over time with its own aesthetic appeal. Contour mowing replaced the straight-line fairway mowing of the Golden Age when designers were focused more on strategy than aesthetics regarding grassing patterns. It became more common with the rise of professional golf, leading many amateurs to conclude that golf was a game best presented as a difficult challenge rather than an enjoyable experience. Contour mowing widened certain areas off the tee and narrowed other areas. The inconsistency of golfers – and deep rough – led to penal playing conditions.

Contour mowing became a dominant mid-twentieth century aesthetic feature that eventually helped lead to added difficulty due to its dependency on deep rough.
(Courtesy: Richard Mandell Golf Architecture)

In recent years, design has moved away from contour mowing and deep rough, maintaining lower rough or just one cut of height for playing surfaces beyond the green. The goal is to make the game more fun and enjoyable with less focus on aesthetics. One height of cut reverse-engineers the negative effects of aesthetics that slowly crept into the game of golf. Despite the lack of a visual relationship between the positive space of the fairway and the negative space of the rough, the hole is indeed more playable, yet somewhat homogenous.

Hole #16, The Reserve at Pawleys Island in Pawleys Island, South Carolina. The positive space of the fairway and the negative space of the adjacent native area create a strong visual statement with one cut of grass from tee to green. (Courtesy: Richard Mandell Golf Architecture)

There is a happy medium where one can utilize the negative space of a reasonable height of rough to promote strategy and aesthetics on equal terms. It requires wide fairways that incorporate natural features or man-made hazards to create strategic options. Weaving fairway lines around hazards or cutting fairway lines tight around putting surfaces creates visual movement with the intention of offering choices for an advantage. The space defined by the lines of a fairway around hazards and contrasting rough is not only strategically functional, but pleasing to the eye as well.

Hole #17, Monroe Country Club in Monroe, North Carolina. Space defined by the fairway wrapping around the bunkers is both strategic and aesthetic. (Courtesy: Richard Mandell Golf Architecture)

Space as a continuous area within lines is as broad a definition as one can consider yet it's the primary element that develops cohesiveness in design. In golf architecture, the full use of space allows for all portions of a golf hole to work together seamlessly. These parts are all tied together through the glue of negative space. The better golf course designers make great use of the negative space within a property, efficiently weaving all portions together for strategy, aesthetics, and a sense of place.

Hole #2, Isla Del Sol Yacht & Country Club in St. Petersburg, Florida. The area between the bunker and putting surface is the negative space that ties both features together.
(Courtesy: Richard Mandell Golf Architecture)

03 The Element of Shape

Shape - A two-dimensional space enclosed by an outline.

Some of the very first things we learn about as toddlers are shapes: circles, squares, triangles, rectangles and others. The shapes we are exposed to at such an early age are shown in two dimensions. The shape of a square, for instance, is represented as a flat image on paper composed of two horizontal lines connected with two vertical lines, all the same length. There is no depth (defined as "*a dimension taken downward or inward through an object or body of material*").

You never physically hold a square or a circle. You may hold a ball or a cube in your hands, but you never hold a square or a circle. You can't, because a square and a circle are not objects with the dimension of depth. They are shapes. A shape is defined as the outside edge (or outline) of a two-dimensional space and it falls into two categories: geometric and organic.

The circle, square, triangle, and rectangle are examples of geometric shapes. They have outlines with perfectly straight line segments from vertex to vertex. A square has four line segments of equal length. In the case of a circle, there are no straight lines. Instead, a circle is made up of a number of points each equidistant from one central point (radius). They are all connected to form one enclosed line.

Most humans recognize the simplicity of basic geometric shapes like squares and circles. In fact, one could say they are very predictable. Although a rectangle may come in many sizes, every rectangle in the world always has two sides of equal length separated by two other equal sides of a different length. Perhaps due to the simplicity of these and other shapes, they are not always considered interesting. The human eye will instantly recognize a triangle and then move on. The predictability of the shape is hard wired into most human's brains and requires little contemplation.

Organic shapes are a much different animal that include both curved and straight segments. They are much more varied and unpredictable. Often times, these organic shapes have segments and curves that point in contrasting directions, are flipped upside down, or even turned inside out as a mirror image. Manipulating segments in these ways (even those that have the same length or radii) creates an infinite number of shapes and nature is full of them.

To many of us, organic shapes are much more interesting to look at. They will often hold our interest simply because we may never have seen them before (or

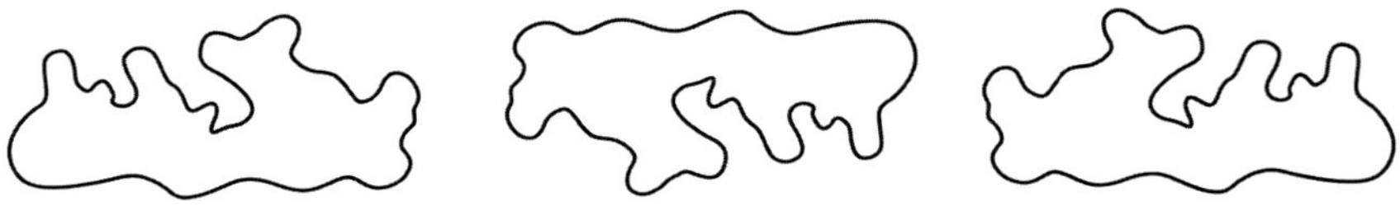

An endless number of organic shapes can be created through mirroring, rotating, and reversing. (Courtesy: Patrick Gainer)

not nearly as often as geometric shapes (which by definition, don't really change) and they can vary in so many ways. Organic shapes that are most attractive to the eye are those that best emulate their natural surroundings.

Geometric shapes are much more useful to incorporate into everyday objects such as a wheel or a chess board. A wheel that's organically-shaped will never serve its function to roll. Instead it will get stuck between the variety of radii and segments as an attempt is made to roll it. An "organic" chess board might consist of boxes with a variety of shapes but that could change the function of the game and possibly create confusion among the players.

Triangular wheels make for a difficult ride. (Courtesy: Patrick Gainer)

The earliest golf courses were developed within the confines of nature along the Scottish coastline as far back as the fifteenth century. The game of golf, then and now, is based on the natural ground. Either we work with it or we change it. It's a very organic diversion. Many, if not most, of the shapes that compose a golf course are organic as well. Fairways, greens, and bunkers all have specifically-defined edges and for the most part, the shapes that define these features are organic.

An exception in modern design is the teeing ground, which tends to be more geometric in practice. Personally, when I am not constrained by topography, I prefer to build rectangular- or square-shaped tee areas. Although I consider myself one who strives to be as natural as possible in my designs, in this case, I am contradictory. The reasoning is based purely on form following function. The name of the game with teeing ground shapes is to utilize as much square footage as possible because the more it has, the easier the wear and tear can be spread out. In other words, if you have to mow a teeing ground, you may as well be able to use it all. Regarding teeing ground shapes, the most efficient use of space comes in rectangles and squares.

The most usable square footage of a circular teeing ground is the square that fits within the circular confines. The outer edges of a circular teeing ground will inhibit a golfer's stance and limit tee marker locations. Yet those portions of the tee still have to be mowed. A more organic tee shape, such as a peanut or kidney bean, has even more wasted space.

The teeing ground is the one geometric golf course feature which gains practical value without losing much in aesthetics. Geometrically-shaped fairways, greens, and bunkers are more efficiently maintained as well because it's easier to mow a rectangular fairway or a round green and simpler to rake a circular bunker with mechanical rakes.

But unlike the innocuous tee box, fairways, greens, and bunkers all convey some sense of aesthete when they are more than basic geometric shapes. Sand bunkers, in particular, are the features that provide the most visual interest and character on a golf course. The overall theme of a golf course is often expressed in the golf architect's chosen sand bunker style, first expressed in a shape, then followed by how that shape is applied - with either a defined outline or one that's broken up by the negative space that surrounds the bunker (grass and sand jumbled together).

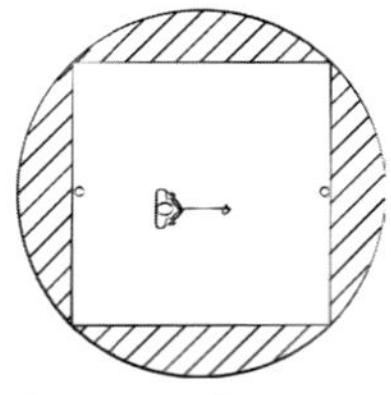

A circular tee shape isn't as useful as a square. (Courtesy: P. Gainer)

Organically- and geometrically-shaped bunkers both have precedence in links golf. The origin of the bunker came when animals burrowed into dunes to stay out of the cold winds at night, over time eroding the grass that covered them and exposing the sand beneath. Many of these earliest bunkers lacked a defined outline.

The geometrically-shaped pot bunker, on the other hand, dominates the links landscape just as much. But most were added by man over the years for strategic purposes (particularly at the Old Course). The more organic, original bunkers of the Old Course such as Hell or Cartgate, have slowly been adapted to possess a more geometric character as well.

Most geometrically-shaped bunkers found on golf courses today exist as a matter of economic function. They require less artistic and construction effort to create. Therefore, they are more economical to build and maintain. Their origins in America, though, were not completely based on finances. Geometrically-shaped bunkers were found more routinely in the early days of golf architecture when there was less emphasis on aesthetics. Function was of primary concern and basic geometric forms served their purpose.

"Hell Bunker", Hole #14, the Old Courseat St. Andrews, Scotland: A couple of centuries old by 1897, the left half of Hell Bunker still held on to its organic origins. (Courtesy: Horace Hutchinson)

Today, Hell Bunker trends toward geometric. (Courtesy: App555 | Dreamstime.com)

The infinite number of bunker shapes that have developed over time all fall into either the organic or geometric categories. In addition to the pot bunker, there are shapes such as the coffin bunker (an elongated pot), cape-and-bay, oval, kidney, and even some with grass islands within their confines. As aesthetics became more prevalent during the Golden Age, more free-form, organic bunkering came into prominence. A primary function of this evolution was the desire to create features that appeared natural, a direct challenge to the geometric fashion of the past.

Efforts to create a geometric shape in the field are simple enough. I am not concerned with what the particular shape looks like from any perspective because, simply put, a circle is a circle. Nor am I worried about sand visibility, because most geometrically-shaped bunkers are historically grass-faced with flat sand. My focus is on maintaining consistent radii or keeping a line straight with the paint gun. Predictably, there is less appreciation of geometric bunkers.

The use of organic shapes for bunkers, on the other hand, results in more visual interest for the golfer and requires more effort from the golf architect in the field. When laying out organic shapes during construction (with a paint gun), I make a concentrated effort to combine straight and curving segments in a free-flowing

Hole # 10, Lake Forest Country Club in Hudson, Ohio. Creating the shape of geometric bunkers requires a steady hand with the paint gun to maintain consistent arcs and segments. (Courtesy: Richard Mandell Golf Architecture)

sequence. This requires stops and starts as I consider its shape from all viewpoints, near and far, left and right, etc. For me, it's crucial to ensure that an organically-shaped bunker is visually interesting from all perspectives. It has to be done with patience and it's where my perfectionist tendencies are on full display. Hopefully the results will ensure the golfer takes notice of the feature and, if done well, appreciates the shape. By combining a variety of straight and curving segments into a pleasing composition, the architect pushes the golfer's eye to follow a longer path, one that requires more cerebral focus yet leads to a higher appreciation of the shape.

Hole # 2, Tanglewood Championship Course in Clemmons, North Carolina (above and below). A combination of straight and curved segments creates a more organic appearance to capture the golfer's eye for an extended period. (Courtesy: Richard Mandell Golf Architecture)

In contrast to bunker shapes, the feature shape I am least concerned with is that of a putting green. The natural lay of the land or the intended shaping of the putting surface itself should drive the design process rather than a randomly assigned outline. Surrounding features, such as mounds bleeding into the putting surface, should contribute to the shape of a green, especially when those features help create visibility of that surface. Greens that sit on plateaus or other natural landforms should always take on the shape of that landform. The shape of a green rarely has any effect on the strategy of a golf hole.

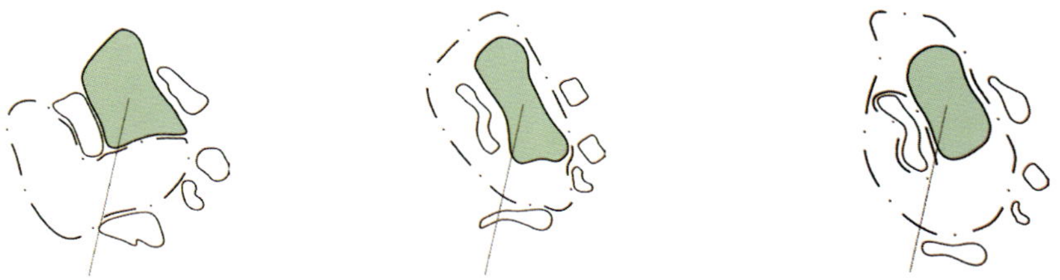

1928 1954 2021

The shape of C. B. Mcdonald's #4 Redan Green at National Golf Links of America in New York has changed over the years but the strategy of the hole hasn't wavered. (Courtesy: Patrick Gainer)

For me, once the detailed shaping of a putting surface is done, I draw an outline of my design work, leaving the outer green shape as an extension of the inner design work and the surrounding landforms. The green edge is literally laid over the putting surface area wherever the designed features tie into the surrounds. As a result, my greens tend toward a modest shape, almost bordering on geometric.

Greens should never stray too far from geometric for fear of creating situations where golfers are forced to putt off the green, through the collar or rough, and then back on to the green in order to get the ball to the hole. In the past, adventurous designers created such organic shapes that had sand bunkers cut into the sides, forcing golfers to chip their ball from one portion of the green to the other.

Yet over the years, a number of greens were designed in such a "geometrically-challenged" way. One of the more famous greens in the world is George Thomas's sixth at Riviera Country Club, a doughnut-shaped one with a pot bunker in the middle. Whereas the surface is designed to avoid putting through the bunker, sometimes it's unavoidable. Donald Ross was known to create a green or two with mouse-ear corners, one of which we restored at Bacon Park Golf Course in Savannah, Georgia. Alister MacKenzie's Royal Melbourne's greens show similar characteristics.

Hole #16, Royal Melbourne Golf Club (East), Victoria, Australia.
(Courtesy: Google Earth)

Hole #6, Bacon Park Golf Course in Savannah, Georgia.
(Courtesy: Google Earth)

Considering the sheer acreage a fairway can encompass, fairway shapes dominate the golfer's view from the tee more than most features. Once the golfer walks the fairway, it's not so much. The shape of even the smallest fairway can get lost when one is within its confines.

Today, many old-line, private club fairways fall into the geometric category with straight lines down both sides. Sometimes these lines waver when a substantial landform comes along, but usually they hold pretty straight. Many call this look "traditional." Yet the truth of the matter was that many Golden Age architects drew more organic fairway shapes on paper. Because of limited irrigation, it was virtually impossible to create a discernible straight line fairway.

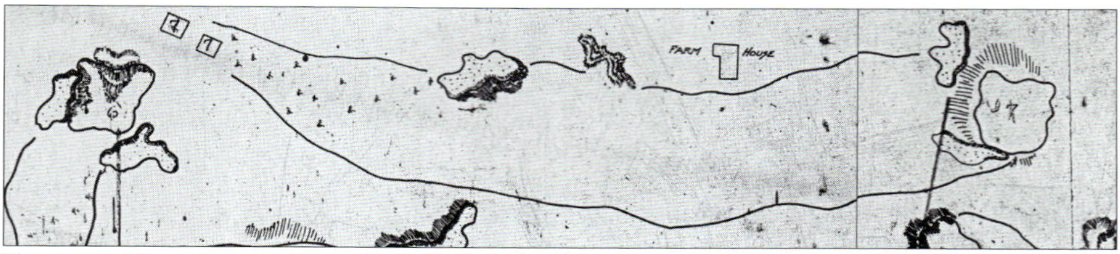

This 1915 Plan of Oconomowoc Golf Club, in Oconomowoc, Wisconsin, shows Donald Ross's tendencies toward organic shapes in his early work. (Courtesy: Oconomowoc Golf Club)

A geometric mowing pattern should only be adopted on ground lacking natural landforms. Straight fairway shapes bisecting natural landforms not only look odd, they diminish the visual effect of the landforms. By the same token, flat holes randomly mowed in a curvilinear fashion have an almost ghost-like appearance. In other words, a sudden turn of the fairway line on flat ground to create a curve leaves one wondering if some feature was removed but the fairway line was never adjusted.

A combination of geometric and organic shapes can work well together provided the correct applications are applied to the appropriate landforms. One should incorporate straight lines only when topography offers no inspiration. In contrast, natural or man-made features - as well as the contour of the ground - shall determine the organic portions of a fairway shape.

Hole # 10, Hooper's Landing Golf Course in Seaford, Delaware. Straight fairway lines combine with organic feature shapes on flat ground. (Courtesy: Richard Mandell Golf Architecture)

Hole # 16, Country Club of Asheville in Asheville, North Carolina. A more organic fairway shape will reflect the natural landforms. (Courtesy: Richard Mandell Golf Architecture)

Strategically speaking, one who adheres to the mantra that the placement of a hazard should challenge and not penalize, will lean toward wrapping a fairway line around a hazard. If the intent of the hazard is to challenge the golfer to play over it to gain an advantage, the golfer should be rewarded by landing in fairway. Therefore, the fairway line should reflect the shape of the hazard line by wrapping around the hazard with fairway on the other side.

Shape is one of the most encompassing elements of golf course design when it comes to aesthetics, but it contributes to strategy on a golf course as well. In the case of golf course design more so than other design disciplines, the precedence of nature has always been an influencing ideal when it comes to the Element of Shape. Following nature's lead will always lead a designer to create organic shapes. This approach will also lead to variety in design, more visual interest, and strategic variations in the art of golf course architecture.

04 The Element of Form

Form – How a particular shape and structure of an object appears or exists.

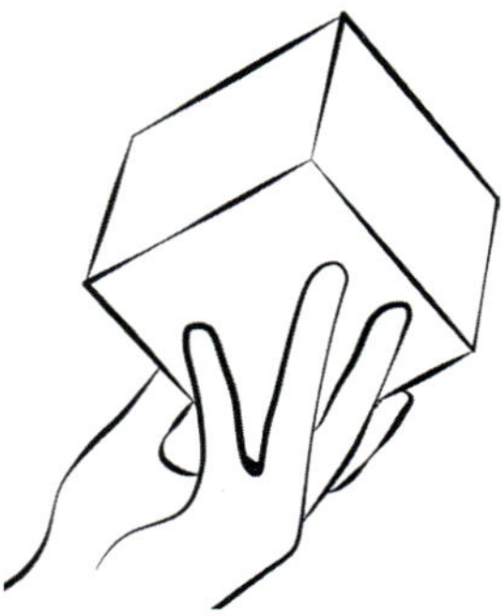
(Courtesy: Patrick Gainer)

The physical difference between balls and toy blocks (spheres and cubes) compared to the shape those spheres and cubes are (circles and squares) is the inability to hold an actual circle or square in our hands, whereas we can physically hold a ball or a toy block. The distinction lies in the dimensional space shapes and forms occupy. Shapes are two-dimensional because they only exist on a flat plane. When those same shapes become three-dimensional objects capable of being held in one's hand, for example, they take on a form.

Although a shape can stand alone as an element of design, the element of Form cannot exist without both shape and mass. Shape is primarily composed of flat lines. But when mass is added to shape, the dimensions of length, width, and depth combine to develop the element of Form. Another way to visualize the element of Form is as the structure of an object.

Unlike shapes, forms take on different characteristics depending upon how and from where they are viewed. Being strictly two-dimensional, shapes can only be viewed one way: looking straight at a flat object. Because form has three-dimensions, it can be viewed from many different angles. One can walk around a form such as a ball, taking in its character on a 360-degree basis. One cannot walk around a circle.

Similar to the element of Shape, Forms fall into the same two descriptive categories: geometric and organic. Geometric forms such as cones, cubes, pyramids, or spheres are consistent in their dimensions regardless of how one views those forms. When one encounters a geometric form at different angles, one's perception does not change. Specific portions may stand out, but the overall form is consistently the same.

Walking around Cloud Gate
Millennium Park, Chicago, Illinois
(Courtesy: Aleksei Glustsenko Dreamstime.com)

Geometric forms don't exist in nature. Most buildings and other architectural elements are constructed, geometric forms. Pyramids are clearly perceived as constructed rather than as forms found in nature. An organic form is more abstract, lacking a consistent set of dimensions. It's either naturally occurring or made to appear natural. One's impression of organic forms can change greatly based upon their viewpoint or position because of the variety in an organic form's detail. Geometric forms, with consistent characteristics of length, width, and depth, do not share this same characteristic. Because of the consistency in the three dimensions of a geometric form, less attention is garnered from the user. Organic forms hold more visual interest than geometric forms through their inherent variety of detail.

The element of Form is one of the most important design elements to a golf course architect because the routing process is dependent on seeking out landscape forms to develop the sequencing of the golf holes. A landform is defined as *"a specific feature delineated on the surface of the earth."* They range from large-scale features such as plains, plateaus, valleys, and mountains to more localized features such as hills, ridges, or swales. Mount Everest, the Grand Canyon, and the White Cliffs of Dover are all landforms just like the eighteenth fairway of Pebble Beach Golf Links, the Valley of Sin on the Old Course, and Rae's Creek at Augusta National. Landforms are the lifeblood of a golf course routing for the designer. Golf architects seek out landforms to create drainage patterns, develop strategy, or simply to stimulate the golfer's visual senses. The majority of memorable and lasting golf courses are those whose natural landforms develop that course's character and strategy.

This ridge/mesa landform at Rocky Mountain National Park can just as easily be a fairway to a plateau green at a different scale. (Courtesy: Richard Mandell Golf Architecture)

My golf course routing philosophy is built around seeking out existing high points for playing areas and existing low points to collect or move runoff away from those playing areas. To illustrate, I often route from high point (teeing ground) to high point (fairway) to high point (green site), leaving the low areas between to divert runoff while not affecting the playing areas. Draws or swales (areas of low ground similar to valleys yet at a smaller scale) are perfect natural conduits for drainage. They are also great landforms to carry in order to gain a strategic advantage.

Many other natural landforms provide golf course functions in a routing based on their individual size. Features such as plateaus and ridge lines are often used for fairways provided they are large enough. These forms are more desirable for fairways than valleys because they allow for water to drain away from the playing areas. If a saddle (a flat form where two high points and two low points converge at a central point) is large enough, it too can be a fairway. On a smaller scale, those same features (plateaus, ridge lines, and saddles), are ideal green sites. For example, the termination of a ridge line can become a green site, particularly when it ties directly into the putting surface as fairway and approach.

Hole #4, Erie Golf Course in Erie, Pennsylvania. This natural bench is a perfect greensite yet is too small to serve as a fairway. (Courtesy: Richard Mandell Golf Architecture)

Scaled down even further, each of those landforms can accommodate teeing grounds. Bench landforms (flat areas naturally cut into the side of a ridge) are also more conducive to tees than full-scale fairways or even greens, depending on the size of the bench. Hilltops or peaks are effective as tees or greens based on their size and potential visibility. Yet a hilltop or peak of the same size cannot function as a fairway due to its lack of space. The size and steepness of a hilltop will determine how playable a green may be because a very small hilltop on a very steep slope can become a very penal putting surface.

The science of golf course routing comes in the knowledge of how much ground is needed for each feature (tees, fairways, greens, etc.) and which landforms best serve that feature. The art comes in how one pieces each landform together in a logical sequence and how each landform contributes to the strategy of each hole. There is also a certain art in dismissing preconceived notions to create the best possible golf holes based on existing conditions. I will always seek out golf holes based on the most intriguing landforms of the ground. If it means developing back-to-back par threes or fives, so be it. Ignoring a formulaic number of par threes, fours, or fives in predictable sequences is always the better path in seeking out the best routing.

Although some golfers may say the eighteenth hole at Cypress Point Club in Pebble Beach, California is a letdown, the three holes that jut into the Pacific Ocean preceding it are well-worth the anticlimactic final hole. In particular, the natural landforms that make up the tees and greens of the back-to-back par-three fifteenth and sixteenth holes lend memorability (and challenge) to arguably the most breath-taking stretch of golf on the planet. The seventeenth hole, a great heroic short par four, sits on the same peninsula utilized by sixteen green and is equally inspiring.

The landforms Alister MacKenzie utilized for all three holes create heroic carries over ocean inlets so the golfer can choose the most direct (and/or aggressive) route from tee to green based on individual ability. The visual stimulus from the tees on each hole equals the strategic challenge. If MacKenzie ignored those natural landforms to avoid criticism based on pre-conceived standards, Cypress Point Club would be far less memorable.

#17 green at Cypress Point Golf Club in California looking back toward the peninsula #16 green and #17 tee. (Courtesy: Richard Mandell Golf Architecture)

Not as dramatic as capes jutting out into the Pacific, but just as important to strategic golf, is a series of existing ridges I incorporated into the thirteenth and fourteenth holes at Skydoor Golf Club in Zhangjiajie, Hunan Province, China. Back-to-back par fives, the holes fell into place during the routing process along existing ridge lines perfectly spaced for each landing area. A single ridge with plateaus at precise intervals for multiple landing areas define the rise to the thirteenth green placed on an existing tabletop surrounded by sheer cliffs. A pair of ridges separated by a lengthwise steep slope called for a split-fairway strategy for the second shot on the fourteenth hole. Both holes would have been less than their full potential if one were a par four, leaving imposing landforms under-utilized.

Holes #14 & 15, Skydoor Golf Club in Zhangjiajie, Hunan, China. Back-to-back par fives incorporate two natural ridges (depicted by hatching) to create a high-point-to-high-point routing. (Courtesy: Richard Mandell Golf Architecture)

Another example of natural landforms transcending bias toward the conventional is the third through eighth hole at Braemar Golf Course in Edina, Minnesota, where I adopted a par sequence of 3-5-3-5-3-5. The first par three is placed on a natural shelf from tee to green. Two shelves separated by a steep slope running parallel to the line of play provide the inspiration for the split-fairway par-five fourth. They are followed by a high-point-to-high-point par three with a green set in a natural amphitheater and a par five playing through a valley to a green set on a peninsula. The landforms not only provide character to the holes, but determine strategy as well.

Hole #4, Braemar Golf Course in Edina, Minnesota. A ridge separates the upper and lower shelves of this split-fairway par five. (Courtesy: David Parker Photography)

The last two holes fit perfectly around property boundaries and wetlands, minimizing forced carries and maximizing bunkers cut into natural rises for visibility and challenge. Each of the landforms I incorporated at Skydoor and Braemar fall within the organic category of form, preserved in their natural state.

The most important component of a great golf course is the routing of its holes - followed closely by the shaping of the features within those holes. Just as the very first golf courses came straight out of nature, the features of new courses should present the inherent randomness best afforded by nature as well. That randomness is further attained through the shaping of those features.

The Author with longtime shaper, David Gray.
(Courtesy: Richard Mandell Golf Architecture)

The relationship between a golf course shaper (on a mchine) and a golf architect is akin to a caddie/player relationship. They are a team with one goal: implement the design intent of the architect. The shaper is the one who literally shapes the landforms that make up the features of each hole. As a caddie works to make sure the golfer properly manages his or her game around the golf course, the shaper ensures the architect's vision is properly executed. Sometimes it requires a soft touch and other times it requires creativity. A soft hand is called upon when the task is to enhance the natural forms that exist on the ground. The creativity comes when there is nothing to enhance. MacKenzie put it best stating, *"I have endeavored to conserve the existing natural features and, where these were lacking, to create formations in the spirit of nature itself."* He believed that successful course design depended upon utilizing natural features to their fullest extent yet saw the need to create artificial features that closely imitate nature where none previously existed.

An organic approach is the best way to manufacture golf course features, yet it requires more effort and attention than building geometric forms. Because geometric forms are consistent in their dimensions, a shaper only has to engineer a form with uniform lengths, widths, depths, etc. If one side of a form is intended to have a five-percent slope, then it's easy to match the other sides of the feature by replicating the first side.

Creating natural-appearing landforms is where the artistic hand becomes crucial. The principles of Balance, Contrast, Emphasis, Proportion, and Rhythm contribute to a form that's varied in shape from side to side and from top to bottom. A trained artistic eye utilizing these design principles is the ultimate critic in determining how natural a form appears.

The trick comes in being random, imperfect, and divergent each step of the way. For me, being a horrible draftsman became an advantage. My inability to pull

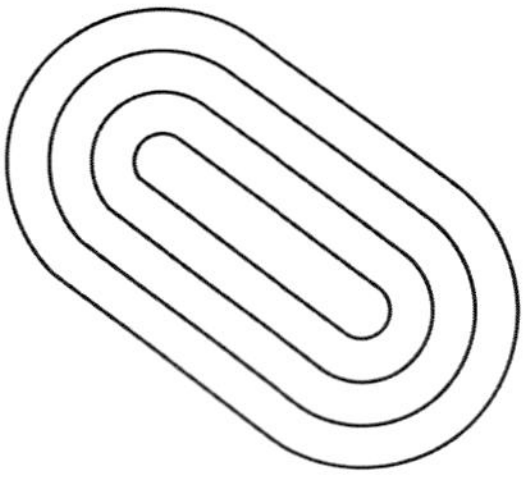

A geometric mound.
(Courtesy: Patrick Gainer)

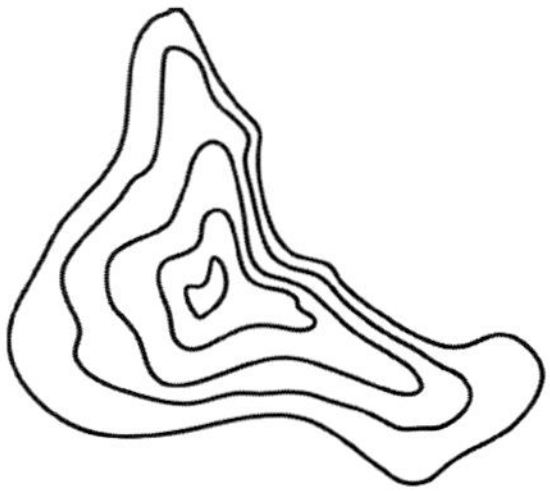

A organic mound.
(Courtesy: Patrick Gainer)

off the necessary precision paired perfectly with my desire to create organic forms in the ground. The imperfect hand instills imperfections into lines that represent a variety of distances and shapes between them. That varied spacing creates varied slopes and angles from top to bottom and side to side. Random shapes derived from each drawn line translates into varied organic bumps and hollows rather than a consistent geometric surface. In the field, I constantly ask my shapers to break up consistent slopes with those same hollows and bumps shown on paper.

The same approach is taken when building adjoining features. Whether we are creating mounds or hollows, the mantra is that adjacent features are varied in all dimensions and slopes. This creates variety in the side slopes and also extends or contracts the base of each feature.

A "mule fart" is what I task my shapers with when I encounter a feature that's too geometrically perfect for my taste. To explain, before bulldozers and other machinery became the primary shaping tools on a golf course, a team of horses, mules, or other equine species (sometimes even oxen) would pull a tool closely resembling a plow directed by a person to move dirt. That person relied on body weight to cut into the ground and relocate that material elsewhere. The use of a shaping plow was not only a time-consuming venture; it was also an imperfect process, far from simply connecting a GPS unit to a bulldozer, trackhoe, or skidsteer and riding along. The "mule fart" breaks a consistent slope with a little bump or dent - an intentional imperfection.

Golf course scraper and mule team circa 1919.
(Courtesy: Charles Scribner & Sons)

Each point has varied slope percentages assigned in different directions. In addition, I avoid trapping water on the greens by showing arrows that delineate specific drainage paths off the surface where high points aren't established. High points, slope percentages, and drainage arrows all contribute to the specific character of the putting surface through the Element of Form.

Sometimes I will create an intentional conflict between the high points and drainage arrows to challenge my shapers to "connect the dots" in a creative way. Once the initial putting surface is roughed in, we expand on the shaper's creativity in connecting those dots, as long as the big picture forms are in place. From there, we massage the fine points of the surface.

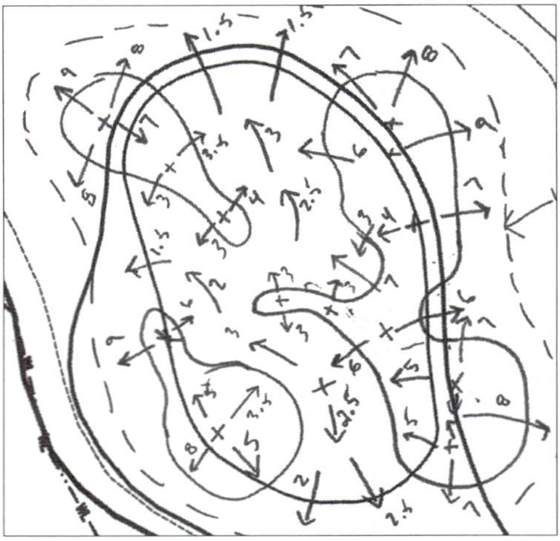

Hole #5, (Legends Nine) Bacon Park: High points (+), drainage arrows, and slope percentage numbers combine to create a putting surface form. (Courtesy: Richard Mandell Golf Architecture)

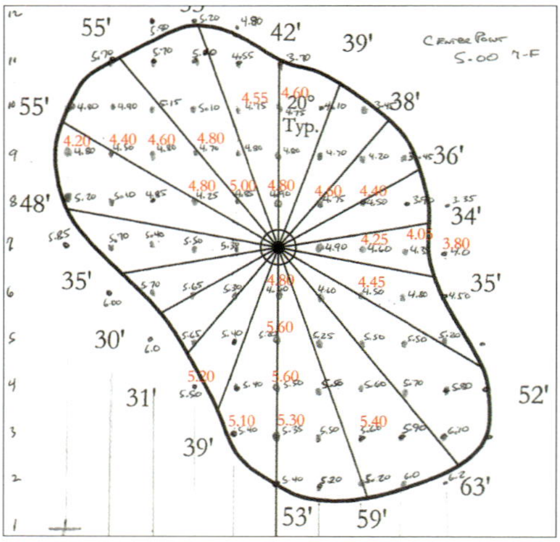

Hole #5, (Legends Nine) Bacon Park: The difference between adjacent grid elevations times 10 provides the slope percentage between points. The red numbers are the architect's revisions to ensure randomness as well as manageable slopes. (Courtesy: Richard Mandell Golf Architecture)

After initial shaping of the green, a ten-foot grid is prepared so we can dial in the slope percentages to tenths of a foot. Yet even at such a precise level of detail in this stage of the shaping process, I consider randomness in form. For instance, I will intentionally break one long slope up into a series of varying slopes. Although the primary task is to ensure no trapped pockets of water, I make sure the numerous slope percentages from point to point on the grid are varied enough so as not to be too predictable, consistent, or boring.

As important as it is to connect smaller forms of a green complex with concave and convex transitions, doing the same while shaping fairways is equally crucial. The most egregious errors in shaping features at this scale are not sizing the individual elements of the fairway correctly and not connecting those elements with concave or convex connection points. The largest features on the course will appear disjointed, manufactured, and haphazard. Using convex or concave connection points will create one flowing landform and promote positive surface drainage.

When working with such broad expanses as fairways (measured in acres), the hand of an amateur is quickly exposed if the elements of the overall composition are not large enough to balance the flat areas of the fairway. In particular, mounds that are not large seem out of place and the flatness of the fairway is more pronounced. It's better to exaggerate the size of mounds rather than underestimate the feature's ability to fill space. Hollows should be properly sized for the same reason. Most importantly, a well-shaped network of rolling features will accentuate the roll of a golf ball and provide more strategic opportunity for the architect to incorporate an interesting ground game aspect. There is nothing quite like the path a ball takes when chasing the lay of the land. This element is what makes links golf so enjoyable and why fast and firm conditions are ideal.

The fairway shaping of one of my favorite golf courses, White Bear Yacht Club in Dellwod, Minnesota, may be the best example of non-links fairways I have seen. Those fairways were almost all completely provided by nature. The land on which it sits (as well as much of Minnesota) was formed by glacial activity of ground moraine till. Ridges, swales, and other landforms were created as glaciers slowly passed over the ground centuries ago, displacing material along the way. White Bear's fairways are the prototypes to study in order to best understand how large-scale landforms can create great challenge and visual interest on a golf course. They are a great example of how the scale of the landforms that make up these features is best produced by nature's own erosive processes, ones we should strive to imitate when creating our own golf course features. In fact, the White Bear fairways are exactly what I directed my shapers to study prior to beginning the work at Braemar.

Slow glaciers are the best shapers as evidenced by the fifth fairway at White Bear Yacht Club in Dellwood, Minnesota. (Courtesy: Richard Mandell Golf Architecture)

The land surrounding the Braemar ground was not quite as inspirational as the White Bear Yacht Club property. It's punctuated by a single moraine drumlin set in the middle. The remainder of the land sits in a bowl surrounded by steep hillsides. The bowl was not flat, though, so I was able to route numerous uphill, downhill, and

Hole #11, Braemar Golf Course in Edina, Minnesota. White Bear Yacht Club's moraine landscape was the inspiration for the fairways at Braemar. (Courtesy: David Parker Photography)

sidehill holes. The success of Braemar's fairway shaping came in how we sculpted the flat areas to resemble the typical moraine landscape, the key of which was tying into existing landforms smoothly. Our guide to the correct scale was the surrounding hillsides, but the *model* were the natural landforms found at White Bear Yacht Club.

Understanding the Element of Form, whether routing golf holes, shaping fairways, or creating greens with plenty of pin placements, is critical to successfully developing the details of any golf course. Following nature's example is always a good approach.

Hole #3 White, Army Navy Country Club in Arlington, Virginia.
(Courtesy: Richard Mandell Golf Architecture)

05 The Element of Texture

Texture - The feel, appearance, or consistency of a surface or substance.

An element most people do not necessarily associate with the design process, particularly when it comes to golf course architecture, is Texture. At first mention of the word, we might think about the texture of food or how a certain material will feel to the touch. Yet, texture is indeed a facet of design that helps to create a connection with the user. Also known as surface quality, texture describes the arrangement of particles in all materials. Terms such as coarse, medium and fine are used to describe texture of materials in design, whether they are building materials such as stone (coarse) or wood (fine), or plants in the landscape.

A combination of coarse (flagstone), medium (brick), and fine (stained concrete) textures.
(Courtesy: Richard Mandell Golf Architecture)

From a tactile standpoint, texture ranges from exhibiting a smooth feeling to the touch or a rough one. For instance, stucco has an extremely rough surface quality; the surface quality of sanded wood is smooth. Texture can also include degrees of firmness of a material such as soft (pillow) or hard (concrete). Texture can even be a visual quality. The human brain converts the appearance of something into a physical reaction based on its visual texture. A painting technique to portray different textures may look rough, fuzzy, or gritty through the use of heavy or bold brush strokes and the use of white space between strokes. The results express feelings of harshness, busyness, or boldness. Thinly-drawn lines, evenly-spaced lines, or a translucent shadowing technique express softness or

Bold brush strokes may evoke uneasy feelings.
Wheatfield With Crows by Vincent van Gogh
(Courtesy: Mrreporter | Dreamstime.com)

serenity. These brush strokes cannot physically be felt but can visually express a feeling.

Smooth brush strokes may evoke serenity now.
The Promenade Poppies by Claude Monet
(Courtesy: Mrreporter | Dreamstime.com)

In landscape architecture, plant materials are chosen for a variety of functions, including as mechanisms to characterize spaces. Coarse-textured plants are best defined as those with large leaves that come in all sizes, from an eighty-foot-tall Bur Oak with eight-to-ten inch leaves to a five-foot Hydrangea with leaves that can reach six inches in size. Fine-textured plants have much smaller leaves that define their appearance yet appear on hundred-foot-tall Willow Oaks just as commonly as an Azalea that's only three feet in height.

When utilized in landscape space planning, coarse - textured plants draw one's eye into an area quicker than finer textures, making a space feel smaller than it physically is or a plant seem closer to the user than it appears. The large leaves of a coarse-textured plant can fill a space quickly with few plants and the user processes the space in a short amount of time – keeping the user's eye from penetrating the space. Using fine-textured plants in a smaller space will do the opposite – expand a tight space by drawing the viewer's eye inward.

Fine-textured plants in this small courtyard at Castle Drogo, Devon, England make it seem expansive.
(Courtesy: Clay Perry)

Coarse-textured plants make a similarly-sized space feel much smaller. (Courtesy: Mick Hales)

So how does texture apply in the world of golf architecture? There are numerous references to textures of sand and gravel in relation to golf course drainage and agronomic applications. An architect is tasked with specifying sand for bunkers that may run from fine-textured to coarse. In this application, the finer sand is usually associated with a bright white color that is desirable at high-end facilities seeking the most visual contrast possible. The coarser the bunker sand is, however, the darker the sand appears and that makes it less desirable from an aesthetic standpoint. The darkest sands are usually used for natural waste areas or cart paths.

From a strategic design standpoint, Texture may apply to those designers who want to use "fool the eye" techniques from tee to green. The French "Trompe l'oeil" (literally translated as *"fool the eye"*) is a painting style of such three-dimensional realism that fools the viewer into believing an object is actually closer than it looks by creating depth through detailed brush strokes. In a similar way in golf architecture, a designer can utilize large, coarse-textured plants closer to a target (such as a green) and fine-textured plants closer to a tee to make the green appear closer than it is. This works in reverse as well – placing fine-textured plants nearer the target to "trick" the golfer into believing the green is farther away than the actual yardage. However, with the advent of numerous digital yardage tools, few golfers would be fooled by such a plan.

A natural "trompe l'oeil" exists within most links courses. I have found that links targets consistently appear further away than their actual distance. The reason for this phenomenon is closely tied to the fact that the majority of plants found on links courses are of the fine-textured variety such as heather, heath, and scotch broom. Woodland trees don't exist in a links setting, furthering the feeling of vastness to links courses that isn't associated with parkland courses. Coarse-textured, tree-lined holes convey more of a sense of enclosure in a parkland setting.

Revisiting how painting techniques create visual texture, those same brush strokes can be applied to golf course design as well. When referencing a "richly-textured" golf scene, it's the variation in "brushstrokes" that one reacts to. Again, links golf serves as a model for "textured" landscapes. Compared to fescue and bent grasses, heather, heath, and scotch broom become contrasting coarse-textured plant materials on a links course. Not only does the texture of the grasses provide visual stimulus, the contrasting textures of sandy blowouts, dunes, and bunkers add to the brushstroke variations experienced by the human eye as well.

The sixth fairway at James Braid's St. Enodoc Golf Club in Rock, England, is the poster boy for a fine-textured links golfscape, accented by its Himalayas bunker.
(Courtesy: Richard Mandell Golf Architecture)

In contrast, a culture of closely-mown fine-textured turfgrasses on a typical parkland golf course lacks the same visual texture coarse grasses provide on a links. An example of this lack of texture was the Pinehurst No. 2 course in North Carolina prior to the 2010 restoration by Bill Coore and Ben Crenshaw. Over the years, No. 2 had become wall-to-wall grass and the result was the loss of Donald Ross's original rolls and hollows in a sea of green. Today, No. 2 can often be found on a magazine cover thanks to the addition of wiregrass, broomsedge, pineweed and other plant material along the edges of the fine-textured Bermuda fairways. The varying brushstrokes come in both the size of the grass fronds and the varying heights of the plants as well.

Pete Dye once said, *"The longer I have been in golf architecture, the more firmly convinced I've become that the contrast of grasses can do as much for a golf course as the undulations of the land."* Dye was one course architect who went through many design evolutions, most seemingly rooted in aesthetic notions. Texture is an element he consistently leaned on in his work.

An influential trip to Scotland with his wife Alice was the start of his first design transformation. Upon his return, he began to incorporate features such as pot bunkers, deep native rough, and railroad-tie bulkheads and it put him on the map for the first time. His work at Harbor Town Golf Links on Hilton Head Island in South Carolina is a legacy of small greens and runway fairways, but also of the textural

The wood retaining wall surrounding the 17th green at TPC Sawgrass in Florida. (Courtesy: Blaircwh | Dreamstime.com).

Rocks surrounding the 17th green at PGA West Stadium Course in California provide more visual texture than wood. (Courtesy: Evan Schiller)

use of wood throughout. His most famous work is still the Stadium Course at TPC Sawgrass in Ponte Vedra Beach, Florida. The design of this course, which many people refer to as Dye's "lunar landscape" style, changed the face of golf architecture for the next few decades. At Sawgrass, as well as at PGA West's Stadium Course in Palm Springs, California, Dye continued the use of railroad ties for bulkheads, bunker faces, or simply embedded in the ground to provide coarse textural contrast to the fine-textured playing surfaces.

Over the years, Dye leaned more toward the use of plant materials for texture. As striking as utilizing ornamental grasses to achieve textural contrast may be, the danger in focusing on aesthetics in this regard is the level of difficulty that's added to the playing experience. It takes constraint as a designer to ensure that playable areas are wide enough and that native areas do not become too penal. Dye's reliance on texture through contrasting grasses is at least one of the reasons many people consider his courses some of the more difficult on the planet.

Yet visual texture can still be created by combining coarse-, medium-, and fine-textured turfgrasses that ensure playability. In the American south, I have specified sand bunker faces with zoysia grasses because it grows slower than Bermuda grass faces. The advantages are mostly practical, yet from an aesthetic standpoint, the coarser texture of zoysia creates a subtle aesthetic in contrast to the surrounding Bermuda fairways and rough. As far south as Florida, a variety of turfgrasses can create a wide range of contrasting textures from the finer Bermudas to the coarser centipede and St. Augustine grasses. The same can be achieved in more cool-season growing environments by utilizing coarse fescues adjacent to medium-textured bluegrasses and fine-textured bents. Within the fescue genus itself, coarse tall fescue rough grass is visually striking against fine fescue fairways.

Hole #2, Country Club of Asheville in Asheville, North Carolina. The coarse texture of zoysia bunker faces contrasts Bermuda fairways. (Courtesy: Richard Mandell Golf Architecture)

Although Texture may not be the most utilized Element in golf architecture, it can be very effective in the consideration of aesthetics. Texture is a component of golf course design that elicits memorable visual reactions more so than influencing strategy.

06 The Element of Color

Color - A perception of light that results in something seen through the eye applied to differentiate otherwise indistinguishable objects.

The human eye acts as a prism for the brain to translate wavelengths of light into color. (Courtesy: Kts|Dreamstime.com).

Similar to the Element of Texture, Color isn't something that can be physically held, only seen. Red, orange, yellow, green, blue, indigo, and violet are the colors of the rainbow, which is scientifically known as the Electromagnetic Spectrum. These colors (as well as an infinite number of colors found within this spectrum) are derived from light that's reflected by the human eyes and translated by our brains. Different wavelengths create different colors based on varying distances between the light source and our eyes. The longest distance wavelength is translated into the color red and the shortest distance produces violet. The term "hue" is often used interchangeably with the word color, yet technically refers to just the pure Electromagnetic Spectrum colors. Whereas "color" refers to all colors. "Value" refers to the lightness or darkness of a hue or color and is also known as "tone."

Color Wheel
(Courtesy: Patrick Gainer)

A color wheel is a graphic organization of colors and their relationship to each other in terms of value. In a color wheel, the three primary colors (blue, red, and yellow) are equally spaced apart. "Analogous" colors fill in those spaces adjacent to each primary color (such as shades of yellow) and "complementary" (contrasting) colors are found directly across from each other (such as blue and orange).

Color evokes emotional reactions in people. They are typically grouped in two categories: warm (reds, oranges, yellows) and cool (blues, greens, purples), all eliciting specific feelings. Cool colors are generally calming while warm colors express activity or uneasiness. Many colors carry both positive and negative implications. For example, red is associated with feelings that are energetic, exciting, or passionate. The downside of red evokes aggressive feelings, suggesting anger or violence. Yellow is optimistic, upbeat, and modern yet can increase uncertainty leading to anxiety. Blue suggests coolness, distance, or spirituality. In its negative mode, we think of sadness, passivity, alienation, or depression.

A yellow brick road evokes optimism and uncertainty at the same time. (Courtesy: Vickifrance | Dreamstime.com).

Similar to texture, the visual quality derived from color can also express a sense of space. Warm colors bring an object closer to the user while cool colors seem to recede into the distance, making an object appear farther away than it actually is.

The Mystery of Golf by Arnold Haultain, and *Golf in the Kingdom* by Michael Murphy, are two books, written more than sixty years apart, rooted in the mysticism of golf and how the game reaches into our inner soul. A key to unlocking this mysticism may just lay in the direct link between the feelings the color green evokes and the fact it's the color most associated with this enchanting game. Green suggests nature, stability, restfulness, and naturalness. It has such a calming effect on a person that golf may truly be a muscle relaxant of the finest order. Yet, at the same time, it can be the most frustrating game imaginable.

When I was a student of landscape architecture, we relied on markers to render our design work. I had thirty-three different green markers to choose from in a list of 130 total AD markers. My collection included most of those green shades, ranging from Blue Green and Viridian to Celery to Jade and Dark Olive. I used Chartreuse for tee boxes, Palm Green for greens, and Linden Green for my fairways because the world of golf architecture was all about the color green, on paper and especially on the ground.

Nowhere in the world of golf is the color green more in the forefront of our minds than at Augusta National Golf Club in Augusta, Georgia. From its green fairways to the Green Jacket presented to each Masters champion, everything at Augusta National screams green. Augusta National is probably the one course most non-golfers know by reputation alone without ever picking up a golf club. With such a high-profile, Augusta National is also often the poster child for everything bad about the game – elitist, difficult, stuffy, expensive. In fact, there is a term for the perceived problems Augusta National has wrought on the game of golf: The Augusta Syndrome. In a nutshell, golf is too expensive – to build, to maintain, to play – and in some minds it can all be laid at the gates at the end of Magnolia Lane and the club's perceived excess. Over the years, the demand for consistency of color in playing surfaces has been a large reason why the game of golf evolved into such an expensive endeavor. The 'Augusta Syndrome' (perfect conditioning and annual changes the club makes for the Masters) is where people point to first as a poor role model for everything else in the golf world. Yet the truth is not that the money spent at Augusta National, for the *membership's* own purposes, is a problem for the game of golf. In actuality, the problem lies with those other golf courses that endeavor to replicate what Augusta National has when they have neither the means nor the clientele to handle such a proposition.

From an architecture standpoint, many course owners or operators have an almost spiritual reaction to the aesthetics derived from perfect conditioning at Augusta National yet brush aside the actual bones of its course – the routing, the strategy, the paucity of bunkers, the putting surfaces. When perfect conditioning is defined by emerald green from tree line to tree line, it's easy to understand why so many golf courses seek to replicate these conditions even though it's often to the detriment of their balance sheets.

The green hues of Augusta National Golf Club in Georgia distracts from the great architectural details of the course, such as the mound in front of #11 green.
(Courtesy: James Fitzroy | Dreamstime.com)

From the onset of the very first Masters Tournament broadcast in color in 1966, the desire for perfectly green golf courses steamrolled toward an unsustainable business model. Almost everything done on a golf course promoted perfect green conditioning and plenty of water was used to achieve it. Golf courses soon became expensive to maintain and just simply too wet. In terms of aesthetics, green was grand and nothing else mattered - not even golf architecture.

Golf courses became longer to play and more calculable. The unpredictability of the ground game was lost. With that loss came the neutralization of numerous course features designed by the great golf architects of the game. Features that promoted shotmaking and utilizing the ground to direct golf balls to a preferred destination were rendered useless in the name of progress. Yearning for the color green may have made golf a relaxing sport but it made it a boring, predictable sport as well.

Golf needed another color to make a triumphant return. That color would be brown – the savior for fast and firm conditions and the return of shotmaking. Although some color theorists say brown and green can be somewhat complimentary colors, many people in the world of golf think exactly the opposite - that green is beautiful and brown has no place on a golf course. Over the past half-century, brown on a golf course was at the wrong end of the spectrum in terms of aesthetics, the right end being green. There was even a time in warm climate areas when course operators were *painting* their dormant, brown fairways green.

Jim Hyler, in his inaugural speech as President of the United States Golf Association in 2010, asked the golf industry as a whole to *"understand how brown can become the new green."* He urged all to re-imagine playability to include terms such as firm, fast, and *"yes, even brown."* The fallout was unimaginable, particularly from golf course superintendents, those keepers of the green. In their defense, they did not necessarily disagree with Mr. Hyler; they just disagreed with the idea of losing their jobs because the members at their respective clubs weren't exactly keen on the color brown dominating their playing fields.

Fallout be damned, the return of brown slowly gained a foothold (although it was even slower at those struggling facilities that really needed a financial break). In addition, an influx of minimalist courses, beginning with Sand Hills Golf Club in Mullen, Nebraska (opened more than a decade before Hyler's words), were developed and the movement was in full swing. A focus on interesting ground features returned, particularly with green approaches. In order to maintain fast and firm conditions, less water was used and it turned courses from a consistent green to a patchwork of greens that leaned more toward brown. An additional result was better agronomic practices. Superintendents focused on creating strong root zones – and a tougher stand of grass to play from – rather than chasing perfectly emerald but weak and unhealthy turf. Form and function once again prevailed.

Accepting the idea that the playing surfaces on golf courses don't need to be perfect, architects began specifying contrasting grasses along the edges of bunkers and in out-of-play areas to minimize daily mowing. Not only were fescue mixes used in no-mow areas, so were wildflowers, wetland buffer grasses, and old-field succession plants such as Broomsedge and Blue Stem. The Element of Color yielded a different type of visual statement, minimizing the use of closely-mown green turf that dominated for so many decades. The contrast between the browns and greens on golf courses contributes to the "richly-textured" scenery more so than plant textures. As a whole, there is much more visual interest when combining contrasting colors and textures rather than a faux-green wash from the first tee to the eighteenth green.

One of the biggest controversies at golf courses is the sand chosen for bunkers. Prior to the "Brown Revolution", bunker sand was often the only source of contrasting color on a green golf course. The most visual contrast came from the whitest sands available, which were typically the most expensive to obtain. Again, Augusta National was the model for the whitest of white bunker sands. The rest of the industry followed suit, sending many other clubs into a financial tailspin trying to get their share. The bunker sand at Augusta National comes from a quarry in Western

The view from the ninth tee at Swinley Forest in Ascot, England, is a tapestry of greens, browns, and purples that balance both the elements of color and texture within a strategic challenge. (Courtesy: Richard Mandell Golf Architecture)

North Carolina. It's known as "Spruce Pine Sand" but it's actually crushed quartz. Augusta National co-founder Cliff Roberts first installed it for the 1975 Masters.

Not every golf course can afford Spruce Pine Sand. Whereas white is the most desirable color for bunkers, many courses use colored sands ranging from grays to yellows to browns. True links courses are limited to the sand on site, which is mostly yellow-brown sand. It's firmer than crushed quartz and most American quarry sands so it requires a golf club with less bounce and a swing with a steeper angle of attack.

The coarser a bunker sand is, the darker the color and less expensive as well. The majority of sands used in Minnesota, for instance, are a native brown that provides much less visual contrast than sand in other locales. The expense to import white sands to Minnesota and other upper Midwest states is too cost-prohibitive for most facilities.

When sand color minimizes visual contrast, one must rely on other strategies to create that tapestry of color. At Braemar Golf Course in Edina, we developed thirty-five acres of Oak Savanna grasses and thirty-two acres of wetland buffer grasses to combat the lack of contrast from the bunker sand. Both areas were dominated by golden and brown hues through a variety of native forbs, sedges, and rushes. The same was accomplished at Keller Golf Course in neighboring Maplewood, where we used a variety of gramas as well as little bluestem, Kalm's brome, and June grass. Although the bunkering did not provide extreme visual contrast, the native areas created an even bolder look when contrasted with the fairways and other playing surfaces.

Trees on a golf course contribute greatly to a variation of color as well. The love that many people have for trees comes from their emotion toward the color green and how it encapsulates calm and rest. It's not just the greens and browns that line parkland golf courses during the summer. The spring and fall seasons bring out a plethora of pleasing flowers and autumnal color as well.

Hole #10, Keller Golf Course in Maplewood, Minnesota. The native areas and fall color of the trees provide visual contrast to the green fairways. (Courtesy: Richard Mandell Golf Architecture)

The implementation of color as an aesthetic element of design is a risky proposition for the golf course architect and almost always comes with a sacrifice in both playability and strategy. Bunkers and water features are penal elements of golf course design, regardless of how they may be strategically used. Covering mounds and slopes with tall grasses can move a golf hole away from strategic and toward a more penal style with limited shotmaking options. An intensive tree planting program will narrow fairways and make recoveries from the rough a game of pinball. The bottom line is that when using color to express one's design intent, one must be careful not to sacrifice the enjoyment and challenge that strategy brings to the experience in the name of aesthetics.

Hole #7, Braemar Golf Course in Edina, Minnesota.
(Courtesy: David Parker Photography)

07 The Element of Scale

Scale - The size of an object relative to the size of the space in which it is located or other objects within that space.

Simply put, scale compares the size of an object in relation to ourselves and the world around us. Scale doesn't determine what is attractive or not but it will elicit feelings of comfort or burden. The result is one's observation that an object is either "in scale" or "out of scale" with its surroundings. How one describes what is in scale or out of scale is a subjective response based on personal feelings. In essence, objects that are considered in scale just look or feel right. When a reference is made to someone who has a "good eye," the inference is that the person, among other traits, can recognize objects which are in scale with each other and/or their surroundings. It's much easier to describe how something is out of scale. When an object is out of scale with the objects near it, that object is too big or too small in relation to the size of those objects. The object doesn't fit our established frame of reference.

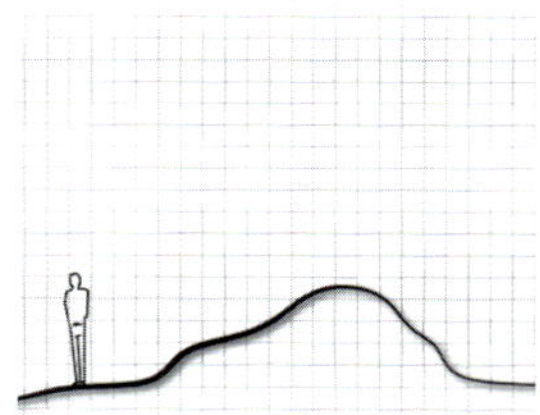

Human Scale
(Courtesy: Patrick Gainer)

There are three generally-accepted terms for denoting the Element of Scale: Human Scale, Monumental Scale, and Shock Scale. All three scale types utilize the human form for distinction. Human Scale is used to design things for the physical and cognitive characteristics of humans. In other words, things are designed - whether they are spaces, vehicles, tools, or computers - so they can be understood and utilized at a level that relates to the limitations of a person.

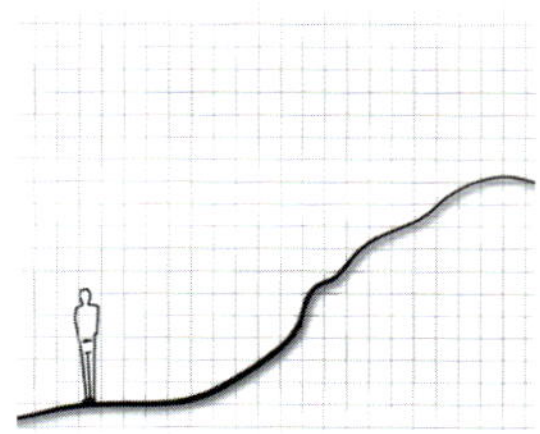

Monumental Scale
(Courtesy: Patrick Gainer)

Human Scale balances the size of a space or object with the size of the user/viewer, allowing the user to feel comfortable more than anything else. Human Scale allows the users to feel themselves in agreeable proportion to what they see and hear so they share a sense of being related to the environment in a pleasing way. When comfort and assurance are desirable traits in a design process, Human Scale must be made evident.

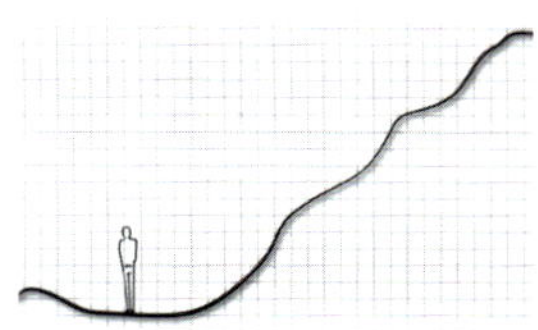

Shock Scale
(Courtesy: Patrick Gainer)

Monumental Scale is larger than us, demanding notice. Human reference points are removed or distorted when design intent is to dominate. Most public buildings are monumental, portraying their importance among humans. The rotundas of both the Pantheon in Rome and the U.S. Capitol in Washington D.C. are of such monumental scale that their importance is unquestioned. Monumental Scale intentionally violates the effort to relate to humans, establishing uneasy dominance.

Monumental scale of the U.S. Capitol is evident in its architecture as well as its site location.
(Courtesy: Alexirina27000 Dreamstime.com)

An element that displays Shock Scale can be either smaller or larger than a human, but in such a dramatic way that it literally takes our breath away. One of the best examples of Shock Scale may likely be Barcelona's unfinished Basilica de la Sagrada Familia by Antoni Gaudi, which broke ground in 1882 and was yet unfinished in 2022.

Basilica de la Sagrada Familia, Spain
(Courtesy: David Pillow Dreamstime.com)

Similar to how color and texture can increase or decrease spaces, scale can also create a distance perspective. For instance, one large out-of-scale object can enclose a space rapidly and draw the user in. Alternatively, an object that's much smaller than its confines can make a space seem larger than its true dimensions and minimize the user.

I am enthralled with the concept of Human Scale in golf architecture. Human Scale is what brings so much joy to my experience on a course. By that, I mean when the features of a golf course are such that I can relate to them; I feel that I can literally wrap my arms around them. There is a certain intimacy that's found in Human Scale, golden-age features that brings the golf course directly to me.

Not only are human-scale features elements I can wrap my arms around, I can also see over them without reaching for a ladder. I can see around them without taking multiple steps in one direction or another. They seem real to me because they fit my own human frame of reference. When golf course features are of Human Scale, I can relate to the golf course and the game on a personal level. Human Scale gives me comfort on a golf course.

Golf courses from before and during the Golden Age were built by teams of domesticated animals and drag pans directed by humans. They were built by

Golf architect Herbert Strong putts through human-scale mounding on the ninth green at Lake Forest Country Club, Hudson, Ohio, circa 1930's. (Courtesy: Western Golf Association Collection)

humans whose only frame of reference at the time was their own physical being. Earth moving limitations impacted visibility from tee to green through the inability to alter large landforms in between. The resultant blind shots were part and parcel of golf course design for centuries, a characteristic of golf that was widely accepted and never questioned. In fact, blind shots and the Human Scale features that defined those shots were a contributing factor to the "sporting" environment of the game. The details that came from humans directing animals are what added character to the golf course, providing a certain pleasure to the golfer that was relatable. Form followed function. Thankfully, the equipment of the day was simply unable to produce fifty-foot tall ridges or other monumental features.

Working in Human Scale allows me to introduce detailed, in-depth forms within my golf course features. In turn, a golfer's challenge increases when confronted with a short-game shot requiring ground-game consideration based on those forms. In a non-Human Scale scenario, if I were to play off a smooth fifty-foot slope behind a green, I would simply need to get it started downhill to the green. There would be very few humps, bumps, or rolls along the way to redirect my shot. If the slope was more Human Scale, however, it would include humps and bumps and the shot would require more thought.

Human Scale features are best created with small, "human-scale" machinery, machines no bigger than a full-size automobile. Larger machines with tracks taller than a person can't effectively create features with enough detail to capture one's attention. Their blades and buckets are so big that the material moved by these tools could bury a person in an instant. Features built to this scale can be overwhelming, often passing straight through Monumental Scale and right into Shock Scale. The transition from Golden Age golf courses to more modern fare came with the introduction of such large equipment. Golf course designers and construction equipment operators had new toys to manipulate the ground as they saw fit. Monumental Scale was introduced to golf course construction for the first time and dominated the next few decades.

While it's true that visibility from tee to green may have been improved with the advent of modern machinery, there were also unintended consequences. Designers and builders soon bypassed the tenet of following the lay of the land to create strategy and interest, opting for "progress" instead. One particular task they undertook was to eliminate the very blindness that created so much interest for earlier players. Twenty-foot-high ridges that previously were unmovable were simply erased by large bulldozers and other machines. The Human Scale details nature attached to those landforms were often collateral damage, replaced by antiseptic slopes. All unpredictability was eliminated from the equation with bigger machines. What emerged were large runways cut through ridges, large hills completely eliminated, and rambling hillsides smoothed out with what seemed like huge rolling pins. The art of shaping the ground was replaced by vanilla earthmoving tasks that were more appropriate for road construction through mountains than golf course shaping.

The broad cut through this ridge is a great example of creating monumental scale to create visibility despite the natural lay of the land. (Courtesy: Richard Mandell Golf Architecture)

Although the Monumental Scale movement that dominated for such a long period of time was a result of form following function, it soon evolved into an aesthetic approach. Bigger became better and so was more: More mounds, more water, more bunkers. Every feature on a golf course took on a Monumental Scale and the golfer became lost among the monuments. The art of shaping features to look natural – as if they were always there - was abandoned. The loss of Human Scale features also made the game of golf a little more impersonal along the way. This newly-accepted approach simply changed sites so much that they began to resemble each other. Specific features were no longer the by-product of the ground from where they came. Designers manipulated sites as they saw fit rather than allow the character of the land to provide the best golf course. What unfolded was a whitewashing of design that made many courses seem the same.

As the twenty-first century dawned, a movement away from the monumental back to Human Scale took shape in the modified approach known as minimalism. Through minimalism, course architects tried to reconnect Human Scale features to the site through the movement of less earth. But minimalism didn't exactly mean moving less dirt. Often, just as much dirt, and sometimes more, was moved to portray a natural appearance.

Nonetheless, craftsmanship was a by-product of the minimalist movement with a focus on detailed shaping of the entire site, even portions of the ground that didn't actually come into play. Small bulldozers, skid steers, and mini-excavators with Human Scale buckets and blades were the preferred paint brush of choice for the shaper. Teams of men armed with shovels and rakes applied detailed brush strokes to the ground as well. No longer was shaping about visibility for the golfer and efficiency for the contractor. It was also about replicating natural landforms.

Hole #7, Country Club of Asheville, N.C.
Final detail work on the green contours.
(Courtesy: Richard Mandell Golf Architecture)

How does one know what's in scale or out of scale on a golf course? It comes down to the eye of the beholder, that is if they prefer Human Scale to Monumental Scale or even Shock Scale, and how the beholder's eye interprets what it sees.

Following nature is my first rule when it comes to establishing scale of golf course features. The connection between nature and Human Scale is that we, as humans, understand our own frame of reference, which is literally the world around us. For whatever reason, it seems to me that natural features always appear to be *in scale*; human intervention is what alters the scale of existing landforms or fails to manufacture features that are in scale. If I try to replicate nature in my design work and ensure my features blend seamlessly with nature, then my work is likely going to be in scale.

I first consider the establishment of scale on paper during the grading process. As I draw contour lines to form a specific golf course feature, I work to see how adjacent natural contours are detailed and use them as a guide. The effort is then extended to the field working with my shapers to logically tie the feature's details into existing landforms. Achieving scale in mound construction is of particular importance. Building multiple mounds coming out of a single base will usually achieve the scale I seek through a smooth transition from the ground. They best reflect nature's erosive processes. In contrast, single mounds rarely exist in nature.

Ailsa Craig, a large rock formation in the Firth of Clyde near Royal Troon Golf Club in Scotland, is one singular landform that comes to mind when I think of Monumental Scale. Its sides, at such steep angles, strongly contrast with the flat plane of the Firth of Clyde. What makes a landform like Ailsa Craig so dramatically Monumental Scale is how the lines formed by the water and the rock virtually come together at a ninety degree angle. The vertical of the object and the horizontal of its base have no commonality other than that one connection point. Yet the balance between the height of the rock and the vastness of the Firth makes the rock appear in scale from a distance. In contrast, single mounds on a golf course often look out of scale because the flat plane from which they rise isn't as boundless as the Firth of Clyde.

Ailsa Craig in the Firth of Clyde, Scotland
(Courtesy: Neil Barr | Dreamstime.com)

Single mounds may be classified as Shock Scale due to their stark individuality yet they may still have a human scale element based on their height and breadth in relation to surrounding features. Even so, I have built isolated mounds to fill a space or emphasize a short-game challenge. In those cases, I still tried to keep them in scale with their surroundings by replicating nature's cues.

The only time I embrace Shock Scale in my work is when I am trying to replicate features that were prominent in the days before scale was a consideration. For instance, my work at Lake Forest Country Club in Hudson, Ohio involves restoration of Tom Bendelow bunkering and mounds. Bendelow was a golf course designer known for a utilitarian look more analogous to the early 1900's than the Golden Age. Chocolate drops, dragon's teeth, and grassed-faced, flat-sand bunkers were the style of the times. These utilitarian era Shock Scale features were either too small or too large for the space they occupied and rarely reflected nature.

Mid-twentieth-century examples of Shock Scale are hillsides that are hacked through with little transition among converging planes or thirty-foot mounds lined along the full length of a hole. Late twentieth-century golf course architects thrived on Shock Scale as well, but with shaping that evolved with better transitions to existing grade and the ability to break up long, flat horizon lines into more natural ones.

Hole #8, Lake Forest Country Club in Hudson, Ohio. Shock scale chocolate drops.
(Courtesy: Richard Mandell Golf Architecture)

Another challenge in establishing proper scale comes in the size of adjacent features such as bunkers flanking putting surfaces. Again, what is most difficult to establish is what may be "in scale." But "out of scale" is much clearer to define. For example, when the size of a bunker is as large as the putting surface it's there to protect. Odds are good it's out of scale with the green.

Hole #12, The Reserve Golf Club in Pawleys Island, South Carolina.
(Courtesy: Richard Mandell Golf Architecture)

On the flip side, a designed waste area that seems so much smaller than an adjacent feature (such as a green) may also be out of scale. By nature, waste areas are utilized to replace large areas of manicured turf and its very form is to function as a feature that isn't turf. A waste area that doesn't serve that function due to lack of size will always be out of scale, not just visually but functionally as well.

Features of a golf course that are on a rolling piece of ground are much more apt to be in scale than features on a flat golf course through the influence of the ground plane. The rolling ground plane changes so often that most features cannot dominate the site, partially because of size restrictions the ground itself creates. The result is features that appear in scale with the rolling landscape. On a flat piece of land, achieving proper scale is a more difficult challenge. Much like the Firth of Clyde or other large water bodies, acres of flat ground appear to run on forever. Short of replicating Ailsa Craig, it's very difficult to get the height and breadth of a feature substantial enough to appear in scale. There is simply not enough topographic restriction on flat land to accomplish the goal. The solution to achieving proper scale on unbroken ground is to avoid building single mounds rising at a ninety degree angle. Instead, a series of mounds connected by a transitional ridge coming out of the ground will appear more in scale. Creating ridge tops or high points that are of human scale is more easily accomplished through a transitional ridge rather than a series of individual mounds.

A single mound (L) appears more out of scale on flat ground than a series of multiple peaks (R).
(Courtesy: Richard Mandell Golf Architecture)

There are times when a golf architect may create out of scale features to introduce distance perspective challenges through "Trompe L'oeil" (fool the eye) techniques. For instance, creating over-sized bunkers can skew one's visual perspective from shot to target when placed adjacent to a narrow fairway or guarding a small green. The size of the bunkers will give the appearance that the green is further away from the golfer than in actuality. Positioning small pot bunkers along wide fairways or fronting large putting surfaces can have the opposite effect as course designer Bert Way demonstrated at Mayfield Country Club (below).

Built in 1911, the 13th green at Mayfield Country Club, in South Euclid, Ohio, displays Shock Scale with huge mounding and tiny pot bunkers flanking both sides of the putting surface.
(Courtesy: Richard Mandell Golf Architecture)

Of all the elements of design, the Element of Scale is the most subjective but it also has the greatest ability to bring comfort to the end user. The best designers have an innate ability to determine how Human Scale delivers that comfort level. They also know when monumental scale may be appropriate. In golf course design, successful monumental scale is achieved by balancing larger features with their surrounds and adjacent human scale landforms simultaneously.

08 The Element of Nature

Nature - The physical world that exists independently of human activities; Humankind's original or natural condition.

"The medium of the artist is paint, and he becomes its master; but the medium of the golf architect is the surface of the earth over which the forces of nature alone are master." - Max Behr

The Element of Nature is not a standard Element of Design but it is a crucial element of golf course design. Nature (humankind's original or natural condition) should unconditionally be the ruling authority in course architecture. The natural ground is the single most important element for the creation of a great course.

The golf course routing is a crucial step in the design process which can make or break a layout, and the difference between success and failure is that the best routings are guided by the Element of Nature first. Everything else is secondary, plain and simple. Routing a golf course is all about adapting the physical attributes of a particular piece of ground for strategy, aesthetics, and drainage. The sign of a talented golf architect is in the use of natural undulation as a hazard rather than copious amounts of water or sand. That same ground must be the determining factor for the location of a hazard, and in turn, a golf hole's strategy. The most natural sites have built-in strategy with little earthwork needed to reveal it.

In my work I always rely on the Element of Nature to uncover subtle rolls, hollows, plateaus, ridges, and mounds to establish strategic challenges for the golfer. Challenge is what all golfers, regardless of ability, seek out in a test of golf and it's best accomplished through a connection to the ground. The key to utilizing ground features to develop strategy is to adapt natural ones along the line of instinct into elements that create a line of charm. If all these elements come together, a great golf hole may be achieved.

For instance, a creek can be utilized as a hazard in either a penal or heroic fashion. Routing a hole perpendicular to the creek will force a carry, making it a penal shot. Positioning a fairway parallel to the creek along the length of a hole is somewhat penal as well. But aligning the hole on a diagonal to the creek and incorporating gently-rolling ridges adjacent to both sides of it as fairway instantly creates an intriguing heroic strategy. Those features locked in place will dictate how the other elements of the hole may come together.

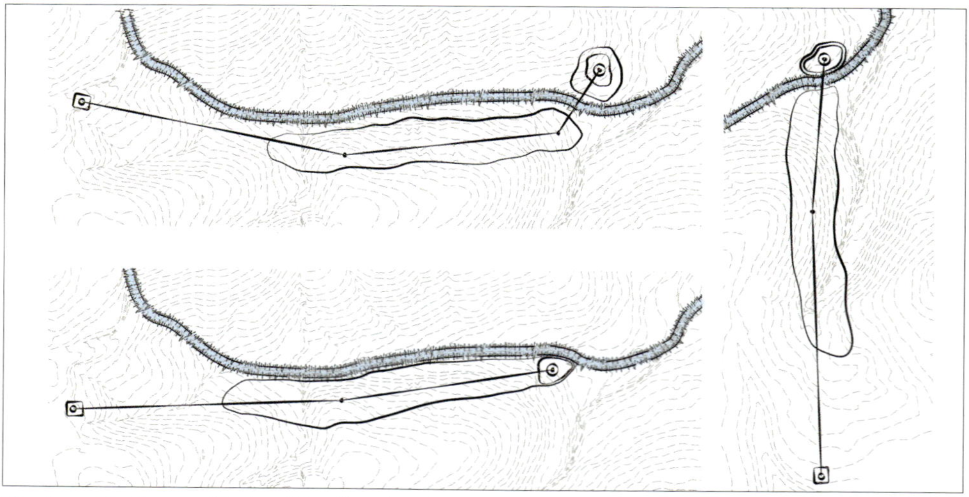

Design Options, Hole #3, Creekside Golf & Country Club in Hiram, Georgia. Three different approaches to strategically integrating the same creek into a golf hole. The top left option is heroic; The others are penal. (Courtesy: Richard Mandell Golf Architecture)

Small, flat areas for tee boxes placed far enough away from the creek will allow it to act as a hazard for tee shots. A plateau juxtaposed at an angle on the opposite side of the creek can be the fairway that provides multiple options to the green. Finally, a natural green site can create a strategy based on it's location. How far away that green site is from the plateau will determine the overall length of the hole.

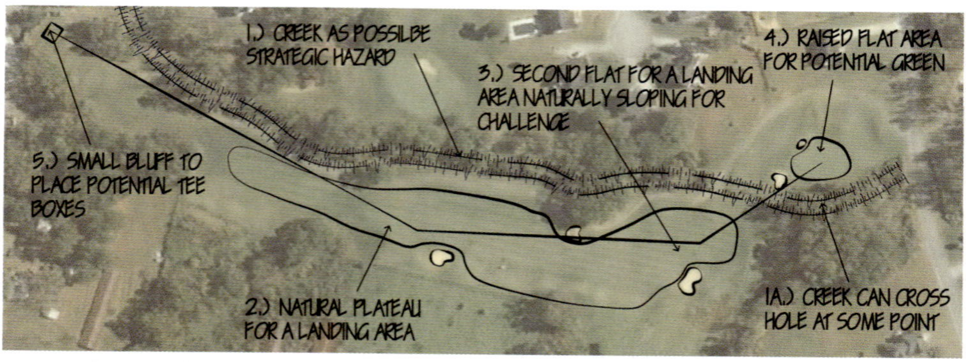

Design Options Itemized, Hole #3, Creekside Golf & Country Club.
(Courtesy: Richard Mandell Golf Architecture)

As I begin the routing process in search of those natural features, I walk the property with a topographic map in hand. Before I do, however, I will study that map in extreme detail. Without first spending some time analyzing the overall shape of the property and understanding the constraints of specific areas (determined by property lines, environmental features, topography, etc.), laying out a course solely on site will be counterproductive at some point. But by knowing how many holes can fit in a certain area, or how the sequencing of holes will be affected by site characteristics beforehand, I can better use my time. It allows me to seek out those site-specific land

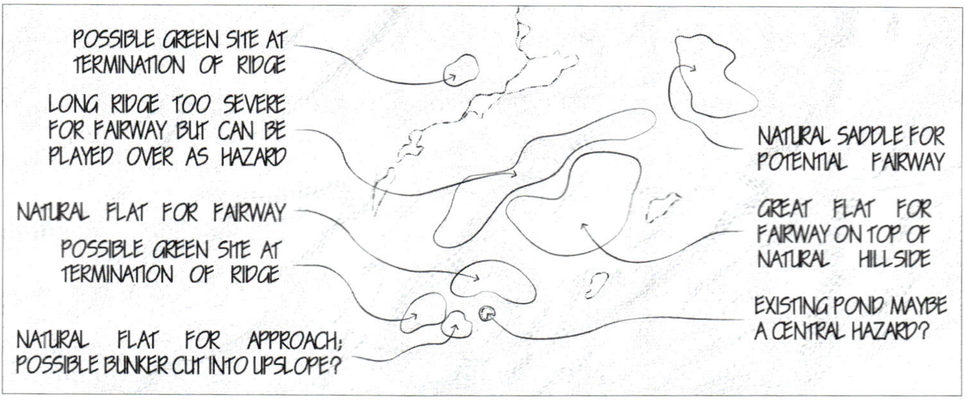

Site Analysis of raw property. (Courtesy: Richard Mandell Golf Architecture)

forms that contribute to the strategy of a golf hole with the full confidence my ideas are achievable within the overall routing. Utilizing those same natural features to set the aesthetic tone of a golf course will rarely invite criticism. The unpredictability of nature is what produces the vast palette of landscapes on this planet, and what makes the playing fields of golf so alluring. Nature dictates the aesthetic character of individual sites, preserving each course's individuality. The randomness of physical features ensures the elements of design come together naturally in a pleasing composition without the repetitiveness and boredom of artificiality.

As for drainage, nature has already determined the best patterns. There is no reason to alter those patterns to force a design idea. Instead, let the natural patterns create strategy because water always finds its original path (or natural condition). Altering that path will require artificial means to redirect drainage. The result will be an unnatural condition and constant maintenance for the life of any course. Internal drainage pipe, accompanied by gravel and other materials, will eventually require replacement. Natural drainage patterns have held up since the dawn of time and have

Hole #3, Creekside Golf & Country Club in Hiram, Georgia. In addition to strategic advantages, the creek fronting the green preserves the natural drainage patterns of the property. (Courtesy: Richard Mandell Golf Architecture)

a pretty good shot at continuing such a low-maintenance trend in the future. Internal drainage pipe should only augment the overall natural drainage of a site; it should not establish new drainage patterns.

Simply put, nature should always override "standards" of golf design and golf architects should not play safe to satisfy expectations. If natural topography provides an opportunity to build a hole that doesn't exist anywhere else, let it ride in the name of emphasizing that physical world. Willie Park Jr. encapsulates the duty of the designer to consider all possibilities, *"A golf architect must approach each bit of country with an absolutely open mind, with no preconceived ideas of what he is going to lay out. The holes have to be found and the land in its natural state used to its best advantage."*

Utilizing the myriad of landforms a site affords to create the best holes possible should supersede any perceived do's and don'ts in today's world as well. Creativity shouldn't be bypassed simply to avoid back-to-back par threes in search of a more "comfortable" sequence of pars. Here's another example: If the lay of the land dictates a phenomenal finishing hole, don't shy away from the opportunity just because the tee might be facing the setting sun for a bit late in the day.

Alister MacKenzie stressed "T*he course should have beautiful surroundings, and all the artificial features should have so natural an appearance that a stranger is unable to distinguish them from nature itself."* So how does one heed Dr. MacKenzie's advice? For starters, as an architect utilizes natural topography to serve as the basis of the course's routing, he or she should respect the Element of Form in designating specific landforms for specific features. In addition, understanding and utilizing the other elements of design properly – Line, Space, Shape, Texture, Color, and Scale – will simply not permit the golfer to distinguish between what is natural and what is made to *"have so natural an appearance."* Recognizing how to connect those artificial features to the natural landscape is most critical. We call this connection the "tie-in" (the physical line where man-made and natural features come together). First and foremost, the greater the limits of disturbance utilized to connect these features, the more indistinguishable the tie-in becomes.

Hole #13, Myers Park Country Club in Charlotte, North Carolina. The tie-in from the right side of this bunker extends thirty feet, transitioning into a fairway roll. (Courtesy: RMGA)

Similar to MacKenzie's approach to replicating waves of an ocean, the broader the connection, the better the tie-in. In other words, the longer the slope that extends from artificial to natural, the more natural the tie-in will appear. It also helps to break up that slope with rolls along the way to replicate the erosive tendencies of the natural world. Conversely, if a constrained area is utilized for a tie-in, there will be an "abruptness" to the shaping, particularly at the connection.

Hole #2, Isla Del Sol Yacht & Country Club in St. Petersburg, Florida. Brian Ross ties a bunker face in to a green edge.
(Courtesy: Richard Mandell Golf Architecture)

Tie-ins must be done with appropriately-sized machinery as well. For instance, if one were to tie the entire side of a golf hole into adjacent woods utilizing a mini skid-steer, the choppiness of the blade work will result in a series of unintentionally-connected landforms that don't relate to each other or the woods. The task will take an extraordinarily inefficient amount of time with such a small blade as well. By the same token, if an architect wishes to tie down a bunker face to existing grade, it would be difficult to accomplish this with a bulldozer blade that's larger than the feature itself.

Seeking out natural tie-ins at the start of the design process minimizes the transition from natural to artificial. When I walk a site I seek out the broadest spaces for landing areas to ensure a natural appearance, plenty of distance, and ample width for strategic play. The need for a broad tie-in is unnecessary in these instances. The most extreme slopes can act as separations between holes (such as from green to the next tee), requiring no tie-ins at all nor affecting play. This approach is a good way to incorporate otherwise unusable land.

Hole #4, Westchester Country Club in Rye, New York
(Courtesy: Evan Schiller)

Many of my hometown Westchester County (New York) golf courses have great examples of incorporating extreme slopes between playing areas with little to no tie-in. The West Course at Westchester Country Club, designed by Walter Travis, is full of such great features. They were the inspiration for many of my own holes at Skydoor Golf Club in Zhangjiajie, where the client's desire to move as little earth as possible on an extreme site was always in the forefront of my mind.

The term minimalism in golf design can take on radically different meanings depending on one's perspective of whether minimalism is either the journey or destination. The final product of a minimalist golf course, hole, or feature is universally accepted as that it looks like it was always there, yet the fundamental debate comes in how one gets to that final product. Over the first two decades of the twenty-first century, many of the most memorable minimalist courses were created on less than ideal property. Architects and shapers worked every square inch of a site to ensure that, in the words of MacKenzie, *"all construction work should follow the irregular lines of nature."* Although not much earth may have been moved (as measured in cubic yards), the constant sculpting of the ground somewhat clouded the definition of minimalism.

So what is the definition of minimalism (as it relates to design) and how does it connect to nature? Is minimalism achieved through a maximum shaping effort to produce a minimalist effect? Or is minimalism in golf design the approach from the start, leading one to minimize design through both initial routing and subsequent shaping in order to preserve or enhance the final product? One dictionary definition of minimalism is, *"A style or technique that is characterized by extreme sparseness and simplicity."* Another definition is *"expressing only the most essential and necessary elements of a product or subject by getting rid of any excessive, unnecessary components and features."* The minimalist movement of the 1950's from where this definition came arose from artists' desire to move away from the previously-dominant expressionist movement, preferring to showcase works in a truer form.

Minimalism reduces form, color, and space to such simplicity as to attain an element's essential nature. Once stripped down to this point, one can't remove anything else from the design to improve it further. Following that train of thought, shaping every inch of a site seems to be the opposite of reducing forms to their essential nature. Wouldn't the ground's initial form be its essential nature? Is it not the architect's job to reveal the ground and preserve its most basic form? For me, true minimalism in golf architecture is an extension of "less is more." In other words, find the essential elements of the ground in their original form and utilize them as course features. Natural flat areas and ridges should be used for landing areas; existing saddles, ridges, and plateaus for greens; knolls and shelves for tee boxes and hazards. These are landforms which I seek out in the ground without any pretense of reshaping beyond what is absolutely necessary for their intended function. The more appropriate the landform for the task, the less shaping required. That said, I do find it necessary to give some extra roll to areas that connect features. That's where MacKenzie's theory of making things indistinguishable from nature is a necessary component of even minimalist design. From my own experience, maybe MacKenzie is really saying that it's the rare piece of ground that doesn't demand at least some push in the right direction.

Khed, Maharashta, India site: Essential site elements in their original form, such as hilltops, creeks, plateaus, and swales, will be transformed into golf course features. (Courtesy: Richard Mandell Golf Architecture)

Or is minimalism simply removing the excesses of nature? Is shaping the site simply removing those excesses? Are those excesses the flat areas I strive to change, smooth slopes, or a straight horizon line? Excess is defined as *"an amount of something that is not necessary, permitted, or desirable."* If so, I would say those flat areas, smooth slopes, and straight horizon lines certainly aren't necessary or desirable. The most successful architects are those that can at least keep the removal of excess to a minimum. I don't believe that there are any golf architects who could resist making at least some adjustments to the ground on even the best sites. But wholesale massaging of the entire property? Probably overkill.

How about the golf courses that just sit on a piece of ground with *no* connection to nature? I'm not referring to the efforts of Monumental Scale. I'm talking about the holes that just sit there, uninspiring in their presentation. Is that minimalism in

Nature had little influence on this golf hole. (Courtesy: Richard Mandell Golf Architecture)

its finest form or is that just lack of inspiration? The difference between the hole that just sits there and the minimalist hole that fits so snugly in its own topographic bed is simply in the quality of the site; whether the hole sits or fits. The less-inspiring hole is clearly in need of MacKenzie's approach that *"all the artificial features should have so natural an appearance that a stranger is unable to distinguish them from nature itself."* That's when a thorough rubbing of the site should be in full throttle. But to call those efforts minimalism may just not be the best description.

One thing is clear. By allowing the natural ground – the Element of Nature - to dictate design, one can incorporate the character of the site to develop a holes' strategic merit. When a site's natural features dictate that strategic merit, a course will be elevated to the highest level of golf course design. The great courses of the past - The Old Course at St. Andrews, North Berwick and Dornoch (also in Scotland), Sunningdale in England, and Cypress Point and Pine Valley in the United States, among others - all derive their character and strategy from the ground on which they are placed with minimal interference by man.

The simplicity of nature's attributes can create the most complex strategic options. For the twelfth hole at Sunningdale (New), in Berkshire, England, Harry Colt wove the fairway between hilltops at an heroic angle to the tees. (Courtesy: Richard Mandell Golf Architecture)

It all comes down to the ground and if nature hands one a site that lacks excesses, lacks flat areas, smooth slopes, or a consistent horizon line, and doesn't need a rubbing, then let it lead your design. Let nature be the driver in your effort to create a great course. True minimalism is utilizing the Element of Nature to reveal the golf course that was already there.

The Element of Nature is the most important Element of Design. The origins of golf are tied directly to nature – from strategy to aesthetics. The remaining Elements - Line, Space, Shape, Form, Texture, Color, and Scale – are each derived from the natural world. As such, the Element of Nature rules these elements of design, particularly in the world of golf course architecture.

09 The Principle of Balance

Balance - The state where elements exist in equal amounts or are of equal importance.

Balance is a simple enough principle to grasp in everyday life. We work daily to maintain physical balance when standing or doing activities. But breaking down the essence of the term gets a bit tough when considering other applications. One interpretation is that balance is a condition in which different elements exist in equal amounts or are of equal importance. Balance can also mean that two opposing forces are in a position where neither is in control or when both forces share equal control.

Balance is generally a positive word. Having a good life balance – family, work, and faith – is a positive thing. The opposite, an imbalance, conjures up uneasy feelings such as a lack of control over life's elements. An imbalance may mean one aspect of life is dominant over others in a negative way, such as work outweighing family. Human nature instinctively appreciates balance yet is suspect of imbalance.

In design, balance helps one achieve visual or physical equilibrium. Whether it's a painting or a landscape, the overall composition evokes a sense of comfort if it's properly balanced. Multiple elements of design such as Color, Form, Shape, and Texture contribute to this balance. For example, a painting composed solely of dark colors may create imbalanced feelings of fear or sadness. Imbalance from the glare of too many bright colors dominating a canvas may convey a sense of unease or tension.

Balance can be achieved through two avenues: symmetry and asymmetry. Purely defined, symmetrical balance can be described as having equal "weight" on both sides of a central axis. This is known as bilateral symmetry (elements on each side arranged equally). These can be physical elements or similar colors, forms, lines, or textures. Radial symmetry is achieved with equal elements arranged around one central point, similar to how a child may draw the sun.

Radial Symmetry
(Courtesy: Agsandrew Dreamstime.com)

The human body is the perfect example of symmetry, particularly if one visualizes da Vinci's Vitruvian Man. The spine acts as the central axis and the human body is perfectly mirrored on each side. Two eyes, two ears, two arms, two legs with each pair separated by one defined line. Symmetry portrays a distinct balance and evokes a strong sense of comfort. Once again considering human scale, one's psyche is comforted by what is familiar and nothing is more familiar to oneself than the bilaterally symmetrical human body. Each side of the body has equal substance. Carried forth in design, each side also has equal substance, requiring little room for interpretation yet a comforting familiarity.

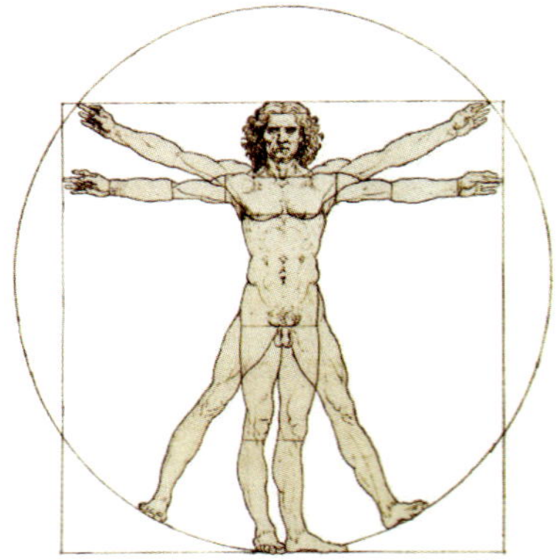

The Symmetry of *Vitruvian Man*.
(Courtesy: Jakub Krechowicz)

Asymmetrical balance is likewise based on a central dividing line. But rather than such a cut and dried example of the human body where each element is represented equally, asymmetrical balance is a more subjective matter. Balance achieved through asymmetry may best be explained through the visualization of a playground seesaw. Symmetrical balance is achieved when two children of equal weight are sitting on each end of the board and are balanced on the fulcrum of the seesaw, resulting in the board being parallel to the ground. Asymmetrical balance will result in the same parallel condition when two children of a certain weight are on one side of the seesaw fulcrum and the other side is occupied by an adult whose weight equals the combined weight of the two children. The board is again balanced and parallel to the ground, yet each side of the board is composed of differently composed elements. Whereas bilateral symmetry requires exact repetition on both sides of a dividing line, asymmetrical balance uses multiple forms, colors, shapes, and textures to obtain balanced attention. Opposites attract to create that balance: bright versus dark; heavy versus light; bold versus pale. Typically a darker, heavier, or bolder side is balanced by more form or texture on the other side. For example, an adult form wearing white balancing on a seesaw with two children on the other side wearing black.

Symmetrical Balance
(Courtesy: Inna Zhukova)

Asymmetrical Balance
(Courtesy: Inna Zhukova)

Another way to describe asymmetry is balancing one thirty-pound weight on one side of the seesaw with three ten-pound weights on the opposite side. The weight is balanced but the sides have one large object contrasted by three smaller objects; visually there is an imbalance, yet physically both sides are in perfect equilibrium..

Successful balance in a composition (whether symmetrical or asymmetrical) is achieved when elements on both sides of a seesaw position the board parallel to the earth. Balancing the visual weight of a design is

Symmetrical Formal Garden, Villa D'Este
(Courtesy: Richard Mandell Golf Architecture)

pleasing to the eye and calming to the viewer and it conveys stability.

In landscape architecture, symmetry is considered more formal and asymmetry is found in more informal settings yet both approaches achieve balance. For example, most Italianate gardens are considered formal. Garden elements found at Villa D'Este (outside Rome) or the Boboli Gardens (Florence) work around a central axis with mirror images of landscape and hardscape materials on each side.

English garden design, on the other hand, is much more informal. English gardeners like William Kent and Capability Brown created an alternate movement resembling a more park-like setting rooted in asymmetry. English gardens such as Stowe or Sissinghurst Castle are characterized by central axes separating contrasting plantings, paths, and outdoor rooms that aren't mirror images of each other. Instead, the elements on each side of the axis are balanced through the use of multiple elements in varying ways. In another era, Kent and Brown would have made great golf course designers.

Asymmetrical Informal Garden, Sissinghurst Castle (Courtesy: Tuan Nguyen Dreamstime.com)

Balance is a Principle of Design few associate with golf architecture yet it is used repeatedly by designers, whether intentional or not. Starting with hazard placement, for example, the mirroring of bunkers on either side of a centerline balances the landing area visually *and* strategically. It conveys a single, clear-cut route for the golfer to take with absolutely no question of strategic intent, providing a certain comfort to those who prefer not to think too much about strategy and options.

Yet this is where symmetry in golf design clashes with how the Principle of Balance conveys a sense of comfort in other applications. Whereas there is a certain pleasure in knowing the proper route to take, there is a competing uneasiness in knowing there is indeed *only* one route to take. There is no question as to how to play the shot, but the question is, *are you prepared for the penalty that comes if you fail?*

In golf architecture, symmetry and asymmetry affect strategy in a very profound way. Symmetrical balance (such as a bunker on each side of the line of play) is more akin to penal design, while asymmetrical balance (such as a central hazard along the line of play) is more reflective of strategic design. The uneasiness of a hazard directly in the line of play is balanced by multiple options to negotiate the hazard. It may not be clearly evident there are various choices but there is some comfort in knowing there is plenty of bail-out area. Whereas the mirroring of fairway bunkers on each side of a landing area creates a runway strategy (conveying unease) and a bilaterally-symmetrical visual (conveying comfort), an asymmetrical design of a bunker placed on one side balanced by a less-imposing feature on the other may or may not convey visual uneasiness. How to strategically approach the shot will be the primary question. The contrasting asymmetrical comfort is that the golfer has strategic options.

Hole #14, Orangeburg Country Club in Orangeburg, South Carolina. The uneasy feeling of the asymmetrical location of the central bunker is balanced by the calming possibility of multiple options off the tee. (Courtesy: Richard Mandell Golf Architecture)

One example of subconsciously implementing the Principle of Balance is when architects create equal strategic options through the use of a central hazard. I think there should always be one strategic choice that's better than the alternatives. The better choice may be different for different golfers but if perfect balance is evident with each option, there is no reason a golfer would choose one over the other. Not that there's anything wrong with that. Yet the essence of strategy is to gain an advantage by making a choice. If there is no advantage to gain, then the choice rings hollow. And so does the balance.

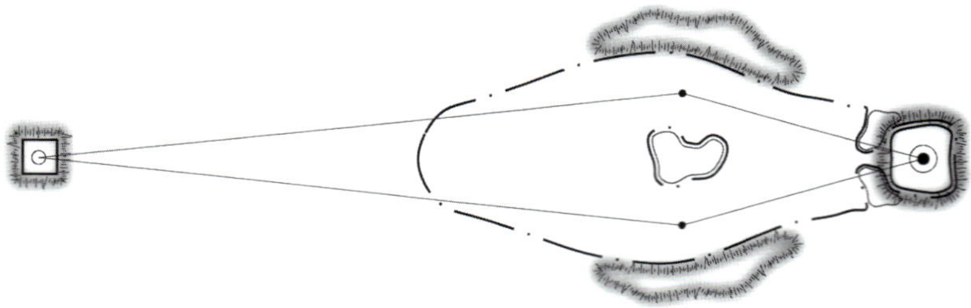

Plan sketch of central hazard hole with symmetrical balance with no strategic advantage. (Courtesy: Richard Mandell Golf Architecture)

Aesthetically, the Principle of Balance is most utilized in the placement of hazards or landforms on either side of a fairway or green complex (the dividing line). I lean more towards the asymmetrical side of things, inherently striving to balance a large bunker on one side of a green with a pair of bunkers or an equally-sized grass hollow, for example, on the opposite side.

Hole #12, Country Club of Asheville in Asheville, North Carolina. Although all three bunkers are similarly-sized, the rotation of the right-side bunker exposes more sand, creating an asymmetrically-balanced composition. (Courtesy: Richard Mandell Golf Architecture)

Many golfers relate Balance to the direction and length of golf holes, noting the number of dogleg-left holes, dogleg-right holes, and straight holes that make up a golf course routing. If there are too many holes of one type, the consensus is the golf course layout lacks a certain "balance." Unless one were routing a course on a flat piece of property, the notion of trying to create a "balanced" number of dogleg-left, dogleg-right, and straight holes forces the principle of Balance upon the Element of Nature, devaluing the lay of the land. This is *not* advisable.

Balance may be more easily pursued through the numbers shown on the scorecard *but it is also not advised.* Most regulation golf courses range in par from 70 – 72. Somehow, over time, a par-72 layout with balanced nines of 36 became the generally-accepted standard (likely through the never-ending pursuit of length). Striving for that balance because it's the "norm" will inevitably result in routing decisions that compromise the natural flow of the ground. Somewhere an existing feature will be sacrificed to ensure a "balanced scorecard." Heed the words of Donald Ross in this regard, *"Each hole must be built in such a manner that it wastes none of the ground at my disposal and takes advantage of every possibility I see."* Not only does Ross *not* refer to the scorecard, he rarely mentions par anywhere in his notes or drawings.

Another way of thinking that has somehow gained a foothold is the premise that if the pars of each nine vary too much, such as 34 - 38, the golf course is considered unbalanced. A protest may erupt declaring one is better (or worse) than the other (take your pick as to which one may be the disappointment). Balanced nines (symmetrical) are the more predictable, the ones that aren't beholden to topographic or environmental constraints. They're easy to flow in any way the architect may choose. This is perfectly acceptable when the site is flat and lacks topographic interest. When the Element of Nature is compromised to balance nines or maximize length on an exceptional site, however, the golf course will be compromised as well. Instead, let the land determine par and length, nothing else.

Golf Architect Tom Simpson said it best: *"Balance nothing, if you can avoid it."* Forcing balance to the point when routing decisions are made that don't maximize the site is something to avoid. Balancing the number of uphill or downhill holes or ones by way of compass direction should be secondary to what the ground is offering. When it comes to difficulty, for example, achieving balance is a more virtuous goal for the architect. A golf course that lacks a balance in difficulty could end up creating improper demands on the golfer (when the difficult holes are bunched together) or boredom (when there too many easy holes in sucession). In a similar vein, too many heroic or penal holes can also create an imbalance in difficulty.

An architect shouldn't, however, avoid utilizing a natural feature in the routing process strictly for the sake of balancing difficulty or strategic concepts. Instead, achieve balance through proper selection and placement of hazards (whether sand, mounding, or challenging putting surface contours). Varying hole lengths is another way. Balancing difficulty can still be accomplished when maximizing landforms for the best possible layout. For example, a hole that incorporates a valley that must be carried with the tee shot and then plays to a high plateau green, should be balanced by few to no additional hazards. Conversely, as Charles Blair Macdonald stated in describing his efforts at National Golf Links of America, *"Where nature was deficient, it would have to be improved upon artificially."* That means adding sand bunkers or other hazards to a hole that lacks natural features of any substance.

So, balancing the number of difficult or easy holes is indeed a task worth pursuing. Granted, this achievement is subjective (no doubt Jack Nicklaus and Tiger Woods will see less difficulty when standing on a particular tee than I would). Nonetheless, eighteen easy holes or eighteen difficult holes will miss the mark almost

Hole #3, The Easton Club, Easton, Maryland. Nicknamed Oxford/Bellevue as a nod to an historic nearby ferry route, the difficulty of a full carry over water on this 174-yard par three is balanced with no additional hazards around a large, receptive putting surface. (Courtesy: Richard Mandell Golf Architecture)

every time. Nine of each is better. Six easy, six halfway there, and six difficult holes may be even better, and that's when the Principle of Balance is worth pursuing.

One of the worst trends in golf architecture, the introduction of the signature hole, is the routing decision that affects the natural balance of golf holes the most. When multiple holes are minimized in an effort to chase that one outstanding hole, the natural balance of the site is broken. The mediocrity that may result before or after the signature hole may not be clearly evident, but rest assured the ripple effect will be profound. Forcing holes into the ground almost always results in demanding carries, challenging slopes to negotiate, and unnatural features – all of which create more difficult playing situations. A routing of eighteen solid holes is always better than fifteen mediocre holes and three great holes.

One instance where the Principle of Balance is valuable in a different way occurs on the construction side of golf course design. The terms "cut" and "fill" refer to how much dirt is being removed from an area (cut) and how much dirt is being placed in an area (fill). The process, known as "balancing earthwork", involves moving a specific amount of cut to fill a different area without having any extra dirt left over. If a golf course routing is done with respect to the site, then earthwork should be at a minimum to begin with. Yet, in many cases, that's not always applicable, particularly when a site lacks natural features. When an architect encounters a flat piece of property, they need to move dirt for drainage, visibility, and irrigation storage in addition to strategy, visual interest and character. This need has its detractors but balancing dirt on site is a noble effort for those who strive to preserve the integrity of a piece of property. To me, it's a bit of a cop-out when dirt is imported to the site or – even worse – the dirt on site is exported. Not only is the cost of either task extremely prohibitive, it just seems like someone didn't try hard enough.

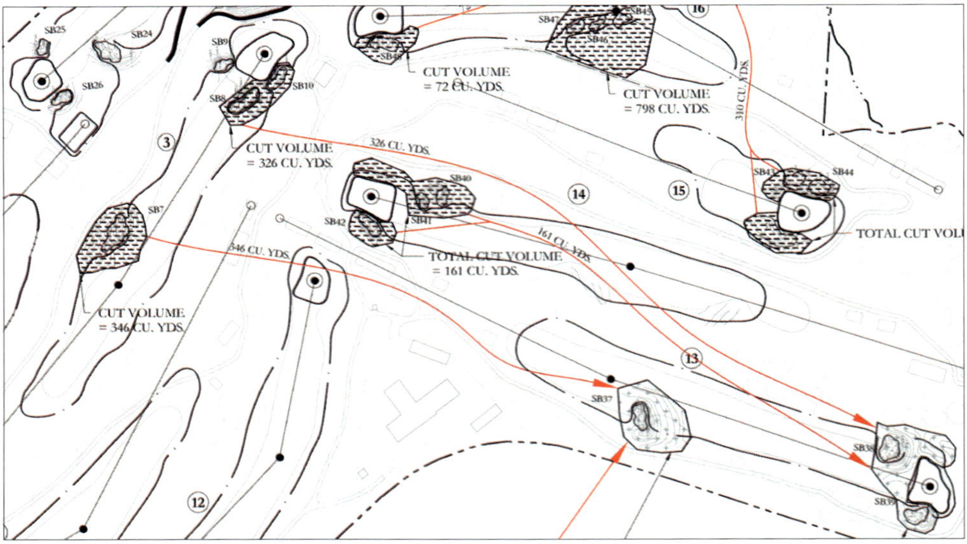

Myers Park Country Club, Charlotte in North Carolina: Balancing one's cut and fill, whether it's entire earth moving of a new course or a Donald Ross bunker restoration project, can be planned out thoughtfully to minimize hauls. (Courtesy: Richard Mandell Golf Architecture)

Balancing dirt can be costly or it can be relatively harmless to the pocketbook. It all depends on how one approaches the task. Balancing many short hauls that add up to more dirt can be less expensive than one or two long hauls of less material. The cost for a contractor is not how much physical material is moved but the number of hours it takes to accomplish the task as well as fuel and wear on the machines.

Hole #3, The Easton Club in Easton, Maryland. Hauling material out of a pond with a single dragpan. (Courtesy: Richard Mandell Golf Architecture)

Hole #4, Hooper's Landing Golf Course, Seaford, Delaware. Pond excavation requiring two machines and operators (Courtesy: Richard Mandell Golf Architecture)

The actual machinery chosen to move dirt will also affect cost. If one can move a certain amount of dirt with a single machine, such as a dragpan, the effort requires just a single machine and a single operator. Yet if transporting the material can only be accomplished by top loading, the cost of the trackhoe, multiple dump trucks, and multiple operators may end up costing more money for less dirt being moved.

Achieving visual balance of golf features is contingent upon balancing dirt as well. Not necessarily a numbers game but more of a subjective observation, moving an appropriate amount of dirt will result in a balanced appearance. The best example is of a golf course feature cut into a hillside. If the feature was completely cut out of the slope, there will be a clear imbalance of material and all the excess material would need to be removed from the area. By the same token, if the entire feature was built on top of the slope, then the dirt necessary to accomplish the task would require importation and the feature will appear overbuilt. Balancing the dirt requires

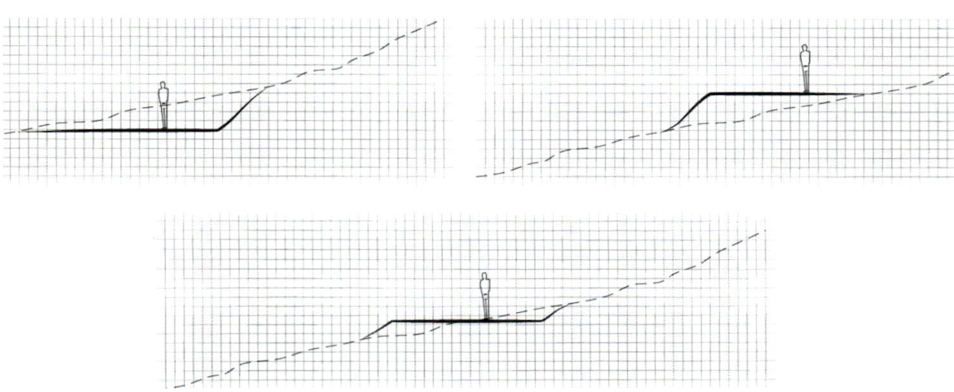

Three ways to balance earthwork for a tee built into a hillside: Top left is completely cut into the slope; top right is material filled on top of the slope. The bottom one is balanced between cut and fill, creating a lower profile. (Courtesy: Patrick Gainer)

establishing a finished elevation of the feature equidistant from the top of the slope to the bottom of the slope. Not only will the dirt balance, requiring no export or import, the limits of work will be minimized. In addition, the slopes above and below will be more maintainable, and most importantly, the appearance of the slopes above and below the feature will be in proportion to the other components of the feature.

Hole #6 Blue, Army Navy Country Club in Arlington, Virginia. The asymmetry of the grass hollow (left) and sand (right) in the approach of this short par five heightens the discomforting challenge of going for the green in two shots. (Courtesy: Richard Mandell Golf Architecture)

For me, balancing dirt on site hearkens back to how our forefathers approached earthmoving. They didn't have the luxury of heavy machinery and a contingent of operators. Rather, they were forced to work with what they had and always found a way to pull it off. The reason why the majority of top courses to this day were built in the Golden Age was because working to keep the ground as intact as possible was the standard of the day.

The Principle of Balance is *sensed* more so than defined by design parameters. It should be revealed as an organic extension of design rather than intentionally developed in the routing process. Strategically speaking, the principles of symmetrical and asymmetrical balance reflect the inherent feelings of comfort and distrust. The comfort comes in knowing what is laid out for the golfer, which to me isn't as fun as solving the puzzle of which way to go. Distrust as a result of asymmetry makes the golfer question what is actually up ahead, demanding them to choose the best route to take. Asymmetrical uneasiness is one of those attributes that makes the game of golf so compelling.

10 The Principle of Rhythm

Rhythm – Movement characterized by the repeating pattern or natural flow of related elements.

Rhythm occurs over time as one moves from point to point in a composed sequence, whether in music, art, or golf course architecture. One does not experience rhythm in the same way as one experiences balance, which is experienced immediately. Rhythm evolves over time. It evolves because pattern and repetition are ingredients that are essential in creating rhythm. Pattern is an arrangement of elements (such as colors, forms, shapes, or textures) expressed at regular intervals. Repetition creates the intervals (or pauses) between patterns. Both elements require timing or spacing to develop before one can experience a rhythm.

Most people associate rhythm as the arrangement of sounds through the repeated spacing of various musical notes. Much like the Principle of Rhythm is musically experienced with one's ears, the same occurs in design through the eyes. In landscape architecture, rhythm happens when the eye follows a regular arrangement of patterns while moving along a specific path or sequence.

Patterns that occur in regular or irregular intervals develop through the repetition of a singular form to create a specific sequence. The repeated spacing of these singular elements is what creates rhythm. For instance: A-A-A-A is a simple rhythm like a single, steady heartbeat. Similar processes to repetition, such as alternation, inversion, or gradation, are used to create patterned sequences as well.

Gradation is a gradual characteristic change in one element. The repeated element in a rhythmic sequence may slowly increase or decrease in size (such as A-A-A-A-A) or another characteristic may vary, such as a steady lightening or darkening of a color. The principle of gradation is a controlled buildup (or decrease) of rhythm without creating sudden changes.

Alternation is a sequence of two different patterns repeating themselves such as A-B-A-B-A-B. The rhythm derived through alternation sounds most like a heartbeat that repeatedly rises and falls. Inversion utilizes opposite elements to create an even stronger rhythm such as A-b-A-b-A-b. Inverted elements change so their characteristics are at the opposite end of the spectrum from each other (such as dark and big to light and small). Each of these examples demonstrate two elements juxtaposed to each other yet there can just as easily be multiple elements stringing together a more intense and longer rhythm, such as A-b-A-c-A-d-A-b, etc. But too many elements spaced out too far can end up losing rhythm altogether. One is then left with just a jumble of sights or sounds.

Nonetheless, through whatever principle of repetition one chooses, everything is connected through pattern and time. When a connection is successfully created through these principles, the eye can move smoothly from one element to another in a pleasing way without interruption. Spacing out elements of design in a specific way creates visual patterns that one responds to subconsciously. Certain elements may form a pattern that's easy to follow, creating a positive rhythm, or the elements may form no pattern and convey a negative experience, lacking rhythm completely.

The left tile pattern has a pleasing rhythm, creating a positive experience horizontally as well as diagonally. The tile pattern to the right lacks a consistent rhythm, creating a negative experience. (Courtesy: Richard Mandell Golf Architecture)

One definition for rhythm is *"a pattern in an activity that makes it enjoyable to watch or easy to do."* This best illustrates why the Principle of Rhythm in golf architecture is often associated with golf course routing. If a routing is pleasing or enjoyable, critics associate the positive feeling with a rhythmic flow of golf holes. Yet because that flow is so difficult to define, the principles of Balance and Variety are often incorrectly cited as a way to define the rhythm.

Because the routing of a golf course is so tied to a site's topography, the rhythm of a golf course is equally tied to the rhythm of its topography. If the topography is varied enough and the golf course architect able enough, the melding of the topography to the routing should be a rhythmic symphony of the highest order. A golf course built on a more topographically-stimulating site has the potential for great rhythm built into the routing. Yet the rhythm of a routing can still be a bit monotonous on a varied site. For example, a course that strictly plays up-down-up-down is repetitive at its most basic. It's the golf architect's job to bring out the topography's rhythm beyond basic repetition.

This is where one must be able to utilize a dominant feature of a site in varying ways to create a rhythm beyond a simple A-B repetition. An example is Seminole Golf Club in Juno Beach, Florida. Seminole is dominated by two ridges that run north-south through the property along the far western and eastern edges. Instead of repeatedly playing up and down from hole to hole, Donald Ross incorporated the ridges four different ways on fourteen of the holes. The three flat holes in the middle of the routing (8, 9, 10) are varied enough to create their own rhythm playing as a par 3-5-4.

Ross's utilization of the ridges is what distinguishes Seminole. He avoided basic repetition by integrating the ridges in a variety of strategic ways, creating a rhythmic symphony through alternation and inversion. He simply never used the ridges the same way back to back. The western-most ridge comes into play from holes 2 to 7 with the following rhythm: B-A-D-C-D-A. Ross repeats a similar rhythm on the back nine through the use of the eastern-most ridge along the ocean from holes 11 to 18: B-A-B-C-A-B-A-C (following is the legend):

A: Tee off the ridge.
B: Green set into or on top of the ridge.
C: The hole tees off the ridge and then plays to a green set within the ridge.
D: Fairway plays along the length of the ridge.

Donald Ross's routing of Seminole Golf Club in Juno Beach, Florida, utilizes two sandy ridges in multiple fashions to create a rhythmic layout. (Courtesy: Richard Mandell Golf Architecture)

It shouldn't be a surprise that some of the best courses in the world have a pleasing rhythm within their layouts as well as the most diversity in their site's topography. The golf architect who takes advantage of the topography by weaving those features into a rhythmically-pleasing way will always be successful.

But how does a designer develop a rhythmic golf course routing on land that lacks any notable topography? The answer is as subjective as one's personal taste in music. For instance, my favorite is Rhythm & Blues. The rhythmic patterns of musical instruments and sounds from R & B artists have specific patterns that entertain me much more than the rhythm exuded from heavy metal or country music. The same specific notes in and of themselves are found in all three musical types but the rhythm of the sounds differs greatly. The same is true of golf course routings. The resultant rhythm the golf course entails may be pleasing to some but not to others.

On a golf course composed of eighteen straight golf holes on flat land, rhythm can only be defined through hole length, which directly translates to difficulty for the majority of golfers. Short-long-short-long may be attractive to some, yet others may want short-medium-long-short-medium-long. Personal preference for a course routing with rhythm may be strong for those who prefer alternating easy-hard holes. Others may prefer easy-easy-hard-hard. Others may not care about difficulty at all. The patterns are endless.

The most intriguing courses are those with a rhythmic order of par that's rarely repeated, such as 3-4-5-3-5-4. Similarly intriguing is when those holes vary in direction as well, such as straight-left-right-straight, etc. The rhythm to one's routing is further enhanced through the placement of hazards and other features on those same holes. For example, a routing in which one hole with a bunker left off the tee is followed by another hole (of a different par) with a bunker to the right off the tee, followed by two more holes repeating the pattern with varying pars, creates repetition through alternation (A-B-a-b). These four holes have a certain rhythm expressed through pattern (bunker placement) *and* spacing (hole par to hole par). There is obvious variety in all of these examples, but how that variety is laid out leads to Rhythm.

Hooper's Landing Golf Course in Seaford, Delaware. A rhythmic routing on flat land.
(Courtesy: Richard Mandell Golf Architecture)

One of my favorite courses is Herbert Fowler's Red course at Berkshire Golf Club outside London. The Red's routing has as much rhythm as a routing can possibly have. Only once is par repeated on the entire course (at the par-four eleventh and twelfth holes). This is one of two places in the entire routing where one comes across parallel golf holes. Every other hole on the course alternates par, creating a rhythm that's far from repetitive and beyond alternating. The rhythm of Berkshire Red is the primary contributor to the joy one experiences there. The property lent itself to such a routing and Herbert Fowler took full advantage of it.

Hole #9 (Red), Berkshire Golf Club, Ascot, England: Golf architect Herbert Fowler found a site with great topographic rhythm, allowing him to create an equally-rhythmic routing. (Courtesy: Richard Mandell Golf Architecture)

A course that offers such a memorable rhythm like the Red is hard to achieve for even a stretch of holes within a routing, let alone all eighteen holes. But when the site allows that possibility, the golf architect must take advantage of it. As I mentioned earlier about Braemar Golf Course in Minnesota, my sequence of holes three through eight runs 3-5-3-5-3-5. Bracketed by par fours, this arrangement is the epitome of an alternating rhythm. Within the realm of golf architecture, where there are only three choices of par, being able to run a string of six alternating threes and fives is an opportunity that must be grasped.

What allowed such great rhythm to happen wasn't my desire to create it but the site features that let me seek out the best holes possible. The rhythm of the pars was just an added bonus. One can easily accomplish such a string of holes on flat land but to achieve it on rolling ground lends itself to a special place.

When it comes to building rhythm to a crescendo through the principle of gradation, the first two places that come to mind are Augusta National Golf Club and TPC Sawgrass. Augusta National's "Amen Corner" (holes 11 – 13) is arguably the most crucial stretch of holes every year at the Masters. The preceding holes all lead up to the strategic decisions made in this stretch. Once through the gauntlet, the rest of the way is a bit less stressful, with holes 15 and 16 being a mini-gauntlet providing a rhythm of their own.

Braemar Golf Course in Edina, Minnesota. Environmental constraints such as ponds, creeks, and wetlands were contributing factors to the 3-5-3-5-3-5 hole sequence. (Courtesy: Richard Mandell Golf Architecture)

From the first tee, everyone playing TPC Sawgrass is thinking about the do-or-die island green seventeenth. Because of its penultimate position on the course, and the potential of disaster that awaits, the tension within the golfers and viewers arguably builds to a greater crescendo than even at Augusta National. Through the use of gradation, Pete and Alice Dye created a steady drumbeat rhythm that leads to the ultimate in high drama.

Sometimes, the rhythmic build-up is pre-ordained like at Sawgrass and yet other times, outside influences such as the Masters allows rhythm to evolve. In the case of Augusta, it was not MacKenzie's or Bobby Jones' intention to reach a high at Amen Corner. Their original plan had the nines reversed. Nonetheless, the annual drama from the Masters helped develop the rhythm of Augusta's routing.

These examples of how rhythm can be experienced in a golf course routing leads one to consider the effects of creating a signature hole at the possible expense of other holes. In this regard, it may be personal preference on the designer's part to create anticipation through rhythm. As long as the other holes do not lack for effect as a result, there is nothing wrong with the idea, particularly if the hole comes naturally. Quite often, though, routing decisions that are made elsewhere just to make a signature hole fit will negatively affect pace of play and disrupt the overall rhythm.

From an operational standpoint, nothing damages customer satisfaction more than pace of play issues. Granted, too many golfers on the course can be the primary culprit. But there are crowded golf courses that don't take nearly as long to play as many less crowded ones. The reason comes in the rhythm of the layout. For example, a long uphill hole that bogs down play may be followed by an easier, downhill hole to balance the pace. Or a hole that has a blind component to it may be surrounded by holes whose features promote a faster pace. Yet back-to-back uphill slogs will cripple pace of play.

Most designers avoid back-to-back par threes for the same reason. But if the site features demand such a stretch, the golf architect should be prepared to augment them with holes before and after that are conducive to pace of play. That way, the rhythm of the overall routing is still enjoyable while the site features are maximized.

Multiple forced carries contribute to pace of play issues as well. To counter this problem, architects must incorporate forced carries wisely and temper them with holes that are more free-flowing before and after. Pace of play isn't about combating slow; it's about creating *flow*.

One example of how to keep the flow going comes from my friend Bill Yates, the "guru of pace." Bill liked to cite the example of a short par four followed by a long par three. Regardless of flow or difficulty, the likelihood of a wait on a par three tee is always greater than on a par four or five because only one group can ever play the hole at one time. If the previous hole is a short par four, taking less time to play than a longer hole, the rhythm of the routing is disrupted by depositing golfers on the par three tee even faster, adding to the inevitable wait.

The pace of play is similar if the short par four follows a par three. If short holes can be balanced on both ends by longer (not necessarily harder) holes, then the flow is spread out more, resulting in less wait time between shots. Creating more pockets where multiple groups can freely move from shot to shot will create a more enjoyable experience. In cases where the natural lay of the land prohibits such routing decisions, the architect must consider the selection and placement of hazards to maintain a good flow.

The distance *between* holes is just as important to flow. A long walk from a green to the next tee may not allow the golfer to establish any rhythm with his or her golf game. Couple that with a string of difficult holes, and the ensuing pace of play will ruin anyone's day. But a routing where the next tee is always a few safe steps from the previous green will create a more positive rhythm to one's round.

When golfers complain about not being able to *"get into a rhythm"* during their rounds, they usually infer that they can't play their own game. This often is due to not being able to hit driver off the tee, forced instead to lay up more than desired. There is a certain rhythm to our golf swings that's usually at full throttle when hitting driver at every opportunity. To stop and consider a lesser club not only halts the flow, it also means forcing a club into a player's hands for the next shot. I am not saying one should never consider a club off the tee other than the one he or she hits the farthest. There are many strategic cases where a lesser club is the club of choice - choice being the critical word here. Strategy is all about options leading to choices but shouldn't forcibly interrupt the rhythm of a golf round.

Putting green design can also create rhythm issues, such as the consideration of putting green size and how it may affect pace of play. One side of the debate favors smaller greens that may mean fewer putts balanced by more short game activity around the green. The thought process is that golfers take less time to analyze and consider a short game recovery shot than a putt, thus maintaining pace. The other side favors larger greens because they will promote more greens in regulation and create a different flow to a round. There is no question as to which club one needs when it comes to putting. But the time taken to read and execute one, two, or three putts can add time to the round and disrupt rhythm for others.

One way to balance this conundrum is to make bigger greens less undulating to promote the pace and leave the more rolling contours for smaller greens. But where is the fun in that? I prefer a variety of green sizes and the chance to create dramatic contours on the larger surfaces. More square footage allows for more dramatic slopes. The opposite is true for a smaller green. The solution to this conflict is to promote challenge and interest in both cases while improving pace of play elsewhere.

In addition to the overall rhythm of a golf course developed through its routing, visual rhythm can be created through shaping of individual golf course features. A visual rhythm is experienced by the path one's eyes travel as they observe a sand bunker outline, a putting surface, or the horizon line of a mound complex through the same principles of repetition, alternation, and inversion. Unlike balance, the rhythm of your eye's path takes time to unfold. Creating bunker lines by alternating patterns of long and short segments with straight and curved segments (all within the same bunker) will create a rhythm that keeps the golfer's interest longer than one perfectly consistent line with no repetition at all.

Hole #12, Skydoor Golf Club in Zhangjiajie, Hunan, China. Arcs (in red) and segments (in black) create an alternating pattern. (Courtesy: Richard Mandell Golf Architecture)

A green or bunker line that's too straight is literally flat-lined with zero rhythm. Even a sand bunker's multiple fingers, repeating the same dimensions, lack rhythm. Yet if one allows the pattern to get too complicated, the look creates a sense of tension in the golfer. Finding the right balance is the artistic differentiator.

The Principle of Rhythm expresses how the golfer moves through a golf course over a period of time and is achieved through the use of repetition, gradation, alternation, and inversion. The rhythm created through these tasks is either an enjoyable experience because it flows in a specific pattern or is not an enjoyable experience because it's a random, broken pattern that stops and starts at different intervals. The specifics of design, from routing to placement of hazards to shaping of features, all contribute to how a round of golf is experienced through the timing and space created through the Principle of Rhythm.

11 The Principle of Contrast

Contrast - To distinguish through the differences of unlike or opposite qualities or characteristics.

> *"The contrast between the vivid green of the grass, the dark green of the firs, the whiteness of the sand, the purple heather, and a vivid background of rhododendrons, combined with the natural appearance and extreme boldness of the contours, gives one a picture probably unsurpassed by anything of a similar kind in nature"* - Alister MacKenzie

Compare and contrast are like peanut butter and jelly or rock and roll. They just go together. Each are directives that require one to analyze two items to determine their similarities (compare) or differences (contrast). Yet only the Principle of Contrast is used within the design process. There isn't a Principle of Compare. That's because contrasting objects (or groups of objects) evoke more discussion or action among users or viewers. The differences, whatever they may be, spur conversation, debate, contemplation. If objects compare favorably there's no compelling follow-up.

Designers use the Principle of Contrast to arrange opposite elements to develop a pleasing visual composition or a functional object. For example, a Phillips head screwdriver and a Phillips head screw are contrasting forms that work well when brought together. Both forms function as one unit to accomplish a specific task.

The juxtaposition of two objects (or groups of objects) with multiple differences is necessary to incorporate contrast. The Elements of Design have opposing characteristics to satisfy this need: Curved lines contrast with straight lines; dark colors contrast with light colors; open spaces contrast with closed spaces. Through these visual differences, contrast keeps the user engaged in their surroundings.

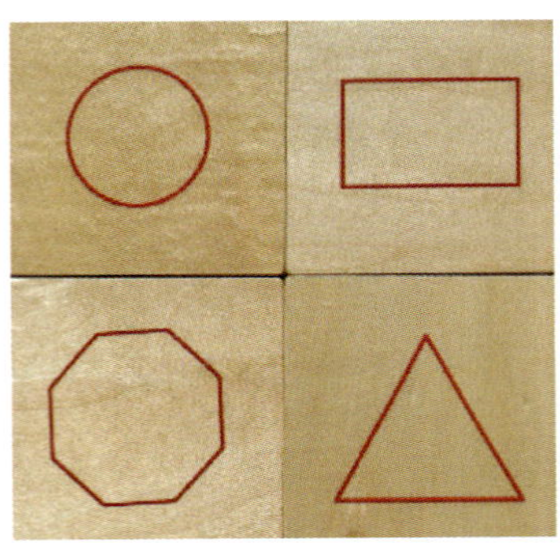

More contrast occurs between a circle and a rectangle than a circle and an octogon. (Courtesy: Antares614 | Dreamstime.com)

Each contrasting pair of elements creates variety, drama, or visual interest by making one object stand out next to the other object. Amplifying the differences between each element creates an even greater separation between objects, further maximizing the impact of the work. A square will stand out next to a circle but not as much next to a rectangle. The contrast between a right angle and a circular shape make each element that much stronger. A black object appears even more black juxtaposed to a white object than if it was adjacent to a dark gray object.

However, even though the principle of Contrast is used to *emphasize* elements of one's design work, it shouldn't be confused with the Principle of Emphasis. The difference between the two is that Contrast involves one object playing off a second object, whereas Emphasis highlights the qualities of one object over multiple objects. Each principle achieves the same goal by augmenting the differences of various objects, yet contrast is strictly applied on a one-to-one basis. For instance, when a Maple tree with purple leaves is standing next to a Maple with green leaves the viewer will immediately notice the stark color difference between the two, garnering each an equal amount of attention than if they were the same color. On the other hand, a single Maple with purple leaves inside a grove of twenty green-leaved Maples will make an even stronger statement. The Principle of Emphasis makes the lone purple-leaved Maple the focus of the composition and it will be dominant in the landscape.

Too much contrast leads to a lack of direction. (Courtesy: Four Seasons Garden)

Contrast is a principle that must be used sparingly, though. If multiple contrasting elements are scattered throughout a composition, each element competes for the same visual attention. When a lack of contrast doesn't accomplish its intended goal, the composition may appear one-dimensional or without clear direction. It's at these points in the design process where the artistic eye successfully utilizes the Principle of Contrast or not.

Developing contrast in course architecture is most often utilized through the elements of line, shape, texture, and color. These elements have contrasting details that specifically engage the golfer visually and strategically. Visually, perhaps the most evident example of the Principle of Contrast is blending straight lines with curved lines to form bunker shapes. Perfect arcs don't exist in nature nor does a perfectly straight line. Rather, the subtle mix of contrasting line types is more organic, keeping the golfer's eyes engaged longer. This is where the artistic eye is critical to visually balance straight and curved lines and the lengths and arcs of each. Too much of either element will tip toward created repetition rather than moving the eye in a pleasing direction.

On a larger scale, the use of contrasting bunker shapes rarely accomplishes the goal of engaging the golfer through visual interest. Instead, it's a one-way ticket to randomness and optical chaos often not noticed by golfers or designers. For instance, after receiving the commission to renovate The Reserve at Pawleys Island in South Carolina, I was struck by its wide variation in bunker shapes. The majority of bunkers had a similar design style of smoothly-connected arcs. Among them lay one or two stacked-sod wall bunkers that could only be interpreted as an attempt to inject a links aspect. There seemed to be no functional reason for stacked-sod wall bunkers and the simple solution was to eliminate them.

Hole #3, The Reserve at Pawleys Island in Pawleys Island, South Carolina.
(Courtesy: Richard Mandell Golf Architecture)

A second aberration at the Reserve was the native red-brown colored sand that was arbitrarily placed in some bunkers while others had brilliant white sand. Because of their random distribution, the contrasting bunker sands created a disjointed pattern instead of visual interest. Our solution was to limit the white sand to all greenside bunkers and the native material to all fairway waste bunkers, which we intentionally bled into the woods line along each hole. The resultant contrast replaced the original approach with clearly-defined visual interest (above).

Mixing bunker styles is one of the most difficult design tasks to pull off, especially through the Principle of Contrast. That said, *successfully* creating contrasting bunker styles on a golf course can be accomplished through the incorporation of common design traits. For example, combining straight and curved segments can still achieve contrast yet avoid a pattern of randomness, even if one mixes grass-faced and flashed-sand bunkers. To further avoid a haphazard look, one may choose to use flashed-sand when visibility is required and grass-faced bunkers when visibility isn't. That way, the contrasting mixture appears less forced and more functional. This approach achieves visual interest through the Principle of Contrast behind the practicality of form following function.

Mixing the same arcs and straight segment types to form modestly-shaped bunkers (as well as elaborate cape-and-bay bunkers) can also create visual interest through contrast. In this case, the cape-and-bay style should be dominant and the more subdued bunkers the contrasting feature. Allowing the simpler style to act as accent will amplify the cape-and-bay appearance, strengthening the visual contrast without over-designing.

At Lake Forest Country Club, I was afforded an opportunity to create visual contrast through Tom Bendelow's original drawing. In it, he uses islands of grass in four of the proposed sixty-two bunkers. In restoring as much of his plan that makes sense for modern golf, I utilized the Principle of Contrast by re-creating all four of his grass island bunkers as contrasting elements. The mixture of arcs and segments that form the islands – as well as all the other bunkers – ties everything together. If I had chosen to flash the sand lines onto the islands or only utilize arcs to form them, the overall design would have lost some integrity. Understanding how to subtly tie contrasting features together with similar design elements strengthens the contrast much more than a jumble of design "tricks" which only weaken contrast.

Hole #7, Lake Forest Country Club in Hudson, Ohio. Similar arcs and segments tie contrasting bunker styles together. (Courtesy: Tom Bolon)

Creating contrast through the Element of Shape is mostly limited to the variation of bunker shapes. One can make a case for creating circular pot bunkers as an overall design theme and use contrasting shapes (such as kidneys or ovals) for visual effect. Using squares and rectangles would also create contrast but the impracticality of right angles may not be worth the effort needed to maintain such effect.

Generally-speaking, bunker shape design is not the best path to incorporate the Principle of Contrast in golf architecture. Over-thinking contrast can have devastating visual consequences or no effect at all, completely neutralizing the effort. The best approach is to avoid such an idea from the start. When I consider Charles Blair Macdonald's advice of *Don't seek an original idea in building a golf course,"* contrasting square bunkers with circular pot bunkers comes to mind. That's an original idea one may not want credit for. A better way to introduce the Principle of Contrast is in size variation of bunkers, a much less complex approach yet very effective. Size variation helps establish the key elements in one's design and a larger design element is naturally emphasized, more likely to draw attention than a smaller element.

As for putting surfaces, they are rarely varied enough for the Principle of Contrast to be evident. The *sizes* of the greens, on the other hand, can definitely stand out if a certain number of them are much larger or smaller than the others. A golfer is certainly more engaged when confronted with a putting surface size that contrasts with the one just played. This hole might require a lag putt, the next hole a short pitch. Just enough of each mixed into a round will make those greens stand out in one's memory. But if there are only one or two greens that differ in size, they may stand out more as a design *flaw* than a use of contrast.

For me, the two elements of the Principle of Contrast that most impress on a golf course are texture and color. Contrasting grass textures - such as the fines of a Bent grass fairway and the coarser Tall Fescues of adjacent roughs - make a strong visual statement from tee to green. From a functional standpoint in warm climates, the use of Zoysia grass for bunker faces requires less mowing and their coarser textures provide visual contrast with surrounding fine-textured Bermuda grasses.

Too many grass types, however, can distract from the overall composition - not only in textural differences but in the intersection of lines that inevitably appear and disappear from view. The architect must carefully lay out grass lines from different viewing angles to ensure they don't become distractions in and of themselves, rendering the subtle contrast of textures lost amid the host of conflicting lines. The easiest way to accomplish this is to roll one grass type over the crest of a framing mound, leaving the connection point on the other side out of the golfer's sight. In addition, they must be sure to over-exaggerate curved lines up close because those same lines observed from farther back always appear straighter than they actually are.

Hole #16, Country Club of Asheville in Asheville, North Carolina. Hiding converging grass lines is crucial for contrast to seem effortless. (Courtesy: Richard Mandell Golf Architecture)

It's wise to conservatively implement contrasting grasses so as not to divert from the primary goal of golf course architecture: create strategically-challenging and fun golf courses. Too much variation draws the focus solely toward aesthetics, calling upon a multitude of agronomic practices for multiple grass types amid multiple growing conditions for a multitude of expenses. Such diversion takes effort away from providing suitable playing surfaces. The primary reason that grasses exist on golf courses is not aesthetics; it's to give the player an aceptable lie from which to hit a golf ball.

Textural contrast can still be achieved on courses that only offer one or two different grasses simply raising the height of the cut for different applications. The utilization of what's known as a "primary" cut exists because there is a "secondary" cut. If visual interest is the intent for multiple cuts, sufficient contrast between fairway and manageable rough is a more sustainable approach. If playability is the intent, a single cut of reasonable height throughout is the more equitable solution.

Similar caution must be taken with contrasting colors on a golf course because the risk of difficulty comes into play more often. The contrast of green grass, white sand, and blue water is the easiest way to introduce visual interest. It's also the easiest way to increase difficulty because the more space occupied by sand and water, the fewer places for a golf ball to land without penalty. The same is true when different-colored grasses are utilized for contrast. By design, such grasses will be taller than turfgrasses, forcing the golfer into excessive challenges.

So, how does the Principle of Contrast affect strategy? By definition, in strategic design, alternate routes are chosen based on the location of hazards. One definition of Contrast is *"the state of being strikingly different from something else in juxtaposition or close association."* The placement of hazards that challenge golfers to consider a strikingly different route than the more direct route is exactly how the Principle of Contrast affects strategy. The most direct line contrasts with the longer route.

Hole #15, Blue Heron Golf Course in Stevensville, Maryland. Letting contrast evolve naturally balances aesthetics and strategy. (Courtesy: Richard Mandell Golf Architecture)

Alister MacKenzie first learned the art of camouflage in the Boer War. Whereas contrast is a design principle used to make things stand out, its absence is the basis for simple camouflage. He adapted this component of warfare to golf architecture, focusing on blending features into their surroundings rather than creating contrast through grass types or bunker shapes. Considering the desire to replicate nature is so prevalent in his writings and work, Contrast was likely a principle he rarely physically sought, because he knew it occurred naturally.

Following MacKenzie's lead, it's better to let contrast evolve naturally rather than make it an intentional design effort. One's interpretation of contrast is subjective; The line drawn from what may be perceived as sufficient contrast to create interest and a random patchwork of design ideas is easy to cross. Contrast, like rhythm, should be sparingly utilized to avoid crossing that line.

12 The Principle of Emphasis

Emphasis - Effort or depth of expression that gives impressiveness or importance to something.

A single red apple is emphasized.
(Courtesy: Diego Vito Cervo)

Contrasting apples have no emphasis.
(Courtesy: Patrick Gainer)

The stone wall is the focal point.
(Courtesy: Hein Schlebusch)

The principles of Emphasis and Contrast are very similar, yet they have different parameters. Emphasis compares a single object (or group of objects) with multiple objects (or groups of objects), whereas Contrast relates to only two distinct objects (or groups of objects), both of which are presented equally. Visual interest may come from either principle, opening things up for interpretation (such as a football team boasting of two starting quarterbacks when, in reality, it probably doesn't have one).

The Principle of Emphasis, though, is more assertive, making a more dramatic statement. It focuses on what is known as a focal point to create its prominence. The focal point can be any one of the elements of design. Common characteristics tie the focal point to the other elements in the composition while establishing an emphatic statement.

For example, an area of turf will stand out among dense plantings, often commanding the landscape; One square (or block) among ten circles (or balls) will draw one's eye emphatically. One blue block, among ten red blocks, will similarly draw attention. Lastly, one smooth ball in a bucket of fifty spiked balls will likely be more desirable to a playful child. The emphasis of any of these elements can be amplified by adding a second contrasting characteristic such as enlarging the smooth ball or making its outer appearance more ornate.

Contrasting different characteristics of specific elements of design is the most obvious way to introduce the Principle of Emphasis. It can also be effective through the Principles of Isolation and Placement. *Emphasis by Isolation* physically separates an object from a group of similar objects, becoming the focal point by its intentional placement within a composition. The opposing principle of *Emphasis by Placement* entails the location of an object as a focal point within a group of the same objects, such as one green maple tree encircled by identical green maples. Although each tree is the same, one stands out because it's the center of attention.

The Principle of Dominance is often used interchangeably with the Principle of Emphasis but there is a subtle difference. Emphasis creates a pattern or movement in order to moderately influence the user. Dominance is used to completely occupy one's focus. A groundcover as a focal point within a lawn is emphasized; the Eiffel Tower as a focal point is one of the most dominant landmarks on the planet. The Principles of Emphasis and Dominance are utilized when the designer wants to make a strong statement within a design and it's the designer's task to create a focal point to aid in establishing that statement.

Donald Ross emphasized intentionally building up greens and *"surround them with mounds, as that is the only way they can be built to stand out distinctly on low, flat, land."*
(Courtesy: Tufts Archives)

By pure definition of *"giving impressiveness or importance to something,"* Emphasis seems most apropos when discussing the broad view aspects of course design, such as a golf architect's design philosophy or a particular golf course's overall theme. A golf course architect's design philosophy is what they repeatedly emphasize in their work. It may be an intentional verbal description such as a set of tenets, or it may be a number of trends they incorporate from course to course. Donald Ross's personal writings, entitled *Golf Has Never Failed Me* (compiled by Ron Whitten), is a rare look into his design approach. There are certain elements of his work he consistently emphasizes, such as visibility of hazards or making the first hole or two relatively friendly. He never uses the terms emphasis or design philosophy. Rather, he shares his design standards such as *Make each hole present a different problem"* and *"Build each hole in such a manner that it wastes none of the ground at my disposal, and take advantage of every possibility I can see."*

In his own words, Ross emphasizes the site over all else in his design work. He doesn't laud penal design over strategic design or use water strictly as an aesthetic feature. He emphasizes that *"each course must be original"* and *"each course must have strategies."* Ross gives priority to establishing green locations that *"give desirable, undulating surfaces."* His personal emphasis is rooted in finding the best golf holes possible.

Over the history of golf architecture, designers have declared specific philosophies as bullet points emphasizing their personal approach, such as John Low's "Principles of Golf Course Design" (as interpreted by Tom Simpson), MacKenzie's "Thirteen Essential Features of a Golf Course," or Macdonald's "Ingredients for an Ideal Golf Course." These writings all clearly emphasize what each designer thought was important in their design process.

Regarding my own design philosophy, I hope that readers by now have determined that I emphasize the natural lay of the land before almost everything else. Hopefully, again, they have also caught on that I strongly believe the placement of a hazard is to challenge, not penalize, the golfer. And, finally, that they have picked up on my embrace of form following function. These three concepts are the basis for my personal design philosophy and I try to emphasize them throughout my work.

But what details would a critic say Richard Mandell emphasizes to support this philosophy? One would notice I emphasize wide fairways that reflect the contour of the ground and provide the golfer with a reward of fairway beyond any successfully-negotiated hazards. I emphasize visibility of hazards and have a particular fondness for central hazards. These are all points of Emphasis that reflect my design philosophy. They are all items of which I give importance.

There is also the matter of using the Principle of Emphasis to *"give impressiveness or importance to something."* As they relate to Emphasis, impressiveness is a visual concept and importance follows along the lines of philosophy or theme. One definition of theme is *"a unifying or dominant idea or motif."* Course designers that choose to develop

Hole #12, Keller Golf Course in Maplewood, Minnesota. I've clearly got a thing for central hazards. (Courtesy: Richard Mandell Golf Architecture)

a theme for their golf course will certainly emphasize elements of design that help to express that theme, both visually and philosophically. One theme could simply be the restoration of an early architect's work. If emphasizing the work of Donald Ross, for example, certain bunkers may be remodeled with the details of a Ross bunker, such as a bulging face or flashed sand in certain instances. The details of Ross's design must take precedent over the restoring architect's personal preferences. Another theme could be a golf course that has been designed to be as difficult as possible, one that emphasizes narrow fairways and numerous hazards. On the opposite end, if playability was the theme, wider playing corridors with minimal hazards would be emphasized.

Themes can be quite literal as well. Replica golf courses promote copies of famous golf holes. Golf designer Bob Cupp once built a course where every feature was built with straight lines. My Easton Club project (in Easton, Maryland), which I co-designed with my former business partner, Mr. Bob Rauch, was based on incorporating historical events or local flora, fauna, and landmarks as a theme for each hole.

One of my favorite holes there, the fifth, is called "Cannonball." The theme for the hole was based on how the locals defended themselves against the British in the War of 1812. To protect themselves, they hung lanterns in the trees of their front yard to give the appearance the town was farther away than it actually was. As a result, the British fired their cannonballs over the town. The Cannonball hole includes a pair of bunker-mound features twenty yards short of the green. Their elevation gives the illusion that the green is closer than in reality. For visual effect, I dropped a pot bunker behind the green to represent the one cannonball that found someone's chimney.

Another Easton Club hole, the par-three eleventh, is named "Oyster Bar." The hole emphasizes one large bunker fronting the green with the mounds and fingers designed in such a way that only the tops of each finger of sand are visible. The visual from the tee is the illusion of multiple pot bunkers, each resembling an oyster.

Hole #5, "Cannonball", The Easton Club in Easton, Maryland.
(Courtesy: Richard Mandell Golf Architecture)

Hole #11, "Oyster Bar", The Easton Club in Easton, Maryland.
(Courtesy: Richard Mandell Golf Architecture)

A focal point utilized for emphasis in a landscape can be as simple as a specimen tree or a building, but the scale of a golf course makes a specific focal point harder to pinpoint. The natural focal point of a course is typically the central geologic or topographic feature of the site and should establish the theme of the routing. For instance, the focal point of Pebble Beach Golf Links is the Pacific Ocean. Through their re-routing of the golf course, Douglas Grant and Jack Neville emphasized the ocean by weaving a figure-eight layout, placing holes for both nines along the ocean.

Another geologic focal point is the quarry found at Merion Golf Club's East Course. Hugh Wilson gave the quarry a certain *"impressiveness and importance"* by routing the last three holes over and around the feature. At nearby Cobbs Creek Golf Course, Wilson emphasized the creek (and a tributary) that runs through and around holes two, four, five, nine, ten, eleven, and twelve, giving it great strategic importance.

At Creekside Golf & Country Club in Hiram, Georgia, I utilized a lake for emphasis in two different ways. The lake runs the length of the left side of the fourteenth hole, challenging the golfer to play as close as possible to the water in order to gain the shorter route. Surrounding the eighteenth hole's island green, the same lake is the determinant to either go for the green in two or lay up.

A more subtle example is the drumlin feature at Braemar Golf Course. That feature became the emphasis for what many would call the most memorable hole on the course, the par-three thirteenth with its green some eighty-five feet below the tee. Due to its location, the drumlin influenced the way many of the other holes unfolded as well. Simply put, I placed great emphasis on that one landform as the focal point for the entire routing.

The Principle of Emphasis utilizes specific hazards as focal points to grab the golfer's attention to possible opportunity or danger through strategic and heroic schools of design. By virtue of definition, emphasizing a specific hazard gives *"special importance"* to the architect's strategic intent. A bunker in the corner of a dogleg, for example, emphasizes the advantage of cutting the corner.

The 17th green at Merion Golf Club in Ardmore, Pennsylvania, sits at the base of a quarry. (Courtesy: Richard Mandell Golf Architecture)

Yet the penal school of thought does not strategically emphasize a specific hazard. In penal design, a bunker on both sides of a landing area compete for visual attention. They offer equal penalty as well. Consequently, the emphasis shifts to playing between the two hazards without a focal point to hone in on. Strategically, the architect doesn't emphasize either bunker.

Donald Ross made sure to emphasize natural water bodies in his work. *"Should your property happily have a brook running through it,"* he wrote, *"choice treatments can be secured by arranging one hole parallel with it and another so the drive or second shot must cross it."* Ross often used creeks as focal points to develop strategy, emphasizing a specific route to gain an advantage. He did this multiple times at the Country Club of Asheville in North Carolina, running holes parallel to creeks (such as five and seven) as well as playing over creeks (such as four, six and sixteen). I restored the previously piped creek diagonally crossing the tenth fairway to specifically emphasize the heroic nature of Ross's intended tee shot.

Hazards set at an angle to the line of play created by Robert Trent Jones, Sr. were the emphatic features in his promotion of the heroic school of design. These focal points lead the golfer to "bite off as much as one can chew" to gain the shortest route to the green. In most cases, the hazards that RTJ emphasized in his work are large lakes, emphasizing the risk-reward strategy of the hole to the golfer.

Throughout design and art, a focal point is utilized to draw visual attention. In golf architecture, a distant tree or landmark serves the same purpose, especially to aid a blind shot. "Son of Nylon Hill," a large mound that I created at Seaford Golf & Country Club's par-five ninth hole in Seaford, Delaware (now known as Hooper's Landing Golf Course), is a visual and strategic focal point. Visually, it pierces the horizon twelve feet above the flat landscape. Strategically, it's the landmark along the line of instinct if a player chooses to go for the green in two shots. For those laying

Hole #10, Country Club of Asheville in Asheville, North Carolina. Restoration of a creek that was piped for decades. (Courtesy: Richard Mandell Golf Architecture)

up, it's imperative to play the second shot far enough past the mound to gain a view of the green for the approach. The nickname comes from a similar mound on the course's original Alfred Tull-designed nine, and both are a nod to the adjacent DuPont textile fibers plant where nylon was first developed.

A more human scale mound that epitomizes the Principle of Emphasis is the one in the center of the seventeenth fairway at Yale Golf Course in New Haven, Connecticut. Not reachable from the tees, it visually bisects the green, creating a vertical break in front of a flat putting surface. The Principle of Emphasis is utilized by C.B. Macdonald and Seth Raynor through this simple feature as an aiming point for the approach. The mound is a perfect example of simplicity, yet it emphatically contrasts with the more manicured elements of the hole.

Early golf architects often emphasized a single mound as part of their green designs as well. Prior to the remodeling work that Robert Trent Jones Sr. did at Augusta National, the eleventh green was fronted with a mound on the right side of the approach, concealing much of the putting surface when played from that side. At North Oaks Golf Club, north of St. Paul, Minnesota, Canadian architect Stanley Thompson incorporated a similar mound at the front left of the first green. Smaller in scale than the one at Augusta's 11th, it's a great example of emphasis in design.

I can go on and on about singular mounds that speak to me (not literally) and enjoy placing them, scaled-up, in the middle of fairways or approaches. Although the ground game is harder to establish in the twenty-first century, the "specimen" mound placed along the line of play can still alter a golf ball upon landing, deflecting a slight miss in a variety of directions. Connecting a mound to an adjacent feature such as a putting surface further entrenches the hazard within the hole, adds an element of slope to the green, and provides some unity as well.

One of my favorite golf pictures that I have ever taken is of this mound visually bisecting Yale Golf Club's seventeenth green in New Haven, Connecticut, circa 1992. Two original bunkers at the base of this feature have since been restored, yet I like the emphatic appearance of the grasses better. (Courtesy: Richard Mandell Golf Architecture)

I incorporate the Principle of Emphasis differently (and more often) than the Principle of Contrast. For aesthetics, my use of emphasis incorporates the Principle of Balance. One example is visually balancing a single mound with a pair of bunkers on the opposite side of play. The mound is the clear point of emphasis, but it's balanced by two contrasting features.

Emphasis is the principle of design that forces the golfer's consideration strategically and visually. Recognizing which hazard the architect places the most emphasis on within the canvas of the golf hole will usually unlock the strategic intent for the shot at hand. Visually, it's used to develop aesthetic impressiveness in a more dramatic approach than the Principle of Contrast.

Yet the concept of emphasis stretches beyond the specifics of golf course design. Each designer's philosophy places emphasis on different aspects of the game, whether it's the influence of the ground, placing a premium on iron play over tee shots, or putting prowess. Whatever it may be that architects emphasize, the details of the architectural work support their approach.

13 The Principle of Movement

Movement - The process of moving or being transported from one physical location to another.

The Principle of Movement captures the eye at a particular point and conveys action along a specific pathway to another point. Designers and artists express Movement through the visual continuation of a line, whether it's literal or implied, to convey a sense of motion. In particular, the use of a diagonal line is most effective in establishing movement by diverting one's eyes in an unexpected direction rather than more predictable vertical or horizontal directions.

(Courtesy: Robert Keenan | Dreamstime.com)

Literal Movement occurs over time as the designer arranges certain elements in such a way as to move the user through a space. The eye will travel along an actual course such as a serpentine path or a straight line of trees (called *Dynamic Literal Movement*) or the eye will subconsciously connect comparable elements, acting as directional arrows, to move from point to point (called *Static Literal Movement*). Modifying certain Elements of Design (such as from large to small forms, dark to light colors, or square shapes to round shapes) can each act as directional arrows.

(Courtesy: Satori13 | Dreamstime.com)

Compositional Movement is to artwork what Literal Movement is to spaces. A photograph of children running through a park has movement built into the story being depicted; the viewer literally follows the same path the children are running along. This is *Dynamic Compositional Movement,* connecting elements of a composition through physical lines. In contrast, Leonardo da Vinci's Mona Lisa also expresses Compositional Movement.

The Element of Space directs the viewer from Mona Lisa's face downward and then toward the open landscape behind her. Known as *Static Compositional Movement*, the voids are connected with lines and forms expressing Mona Lisa's face.

In Static Compositional Movement, the separated elements' similarities make a connection regardless of their position in the arrangement. A composition of five rows of black squares and five columns of black squares needs just three or four red circles arranged in a specific pattern for the eye to move from the first red circle to the last red circle, regardless of their placement.

(Courtesy: Mrreporter | Dreamstime.com)

A case can be made that Movement is the primary principle of design with Balance, Contrast, Emphasis, and Rhythm all supporting principles. These devices allow the user to experience aspects of a composition differently, yet with the overarching goal of moving from one point to another. The movement of one's eyes between similar elements reveals balance. That same movement between disparities reveals contrast. Movement sends the user on a path toward focal points necessary to establish emphasis; and Movement leads the eye from the beginning to the end of a repeating pattern and that reveals rhythm. Almost all design involves the Principle of Movement, visually or literally.

When golf architects speak of movement of the ground, they are referring to how the landforms rise, fall, roll left and right, dip and tumble, etc., whether naturally occurring or manufactured. The primary failing of manufactured movement comes in too much landform repetition. In other words, constructed rolling ground often lacks variation in the height of peaks, depth of valleys, and breadth of each. An A-B-A-B manufactured repetition does not move as rhythmically as an A-B-C-D repetition in terms of natural land movement. In the case of replicating natural landforms, more variable repetition is better than less.

In golf design, Literal Movement applies to the tools an architect uses to move the golfer *strategically* from tee to green. Compositional Movement defines the *aesthetic* approach to the golf course landscape. It moves the golfer's eye from one point to another. For many golf course designers, visuals takes a front seat to strategy, utilizing the principles of design to highlight natural features or develop man-made features strictly for artistic value. Static Compositional Movement is developed by visual directional arrows that lead the golfer's eye through specific "snapshots" taken at different points of the golf hole. The arrows that create visual interest are usually sand, mounds, and water.

Compositional Movement directs the golfer's eye from tee to green through hazards at Interlachen Country Club's sixth hole in Edina, Minnesota. (Courtesy: Richard Mandell Golf Architecture)

Many designers use a heavy hand to make their statement, following a "more is better" philosophy rather than relying on subtle, discernible connections for visual interest. The aesthetics created through Compositional Movement may be great, but elements that make the game of golf interesting – risk/reward for certain shots, a variety of shot options, alternate routes of play – are neutralized. In some cases, the aesthetics are so overwhelming that the fairway itself is the device that moves the golfer from tee to green.

Hole #7, Keowee Key Golf & Country Club in Salem, South Carolina. Literal Movement, formed by static hazards along the line of instinct, move the golfer along multiple lines of charm. (Courtesy: Richard Mandell Golf Architecture)

Literal movement in golf course design is best created through connection. Standing on the teeing ground, a golfer relies on the architect's use of Dynamic Literal Movement to determine the best strategic route to take. The implied centerlines of the golf hole - from the straight line of instinct to the meandering line of charm - provide the range of options at the golfer's disposal. The line of instinct is a static continuous line moving from tee to green. The hazards that form the line of charm are also static, serving as visual cues for golfers to determine their own strategic path to the green. Yet the line of charm itself is a continuous connection of ground from tee to green defined through Dynamic Literal Movement. Literal Movement of the ground literally directs the ball from point to point, sometimes in a positive way and sometimes in a negative way.

Ground game challenges come through the literal movement of the ball along the landscape.
(Courtesy: Richard Mandell Golf Architecture)

An aerial game is quite literal in its meaning as well. From initial club contact to when the ball comes to its final resting spot, there is little contact with the ground. Equipment advances have allowed more and more golfers with less and less skill to hit the ball longer and longer and stop it quicker and quicker, rendering the movement of the ground irrelevant. We don't care how much traffic is on the roads during rush hour if we are flying over it 30,000 feet in the air, do we?

The distances golf balls can travel these days isn't what has caused challenges in course design; it's the carry of golf balls that has eliminated the ground game from the art of course architecture. In turn, the movement of the ground from a strategic perspective (literal) has become less important as the game moved to more of an aerial game (and more compositional).

Shotmaking is the ability of a golfer to be creative - in the face of architectural challenge - in order to control the flight of the ball through trajectory and the amount and direction of roll. An architect who considers shotmaking starts by creating movement on the ground plane, challenging the golfer to play a ball from a variety of lies and stances. Flat golf courses lack the variation in lies and stances necessary to develop a shotmaking repertoire. If every fairway is basically flat there are few, if any, uphill, downhill, or sidehill lies and stances for a golfer to deal with.

Charles Blair Macdonald once said *"The secret of most great golf holes is they all have some kind of a twist."* Whether he was talking about a figurative deviation from the norm strategically, or a literal twist in the contours of the ground, movement of the ground is crucial to his thesis. Shotmaking allows choices for covering a particular distance in different ways, such as fading or drawing the ball right or left. A golf architect who considers these opportunities along the way is using the Principle of Movement in a literal, yet strategic, way.

Unique characteristics of a golf hole, such as the contours in a fairway, that don't always allow the golfer to hit a standard shot demand creativity in shotmaking. The general direction of the land may require a left to right shot to avoid hazards and still stay on the fairway rather than a straight shot which may carry the hazard but end up in the rough. Targets which fall away from the intended line of flight in multiple directions promote shotmaking. Rather than a full seven-iron, for instance, bouncing a half-six iron into the green may be the better strategy to keep a ball from rolling off the back. A hole where judgment in distance is needed also favors shotmaking - playing as close to the target as possible for the next shot may not be the best approach.

Modern agronomic conditions that promote slow and soft playing conditions means the ball does not roll very far in the modern game. But with a comeback of fast and firm conditions, hazards which were strictly encountered from the air are coming back into play along the ground, corralling stray shots into hazards and bringing shotmaking back into the game.

Macdonald used sand bunkers as the center of larger collection areas, increasing the effectiveness of his hazards to catch shots that didn't directly land within the confines of a bunker (i.e., they rolled along an adjacent slope that fed the ball into the sand). Stray shots which were held up by wet, deep grass in recent decades again run hot through fairways into sand as he originally intended. Donald Ross incorporated "wing bunkers" to serve the same purpose around greens.

Hole #16, Raleigh Country Club in Raleigh, North Carolina.
Restored Ross wing bunkers corral stray shots. (Courtesy: McConnell Golf)

Ross did a great job of juxtaposing sand bunkers along the length of a golf hole both strategically and visually. A bunker left of the first landing area of a par five was contrasted with a fairway bunker to the right of the second landing area. He would then often place a bunker at the front left of the green and one to the middle right, moving the golfer's eyes from left to right and back again, using Movement to create Rhythm and Balance. That same bunker configuration creates an effective strategy as well, introducing Dynamic Movement to the design.

By contrast, a strategic tenet of Australian golf course designer Walter Travis was to tighten up his targets the closer a player got to the green. He would use bunkers as elements to point the golfer toward a target that seemed smaller from farther away. A wide fairway would be visually reduced by converging bunkers past the landing area on both sides. Travis's use of the Principle of Movement created a two-point visual perspective using hazards and the fairway as vanishing points to create a diminishing target.

Hole #15, Tanglewood Championship Course in Clemmons, North Carolina. Like Walter Travis's approach, this restored Robert Trent Jones bunker configuration moves the eye to the green by diminishing the perspective to the green. (Courtesy: Richard Mandell Golf Architecture)

The Principle of Movement is possibly the most visual principle of golf course architecture. Yet it can also be the one that creates the most clutter on a golf course. Utilizing hazards such as bunkers or water to create visual movement can easily cross the line to chaos. The golf course architect with that "eye for design," however, understands when too much movement overwhelms a composition versus just enough movement for visual interest *and* strategic challenge. Over-manipulation of the ground plane will visually stifle the golfer's senses, whether through shaping of the land or with numerous hazards that shift one's eyes among multiple focal points.

Equal measures of literal (strategic) movement and compositional (visual) movement is the exception rather than the rule. It's the highest level of exception, though, reserved for the best golf courses in the world. Successful incorporation of both strategic and visual movement as ranking criteria would separate the better courses. Utilizing the Principles of Balance, Contrast, Emphasis, and Rhythm to develop Movement in golf course design will create a golf course with just enough visual interest to avoid distraction yet encourage challenge at the same time.

14 THE PRINCIPLE OF PROPORTION

PROPORTION - A COMPARATIVE RELATIONSHIP BETWEEN ONE PART OF A WHOLE TO ANOTHER PART OF A WHOLE OR TO THE WHOLE ITSELF.

Most people accept that scale and proportion are one and the same because they are comparative relationships, yet they are actually distinct. Scale compares the size of one object specifically to other objects within the same space. Proportion compares the various parts of an object to other parts of the object or to the entire object itself. For example, a 250-square-foot galley kitchen would be out of proportion within a 4,000-square-foot house. Inversely, a 2,500-square-foot kitchen within that same house may also be out of proportion.

Designers use the Element of Scale as a tool when placing different objects in a composition. Proportion is a principle that designers follow to express a specific message. For instance, determining what size of a kitchen would be in proportion makes this principle a challenge to properly express. Proportion is mostly a comfort-inducing visual concept not even noticed until something "seems" out of proportion.

Proportion relates why there is too much kitchen (red) in a house or not enough, for example.
(Courtesy: Patrick Gainer)

Human Proportion relates how the size of certain body parts relate to the body as a whole. It has been the standard to evaluate design proportion through mathematical relationships for centuries. The Roman architect Vitruvius was the first to study human proportions from an aesthetic standpoint and incorporate them into his design work. He observed that although there was a great difference between the size of people's legs, arms, and torsos, a relationship was established between body parts that was consistent from person to person regardless of specific measurements.

Vitruvius believed proportional relationships of human body parts to each other - and to the entire body itself - were the best examples of proportion on earth and should be the standard when evaluating proportion throughout nature. Da Vinci expressed his ideal proportions of the human body through his "Vitruvian Man" sketch, giving credit to his Roman predecessor.

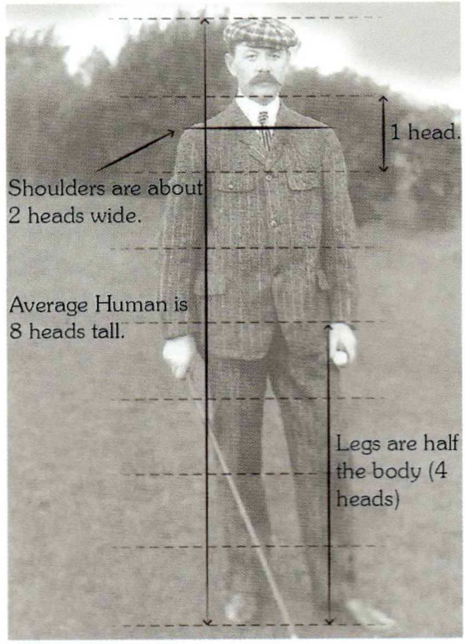

Body proportions are consistent from person to person regardless of measurements. (Courtesy: Patrick Gainer)

Using natural proportions such as those suggested by Vitruvius will convey shapes and sizes accepted by most as realistic expressions of a subject. For example, a person's overall height averages out to 7.5 times the length of one's head. Because this is the average, we condition ourselves to find this relationship proportionately pleasing. We are most comfortable with the appearance derived from this relationship because we have seen it more often than not. Those who choose to deviate from these universal ideals will create an unrealistic composition. Picasso often manipulated the rule of proportion to express his subjects in an abstract way; Renoir stuck to the more Vitruvian example to express more realistic subjects in his impressionist paintings.

A few centuries before Vitruvius' work, the Greek mathematician Euclid devised what came to be known as the "Golden Ratio", a formula stating that **A + B is to C** just as **A is to B** to create the perfect proportional ratio of 1.6810:1. In other words, when the longer segment of a line constitutes 61.80% of the line and the smaller segment of the line is 61.80% of the length of the larger segment, these line segments are in the perfect proportional relationship to each other and to the entire line. The Golden Ratio eventually became the gold standard for creating perfect proportions in design, art, architecture, etc. Based on that success, Euclid followed up with his Golden Rectangle, in which the ratio of the longer side to the shorter side is the same ratio as the Golden Ratio.

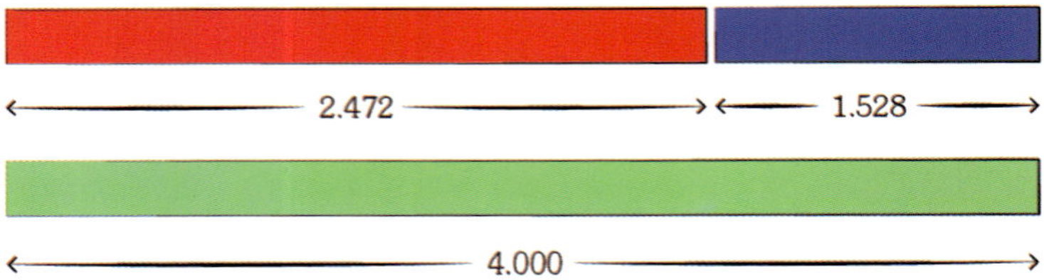

$$\frac{2.472}{1.528} = \frac{4.000}{2.472} = 1.618$$

The Golden Ratio Illustrated (Courtesy: Patrick Gainer)

Universally, artists and designers alike have concluded that the Euclidean Theory of proportion is as good a litmus test for "proper proportion" as any. For example, to create proportion in a landscape design, rather than randomly assigning dimensions to a rectangular outdoor space, a landscape architect may choose to determine one dimension based on site constraints and adjust the secondary dimension to 68% the size of the first dimension in order to develop the best visual proportions.

So how does one recognize *good* proportion versus *bad* proportion beyond simply accepting theories passed down from theorists like Euclid and Vitruvius? Beyond their approaches, determining "proper" proportion falls into the category of "Beauty is in the eye of the beholder." Once again, those with a good eye for design usually have proportion figured out in their artistic efforts. Through transitive logic, someone whose design work is accepted as successful (meaning: people like it) has most likely conquered the challenge of creating a well-proportioned object, work of art, sculpture, outdoor space, etc.

Using the Golden Ratio to break a subject into minor and major areas of design creates visual interest through pleasing proportions. When the differences are vast, proportion isn't achieved. A 10:1 ratio is too great of a difference to overcome.

At the end of the day, the difference between scale and proportion is subtle, yet absolute. Objects are either in scale or they're not. The Principle of Proportion, though, allows a designer to manipulate an object's dimensions to convey a certain message. Designers who utilize proportion to express realism or abstraction are simply expressing philosophy, with no right or wrong approach.

Alister MacKenzie once said that to be a great golf architect one *"Must have a sense of proportion above all else."* MacKenzie definitely did. A case can be made that the evolution of golf architecture is defined by the utilization (or lack thereof) of the Principle of Proportion. The utilitarian period of golf course design spanned roughly the last two decades of the nineteenth century, leading to what golf architect Tom Simpson referred to as the "dark ages of golf architecture." This period was the first time golf courses were intentionally designed and built. One of the qualities those early layouts lacked was a sense of proportion.

Many feel the Victorian design aesthetic was an influence on early courses. The addition of superfluous ornament to buildings (with no connection to the building on which it's placed) is the architecture equivalent to random placement of penal hazards (with no connection to the ground on which they are placed) in course design.

Many of the late nineteenth-century courses were created by Scottish golf professionals without qualifications for doing so, such as Tom Dunn and Willie Park, Sr. They were pioneers in the field of course design. Simpson describes the first manufactured golf course greens as *"invariably oblong, round or square, supported by railway embankment sides or batters" and* guarded by rectangular bunkers resembling coffins.

If these golf professionals sought inspiration in design, they most likely turned to commonalities of the Victorian period in which they lived. Platform greens and coffin bunkers undoubtedly mirror the rectangular flower beds that were the dominant feature of the Victorian style. Because the Victorian element of the gardenesque style focused on single plants for emphasis, there was little unity among plant materials and geometric beds overpowered the landscape.

One cannot be certain the Dunns and Parks were actually influenced in this way. But their connection to Musselburgh, a suburb of Edinburgh, most likely exposed them to the Victorian gardenesque style more so than the grand parks of Capability Brown and William Kent evolving in England at the same time. Less than a mile from their home course of Musselburgh Golf Links is the very gardenesque-style Inveresk Lodge Gardens, established in 1683. Another gardenesque influence is Harmony Garden (1807), found thirty miles to the south in Melrose. Both landscapes are dominated by geometric forms, which may explain the utilitarian design style adopted by these early Musselburgh professionals.

Rectangular flower beds of Inveresk Lodge Gardens.
(Courtesy: National Trust for Scotland)

Again according to Simpson, sand bunkers possessing *"rectangular ramparts of a peculiarly obnoxious type, stretching at regular intervals across the course and having no architectural merit whatever"* dominated the world's first designed courses. The possibility that Dunn and others may have taken exact measurements of such geometric forms within an enclosed property such as Inveresk, just to transpose them to open landscapes, may explain the lack of proportion in their work. But those dimensions that fit so well within a residential setting as plant beds are conversely swallowed up within a wide open space and a never-ending horizon line as sand bunkers.

Bunkers laid out by J. H. Taylor at Cassiobury, circa 1906, known today as West Herts Golf Club in Rickmansworth, England. (Courtesy: Country Life)

Golf Architect Charles Alison confirmed that hazards were built to exact specifications and passed on from designer to designer in those days: *"The construction of these courses was simple in the extreme. There was only one form of bunker. This consisted of a rampart built of sods with a trench in front of it. The face of the rampart was perpendicular. It was precisely three feet, six inches in height throughout, and ran at an exact right-angle to the line of play. The fairways were invariably rectangular, and the putting greens were square and flat. It will be realized that this stereotyped placing of bunkers rendered the game monotonous."*

Tom Dunn and his contemporaries had little to go by at the time (other than, one would like to think, the links courses they learned the game on). Restricting themselves to specific dimensions and shapes without any site adjustments (adjusting scale) meant proportions could not be consistent from feature to feature or site to site. They simply lacked the ability to translate the space-constricted Victorian gardenesque details to open fields for golf.

The concept of proportion wasn't a consideration in the United States originally, either. But as the golf architecture profession developed, the Principle of Proportion developed as well by following nature's lead and adopting Euclid's theories. Geometric features as a design trend faded away as architects like Willie Park, Junior, Herbert Fowler, and Harry Colt arrived on the scene. These "heathland" designers were the first to create features in proper proportion to a wooded setting, something much easier to accomplish than developing pleasing proportions on open linksland.

The enlightenment of the Golden Age of golf architecture introduced the Principle of Proportion in equal measures of strategy and aesthetics. By this time, use of the Golden Ratio to develop pleasing proportions (in a subconscious way) was standard fare in designing courses that appear pleasant to the eye. The use of the Golden Ratio is as good a reason to crown this era as the "Golden Age" as any other.

James Braid's bunkering on the par-three 9th at Stinchcombe Hill Golf Club in Dursley, England, circa 1933, is in proportion with the surrounding countryside. (Courtesy: Sutton and Sons, Ltd.)

MacKenzie sized his bunkers to be in proportion with the sandy landscape at Cypress Point Club in California, as evidenced by the green complex of the seventh hole. (Courtesy: The Bancroft Library)

Yet by the mid twentieth-century, architects like Robert Bruce Harris and James Harrison focused more on aesthetic balance than proportion, equally locating bunkers of the same size on either side of a target. Unsurprisingly, they were not considered very visual designers and while not on the level of Tom Simpson's "dark ages," they didn't produce many memorable layouts. Whereas golden-age architects utilized proportion to convey a sense of naturalness, many subsequent architects expressed proportion from a compositional standpoint, much like a painting.

Hole #10, Beechmont Country Club in Beachwood, Ohio. Not exactly the Golden Ratio, but Euclid may say this composition of green and bunker has good proportion. (Courtesy: RMGA)

The Principle of Proportion may be the most difficult one to master. That's because when proportion is off, someone notices and when it's not, it usually passes undetected. In that regard, the user is always the subjective judge. The absence of proportion in golf design is the loudest indicator of a poor designer, one who has yet to develop the ability to implement the Golden Ratio through sheer awareness or even measuring out some multiple of 1.6810 as part of the process.

15 The Principle of Unity

Unity – The wholeness or completeness of a composition; the state of being one.

Unity and harmony are very similar principles of design, often considered interchangeable. Although "completeness" can be used to characterize both unity and harmony, there is a subtle difference: Unity is defined as *a state of being one* and Harmony is *a pleasing arrangement of parts.*

The elements of form, shape, line, texture, pattern, and color all work together to achieve unity. The Principle of Movement often takes the lead through repetition of elements to create a sense of order, consistency, and completion. When the repetition of elements is connected successfully, the eye moves smoothly from one element to another without interruption. For example, unity loses its impact when multiple groups of plants are spread out so far that the eye cannot make the connection. Yet filling the gaps with similar elements creates a unified composition.

Separating groupings of plants too far apart establishes a clear division of elements. Adding additional elements in between will create enough movement to ensure that unity is achieved. (Courtesy: Patrick Gainer)

Like much in design, the subjectivity of harmony may be argued, yet the subjectivity of unity can't be argued; There is either the state of being whole or not. If all the parts of a composition relate to each other they create a unified whole, making the sum greater than its individual parts rather than an assortment of parts that are disconnected from each other. Harmony occurs when the parts that make up such wholeness are "pleasing to the eye." A composition may be unified, but it may not be all that pleasing.

The Principle of Harmony is simply the Principle of Unity done well. It engages the user just enough to avoid over-stimulation, resulting in a sense of calmness and satisfaction that can also express a positivity that eases tension. Absent harmony, human reaction is one of unease. Harmony achieves equilibrium between variety and unity that's neither chaotic nor boring. The key to harmony is an added dose of variety that moves a composition from simple unity to one that has its own personality through visual and intellectual interest.

The stairs above are unified through color but lack harmony.
(Courtesy: Socrates | Dreamstime.com)

The stairs below achieves harmony through color and shape of the stairs.
(Courtesy: Sergiy Mashchenko)

Color is the Element of Design that's most associated with the Principle of Harmony. Colors sitting side by side on a color wheel are considered in harmony with each other. In an overall composition, be it a painting or the interior of a house, color harmony is created through no more than six or seven that develop a single palette (a range of colors). The repetitive use of a single color a few times throughout a composition also creates harmony. This is called "Color Jump," leading the viewer to move from one point to another through a unified element. Harmony can also be achieved through the Element of Shape, stressing the similarities of all parts or how the shape of one feature fits or mirrors the shape of an adjoining feature.

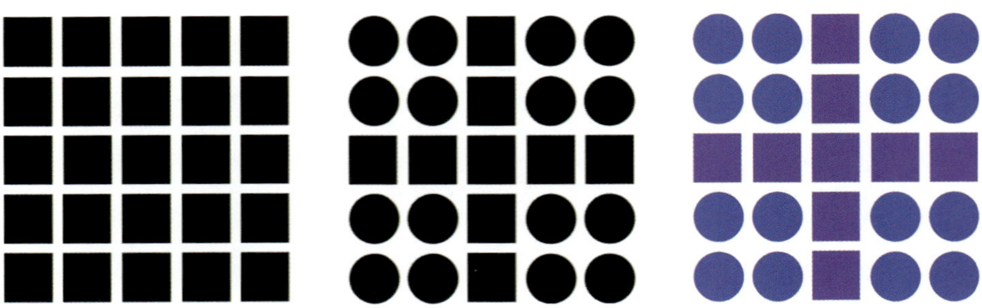

A composition can be simply unified by a single repetitive element (left); The same composition can be unified *and* pleasing to the eye (harmony) by adding additional shapes, such as circles (center); Adding a third element to the composition (color) can achieve even more harmony.
(Courtesy: Patrick Gainer)

Unity and harmony, however, don't just happen by accident. A good designer knows that unity is achieved when none of the individual elements within a composition seem to compete with each other. The overall goal of the design is clearly communicated and a feeling of completion and organization is achieved. When there are no distractions, either through inclusion or absence, harmony is achieved and a satisfying sense of belonging and relationship is created.

The most challenging conundrum in golf course design is the conflict between designing holes that are distinct from each other yet inherently connected as part of a complete golf course. In golf architecture, the Principle of Unity is the tool that the golf architect uses to tie each hole's individuality to all the other holes.

Hole #7 White, Army Navy Country Club in Fairfax, Virginia. Unity is achieved through the consistent bunker style from hole to hole as well as the connection provided by Daniel's Run Creek through the grounds and its plantings. (Courtesy: Richard Mandell Golf Architecture)

Consistency and connection are the keys to establishing unity on a golf course. By default, the Element of Nature is what unifies a golf course. Every hole sits on top of the land and relies on the landforms for strategic and visual interest. The land physically connects the previous green to the next tee. Although the land logically (and literally) unifies the holes, whether it's done well or not is another story. Harmony exists between the land and the golf course when holes are natural extensions of the topography. In other words, when the land dictates the design, the entire golf course is connected to the ground through harmony. But if the design dictates the land and one must alter the ground so much to make the holes fit, there is a lack of unity and harmony. For example, when one hole takes on such special focus that the topography is changed so drastically to awkwardly fit all the other holes, the course loses its connection to the ground and loses unity.

The most direct way to create unity in golf architecture is by developing one specific design style, sometimes as underlying trends and other times capturing the spirit of the place, such as links or parkland design. Yet these styles are often erroneously implemented, such as an American links-style course that isn't actually on linksland. Typically attributed to a wind-swept, treeless site, a course described as a links that isn't on sandy soil is technically not a links course. Often overwatered and lush to attract golfers, its ground game options are muted, missing the fast and firm conditions that are the very essence of links style. In reality, the openness of the site is the unifying characteristic, not the links concept itself.

Pebble Beach Golf Links is not actually a links course because of the presence of trees and its setting far above the Pacific Ocean. (Courtesy: Richard Mandell Golf Architecture)

One of the lesser-known facts about Augusta National Golf Club is the naming of each golf hole for a tree or shrub, preserving its heritage as a plant nursery prior to its conversion to a golf course by Bobby Jones and Alister MacKenzie. But the concept is ineffective as a theme because eighteen different plants do not create Unity as much as the azaleas and rhododendrons throughout the course. The conditioning of Augusta's holes is what achieves Unity more than anything else, followed closely by the appearance of the bunkers.

The utilization of replica golf holes (copies of famous golf holes) is a great example of a lack of unity. It should come as no surprise when one encounters playing a replica of Amen Corner followed by the island green seventeenth of TPC Sawgrass that a feeling of unease and disconnection occurs. But when a famous hole is replicated in such a way that the hole's elements are found on other holes, unity can still be maintained.

C. B. Macdonald's National Golf Links of America is the first example of replication and may still be the best. He incorporated copies of many of his favorites in the British Isles, such as the Road hole, Sahara hole, and Redan hole. He also created a few that have become famous in their own right, such as his Cape hole. Yet his work at National is far from disjointed. Knowing full well that his inspiration came from numerous sources far from Long Island, he did not exactly replicate his golf holes. Rather, he modeled each of his holes at NGLA to be *"representative and classic in itself."* Macdonald tied his original holes to the replicated holes through common elements such as similar bunkering. More natural-appearing than his subsequent efforts, the consistent use of simple bunker and bunker-island shapes helped unify the holes.

Whenever Macdonald built replica holes, the design concepts of his copies were consistent yet fitted into each landscape, utilizing the existing topography to unify each course despite adapting foreign features. The locations of hazards were always in the same relative locations strategically, but the details were adapted to fit within the golf course site. At NGLA's fourth hole, for example, he didn't replicate the wooden retaining walls that support the bunkers on the original Redan hole found at North Berwick. And at the seventh – a replica of the Road hole at the Old Course at St. Andrews (17th) – Macdonald placed sand behind the green instead of something similar to the Old Station Road behind the original. He also built his replicas to fit the elevations of each site rather than undertake a massive earthmoving operation to create exact copies.

The geometric design style Macdonald eventually moved toward is the most consistently distinct of all golden-age golf architects, which allowed the implementation of his own replica holes at each course to be so seamless. Adopting an angular, grass-faced look to his bunkering (which effectively conceals the sand from view) and the right-angle slopes amid squarish greens, unifies each of his courses. Macdonald's proteges, Seth Raynor and Charles Banks sometimes used similar approaches.

Sand behind the seventh green at the National Golf Links of America in New York represented the road behind the Old Course's #17 green. (Courtesy: Richard Mandell Golf Architecture)

As illustrated by Macdonald's and Raynor's efforts, the most evident way to create unity throughout a golf course is the connection of specific sand bunker styles from hole to hole. A golf course which limits itself to even a single bunker style (such as pots) with subtle variation in line, shape, and even form can develop unity successfully, leading to harmony. Varying the radii of each pot bunker or their overall shapes is a strategy that can achieve that harmony. But if the pots are all the same size, shape, and depth, or they are limited to just front left and front right of every green, monotony will overtake unity.

Seth Raynor wasn't as beholden to right-angled features as his mentor, yet his geometric leanings still brought unity to his design work such as the 12th at Shoreacres Club in Lake Bluff, Illinois. (Courtesy: Richard Mandell Golf Architecture)

One style that creates strong unity is minimalist design. Blowout bunkering seems to be in vogue everywhere - cut into stark landscapes of roughly-graded ground dotted by wild grasses. An attempt to recapture the links roots of the game (to its detriment), the same look is adapted on sand and clay, in the south and north, on open land and even on parkland sites.

What should be a great example of the Genius of the Place turned into a different vanilla-ization of golf architecture, albeit much more visually impressive and distinct than the mid-to late twentieth century attempts at large-scale design shrouded in perfect conditioning. The minimalist movement's attempt at unity works, but harmony falls short because a false landscape is created many times over.

Because the ground is the primary unifying element for individual holes, it's not so imperative that hazard, fairway, and green shapes have unifying forms, especially because they all have different functions. But a hole loses unity when each tee varies in shape, unless that variation comes from those topographic constraints. For instance, it's poor design to have a square tee, a rectangular tee, a round tee, and a free-form tee all on the same hole, particularly on flat ground. But if each tee box varies in shape because of topography, unity is maintained through that connection to the ground.

Hole #7 Blue, Army Navy Country Club in Arlington, Virginia. Incorporating square and rectangular teeing grounds from hole to hole is one example of achieving unity. (Courtesy: Richard Mandell Golf Architecture)

With almost any flat piece of property, the golf architect is faced with the prospect of monotony. For instance, each green may need to be raised the same elevation above grade for drainage purposes, rendering every approach identical. The same may be said of tee boxes and bunkers. In those cases, the land cannot be relied on as the primary element to unify golf holes so a creative design touch is critical to avoid what may appear to be necessary sameness.

Creating unity through the Element of Line is achieved most effectively when grassing lines tie features to each other. A fairway line unifies a golf hole by simply connecting the tee complex to the green complex, even if there is an interruption of rough between. When a fairway line flows seamlessly around a bunker line, both features create visual unity.

Strategically, a fairway line should run to the outside of the bunker as it approaches, swing tightly around it and then turn back toward that same outer edge on the other side. That way the fairway and bunker are working together to challenge the golfer. But when a fairway line simply runs straight past a bunker mired in rough, there is both a lack of visual and strategic unity.

The color palette on a golf course never really goes beyond four or five shades of green or brown, making color an essential element in achieving unity (and harmony). Although each golf course feature may possess a different shade of green from hole to hole, unity through color is still achieved. Utilizing the same grasses for each golf course feature not only makes for consistent playing conditions, it also assures a seamless connection for all eighteen holes. Individual native areas full of browns and creams connect golf holes as well. They unify even more effectively when they span multiple holes. That said, inconsistent playing conditions can disrupt

Holes #2 & 3, The Country Club of Asheville in Asheville, North Carolina. Creating one fairway for two holes is one way to introduce unity. (Courtesy: Richard Mandell Golf Architecture)

unity just as easily. If one hole has no rough but the next one is surrounded by U. S. Open-like rough, the golfer may exhibit the feeling of unease that comes with a lack of order and consistency. Erratic green speeds and varying bunker sand conditions can lead to frustration and unity is lost.

The enjoyment a golfer experiences on a golf course can often be traced to the Principle of Unity. If the golfer enjoys the day, some sort of unifying element helped formulate that opinion, even if they can't specifically pinpoint what it was that made the round so enjoyable. The odds are high that the Principle of Unity applied to the Elements of Design led the golfer to that conclusion. The phrase "the sum of the whole is greater than its parts" certainly applies to such an experience and the Principle of Unity paves the way to achieve that sum. Similar lines, forms, and shapes applied differently from hole to hole create unity and if done well, the golfer has another reason to enjoy the day from the from the first tee to the eighteenth green.

Hole #2, Orangeburg Country Club in Orangeburg, South Carolina.
(Courtesy: Richard Mandell Golf Architecture)

16 The Principle of Variety

Variety - The quality or state of being different or diverse; the absence of uniformity, sameness, or monotony.

Variety comes from the word vary, meaning *"to change or alter, as in form, appearance, character, or substance."* The concept of variety is simple enough: Creating multiple lines that are different, multiple circles that are different, multiple balls that are different, multiple colors that differ, or multiple patterns that are different. Creating those differences in the Elements of Design comes through the application of the Principle of Variety.

Variety is the easiest principle for artists, designers, lawyers, actors, athletes, teachers, and every other walk of life to understand. Its simplicity and versatility is why *"Variety is the spice of life."* Variety makes everything feel good, taste good, look good. Without variety, boredom can set in as one's eye repeatedly makes the same observations. With no change from object to object, the eye ceases to engage in the process and a composition loses visual interest.

Variety is derived through juxtaposition: Placing elements with contrasting characteristics side by side. But isn't that what the Principle of Contrast does? Or Emphasis? Doesn't Rhythm happen when a variable breaks up the repetition in a pattern? Variety is the tool that executes *all* those principles. Variety provides the varying elements among objects for contrast and emphasis to succeed. Although emphasis is used to lead the user from point A to point B, variety keeps them engaged in the process. Variety makes rhythm happen as well. A-A-A-A A-A is not a rhythm; it's a sound. A-B-A-B A-B adds a different sound, creating a rhythm, but one that has little staying power. It's a "tick-tock." Adding a third variant to create A-B-C-A-B-C provides a more defined rhythm and better engagement with an audience. One note is emphasis; two notes is contrast; three notes is variety.

Rhythm and contrast can work hand in hand to allow variety to do its best job. Repeating two elements through alternation establishes a rhythmic base for a design and ties things together for unity's sake. Adding opposing elements for contrast is the variable that creates enough visual interest for variety's sake.

When the principle of Variety is applied to specific forms, the intellectual interest of its function increases also. For example, a child will quickly become bored of a game which involves just one task. A restaurant will fail if there is just one menu item. Creating variety in the way a specific object performs will provide more value.

When designers place juxtaposed elements together, they are developing variety for visual interest. Straight lines working in conjunction with curving lines will engage the audience more than straight lines alone. Yet an assortment of line weights, angles, or lengths can still lend variety to a composition of straight lines. A mix of shapes that vary in color or size attracts more attention than an assortment of shapes of the same color and size.

At some point, though, too much variation ceases to create variety and moves toward chaos, which is where mastering the Principle of Variety becomes the challenge. Whereas too much repetition will lose one's audience to monotony, too much contrast will dilute repetition, moving variety closer to chaos. Moving in either direction results in a lack of focus.

Each person's capacity to avoid chaos is different, so the cross-over from variety to chaos is somewhat of a moving target depending on the audience or medium. The best designers understand how to avoid that crossover. An artist who flourishes in abstract art can get away with more variety than a school building architect who must create a relaxed atmosphere to promote focus and concentration among students.

The "eye" for design takes over when discerning how and when to avoid variety for variety's sake. One doesn't just incorporate differing elements to a design just to mix it up. Rather, the best designers intentionally utilize variety to develop contrast, emphasis, rhythm and unity for a specific purpose. They understand how to straddle the line between variety and chaos.

A variety of curved lines (left) turns to chaos with too much color (right). (Courtesy: Patrick Gainer)

Baseball, basketball, football, soccer, and tennis all have specific dimensions for their playing fields. Other than the number of holes, there are very few hard and fast dimensions found on a golf course. In fact, there may be only one: the four and one-quarter-inch diameter of the cup. Beyond that, anything goes, meaning the Principle of Variety is in all its glory when it comes to golf courses.

That said, it's difficult to cross the line from variety to chaos in golf architecture. That's because there are a finite number of holes per course, precluding a golfer from experiencing such variation that it becomes a distraction. There are also only par threes, fours, and fives (with a very rare six). The playing fields of golf can be as varied as one's imagination, but that variety will always be tempered by these limitations, balancing endless design possibilities with the structure of the game.

In describing exceptional golf course sites, the common denominator they all possess is variety. Every great golf course has its own rhythm derived from the variety of golf holes it possesses. The fantastic rhythm of Donald Ross's routing of Seminole comes in the various ways he uses the ridges across the property. A variation in topography far outweighs deserts of sand or oceans of water. Wholesale earthwork simply cannot replace the variety of land forms that come from nature. An assortment of knobs, knolls, plateaus, swales, saddles, hollows, and ridges stretching across a piece of ground are the features that the best courses possess.

Herbert Fowler's sixth hole at Eastward Ho! Club in Chatham, Massachusetts, has a great variety of landforms as well as vistas. (Courtesy: Richard Mandell Golf Architecture)

The greats of golf architecture all consider the Principle of Variety as the most important one of all, especially when considering the land itself. Alister MacKenzie was among those that led the way: *"Variety in golf is everything and undulations provide this variety."* He is not alone:

> C. B. Macdonald: *"Variety is not only the spice of life, but it is the very foundation of golfing architecture - diversity in nature is universal."*
>
> Harry Colt: *"What we want to have is variety, gained by utilizing all the best natural features of the land, and alternating the holes of various lengths."*

Variety in golf architecture always starts with site selection. It's the step in the process when a designer can lean more toward chaos because more variety in landforms ensures that the best golf holes can be discovered. The potential for strategy created by the natural details of the ground will increase proportionately.

A variety of uphill, downhill, and flat golf holes, a variety of straight, dogleg-left, and dogleg-right holes; even a variety of hole distances, can all be realized within a site, provided one takes full advantage of the landforms. A variety of landforms not only allows for eighteen distinct (and varied) golf holes, it ensures many natural opportunities for drainage as well.

A site varied enough in size and shape allows for a variety of hole directions, the incorporation of wind, and the avoidance of the sun when needed (beginning and/or finishing holes played into the sun). Four par-three holes that play in four compass directions elevate a routing every time. The same is true of par fives. Generally speaking, a square-shaped property will yield more variety than a more linear piece of property.

In golf architecture, visual interest comes through aesthetic variety and intellectual interest comes through strategic variety. In fact, the very concept of golf course strategy is based on the Principle of Variety: Architects juxtapose alternative routes for the golfer to choose. The formula I utilize to describe the value of strategic variety is:

Strategy = Challenge = Options = Choices = Repeat Play

It's a simple enough mantra to follow. If strategic options exist, the golfer will have a variety of choices to play a particular hole. If one approach fails on a Monday, there is every incentive to try another route on Tuesday. With plenty of width to a golf hole, the odds are good that another crack at the hole on Wednesday and yet another on Thursday will be in the cards as well. Without strategic options, a lack of intellectual interest will discourage repeat play, something all successful golf course operators thrive on. That incorporation of width is the most important requisite to create intellectual interest in golf architecture. MacKenzie's sketch of the fourteenth hole of the Old Course at St. Andrews is a textbook example.

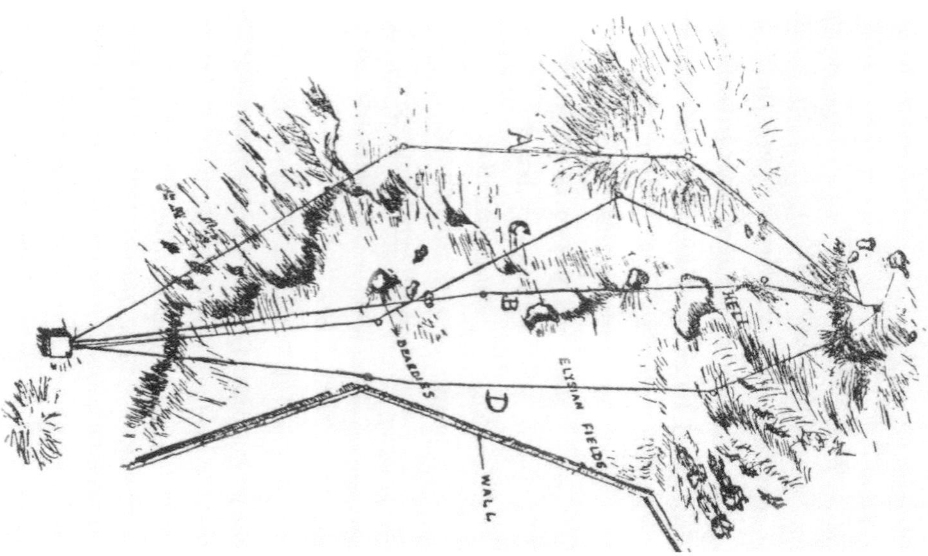

Sketch from MacKenzie's *Golf Architecture* from 1920.
(Courtesy: Simpkin, Marshall, Hamilton, Kent, & Co.)

Two of MacKenzie's "Essential Features of a Golf Course" directly address the Principle of Variety. The first addresses hole lengths: *"There should be a large proportion of good two-shot holes, two or three drive and pitch holes, and at least four one-shot holes."* Variety in hole lengths should be on every architect's checklist. Although difficult to accomplish on rolling ground, a variety of lengths should be automatic on flat land.

Length variety is challenging when trying to maintain variation from each set of tees. Yet that doesn't mean different golfers with different talents can't play from different tee boxes to experience even more variety of options. The traditional limits of a par three, four, and five can be expanded by placing tee markers between standard distances, in essence creating par 2 ½, 3 ½, and 4 ½ holes as a change of pace.

The second of MacKenzie's two features addresses shot type: *"There should be an infinite variety in the strokes required to play the various holes - interesting brassy shots, iron shots, pitch and run-up shots."* Shotmaking promotes variety in golf architecture by offering different approaches to the same length of shot: For example, 150 yards can be covered with a draw, a straight shot, or a fade as well as with a variety of trajectories. Greens perched above a fairway, greens set flush to the approach, and punchbowl greens can add great variety to shotmaking.

MacKenzie's fourth at Pasatiempo Golf Course, in Santa Cruz, California, is a great shotmaker's hole. It's best approached with a right-to-left tee shot to avoid a tough angle from the right when the flagstick is on that side. A left-to-right second shot will be the best way to access the hole location. The opposite strategies are needed when the flagstick is on the left.
(Courtesy: Richard Mandell Golf Architecture)

I'm sure most golf architects, past and present, would claim the importance of variety in golf course architecture. Yet not everyone can execute in the field, carefully straddling the somewhat vague line between variety and chaos. Shaping of golf features is where that line is most evident and crossed the most. By sheer function, the golf course shaper is tasked with altering the land from one condition to another. In describing his work at The National Golf Links of America, Macdonald said, *"Where nature was deficient, it would have to be improved on artificially."* Those in the shaping profession can hardly be blamed for their zealousness to perform the task at hand. On flat ground it's necessity, but on undulating ground one must proceed with caution.

If one is determined to re-shape existing landforms to suit preconceived ideas, natural variety is lessened while chaos is increased. The shaping process becomes the focal point more than the site itself. Shaping simply to *"create"* variety leads to chaos more often than not. Nature's work will always be better.

Shaping of the hillside behind this green distracts from the hole as well as the natural topography.
(Courtesy: Richard Mandell Golf Architecture)

Over-shaping is an issue in the number of features being created as well as in the actual shaping of those features. A line of five mounds standing sentinel along a fairway is overkill. But when the exact dimensions of each are the same, the visual is particularly galling. A course that's full of manufactured features that have no function beyond decoration misses the target. They become too much for the human mind to process and chaos settles in. Chaos and over-production go hand in hand in destroying any attempt at Variety. Yet the same number of natural features

A group of mounds with perfectly round, exact profiles is an unsettling appearance.
(Courtesy: Richard Mandell Golf Architecture)

on a golf course will have a less disturbing effect on golfers because they were already there. Because, to me, nature is the great "differentiator," it's hard to argue with what was on the ground before anyone arrived. Any multitude of natural features on a site can either be softened through tempered shaping or remain between the holes, neutralizing any potential chaos.

I can't think of one golf course where too many natural features created a negative reaction. More variety of natural features will almost always yield a better golf course in both strategy and aesthetics. Sites such as Cypress Point and Pine Valley near Philadelphia come to mind. Similar to the limitations placed by the number of golf holes, there is probably not enough variety of natural hazards in the world that can reach the point of chaos on a golf course.

This site in southeastern Belize has a variety of site attributes from wooded parcels to open ground, creeks running in multiple directions, mountain views, knolls, swales, ridges, and valleys. (Courtesy: Richard Mandell Golf Architecture)

My time on site is full of many details. The most important ones are those spent analyzing landforms to ensure personality and character are in each, with variety the lead principle in my effort. It's a very simple task to develop variety among landforms. The charge to my shapers is simply to change just one element of a designed feature to ensure it stands alone in detail and varies from adjacent features. One of the most important written construction specifications I include with every project directs my shapers to ensure variety in the field with all they do:

"As an act of checks and balances: During the shaping of the golf course features, including greens, attention shall be given to the formations of mounds and undulations. A natural variety in the size and shape of all mounds and undulations shall be accomplished rather than a uniform look to each feature. This concept shall be utilized whenever adjacent mounds, etc. look to be the same size, height, or shape in the construction documents. Some mounds shall vary in an asymmetrical appearance while others may appear more off-center. The finished shaping shall blend into the existing lay of the land and be contoured so that all can be easily mowed with modern fairway mowing equipment. No mounds shall appear exactly as an adjacent mound. Variety in shaping, as in nature, shall be the rule."

On the strategy side, the most variety one can create is eighteen holes that call upon the golfer to perform a different task. Coupled with a mix of threes, fours, and fives, there is no possible way one could have too much strategic variety. Forced and contrived visual features may be revealed through a misuse of rhythm, contrast, or emphasis, but when it comes to strategic challenges, the Principle of Variety can't possibly turn to chaos.

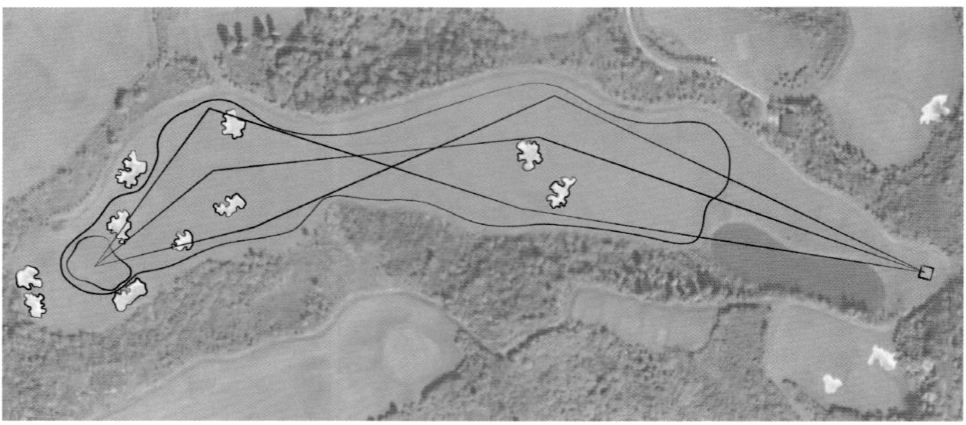

Hole #6, Skydoor Golf Club in Zhangjiajie, Hunan, China. The Variety of strategic choices can never create chaos, only options. (Courtesy: Richard Mandell Golf Architecture)

Because they are such a visible element of any golf course, bunkers should be the one feature that ties everything together. For that very reason, the quickest way a golf course can turn from variety to chaos is through the use of too many bunker styles. In my opinion, a golf course can't stray from more than a few bunker styles before descending into said chaos. Mostly, bunker choices are as follows: cape-and-bays, pots, coffins, waste bunkers, clover shapes, kidneys, sod-faced, bunkers with grass islands, dunes, strip bunkers, blow-outs, and ragged-edges. If one were to utilize multiple bunker styles and then compound that look by mixing flashed-sand and grass-faced variations of each, the resulting look will surely pass the limits of variety.

Sometimes, however, a golf course with just *two* bunker styles can have too much variety simply because their contrasting details clash. A perfect example is a layout with beach-like waste bunkers and cape-and-bay, fringe-edged bunkers. The characteristics of a beach bunker include a generally flat appearance, shallow sand, and large-scale arcs that create amoeba shapes. The cape-and-bay style has a concave bottom, some flashed sand with an elevation change from the floor to the top of the face, and a larger number of sharp arcs that form the capes and bays. The details of each bunker oppose each other in every aspect of design and construction, leading to a great potential for chaos.

My work at The Reserve on Pawleys Island in South Carolina is another example. Because there was no unifying system as to how each bunker type was utilized, it originally created a chaotic appearance. Our solution to set a consistent standard for each bunker style that would limit the chaos: white-sand bunkers were reserved for around the green complexes and any waste bunkers were limited to off the tee, along fairways, and around ponds. To further minimize the chaos, we utilized the same arc radii for both bunker types.

Hole #4, The Reserve at Pawleys Island in Pawleys Island, South Carolina. A pair of greenside bunkers incorporate the same arc radii as fairway waste bunkers on other holes. (Courtesy: Richard Mandell Golf Architecture)

One can comfortably incorporate more than two bunker styles provided that each style shares at least one or two characteristics. For instance, cape-and-bay bunkers work well with pot bunkers and other simple shapes because the scale of the arcs that determine their shapes unifies them. Yet there are a number of common characteristics that can still flip a course to chaos. My initial visit to Keller Golf Course in Maplewood, Minnesota, revealed a chaotic variety of six or seven different bunker shapes. There were perfect circles, long strip bunkers, kidneys, amoebas, pots, boomerangs, and a few "almost" cape and bays. Although the majority of bunkers generally had unifying arc radii, the number of bunker shapes was just too distracting.

Endeavoring to create unity in my proposed bunker style approach, I eventually found the answer when I came across an aerial photograph of the course from 1940. I quickly realized I was tasked to renovate a golf course with a surprisingly well-preserved bunker style, one that I called "early chaos." The 1940 layout had even more variation of these hazards, compounded by exaggerated capes-and-bays, longer strip bunkers, and random, poorly-scaled noses within otherwise simply-shaped bunkers.

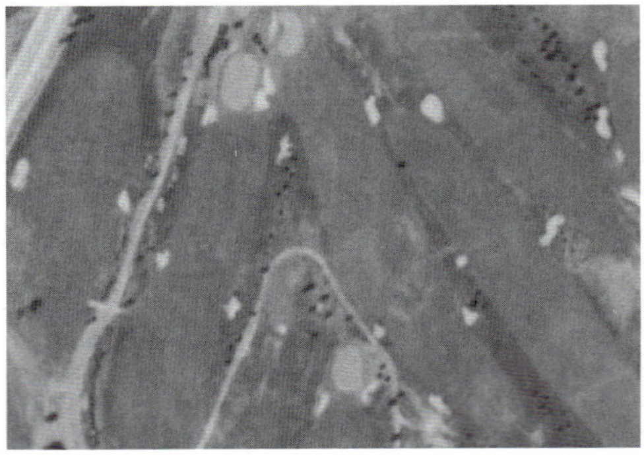

The chaotic bunker styles of Keller Golf Course in Maplewood, Minnesota (circa 1940)
(Courtesy: Richard Mandell Golf Architecture)

The solution of a cape-and-bay style with subtle arcs combined with simple organic shapes, provided just enough variety so as not to distract from the great topography of the layout. By eliminating the more recently-added amoeba shapes and boomerangs, we were able to eliminate the chaos. The bunkers we added were more historically accurate as well.

Hole #1, Keller Golf Course in Maplewood, Minnesota. Similar arcs and radii with cape-and-bay bunkers and simpler shapes ensures the Principles of Unity and Variety work complementary. (Courtesy: Richard Mandell Golf Architecture)

Avoiding repetition is the key to developing variety in golf architecture and the best approach is to master the art of subtlety when creating the details. The smallest of alterations in form, scale, shape, and elevation offers the golf architect every element to successfully develop the Principle of Variety. It is truly the spice of life and the go-to design principle for golf architects.

17 The Principle of Randomness

Randomness - The quality or state of being made, done, happening, or chosen without method or conscious decision.

I have always been in favor of eliminating bunker rakes from golf courses. Practical reasons such as pace of play and reducing maintenance hours provide plenty of incentive. But re-introducing the concept of "Rub of the Green" (defined in the 1812 official Rules of Golf as *"Whatever happens to the ball by accident must be reckoned a rub of the green"*), starting with random lies, is the best reason yet. The great amateur golfer, Chick Evans, considered Rub of the Green as *"even with the elimination of most hazards, 'rubs' of the green remain to cause crazy bounces and cranky lies."* The Principle of Randomness is what the golf architect uses to create those crazy bounces and cranky lies. This was how the game originally captured our hearts: Random acts of frustration to overcome.

Randomness is one word people may not associate with golf course architecture. But without it, great design can't be achieved. The Principle of Randomness is what creates exciting opportunities; reacting to the unexpected with a specific shot that isn't usually called upon.

In the early days of American golf architecture, random placement of multiple bunkers to catch as many different shots as possible was a major theme. This method was a great example of how the first designers approached their work - by

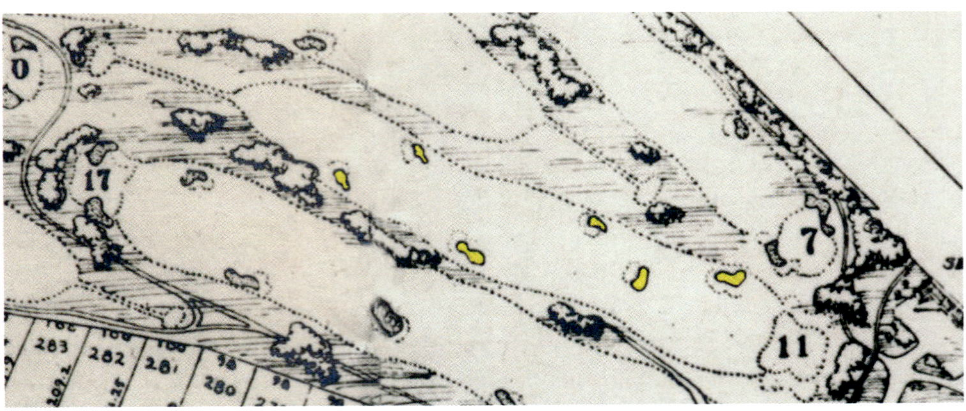

Hole #11 (today's #2) from Tom Bendelow's Routing of Lake Forest Country Club in Hudson, Ohio. Random bunker placement from tee to green was a standard practice in the early days of American golf design. (Courtesy: Hudson Historical Society)

utilizing the Principle of Randomness proudly. Over the years, though, this approach fell out of favor for a variety of reasons: maintenance costs, playability, strategy. Yet as the number of hazards diminished over time, the placement of hazards at random distances from tee to green continued. Eventually, engineered positioning of bunkers on both sides of a landing area at precise distances challenged just a chosen skill-set of accurate golfers, effectively penalizing everyone else and making the game tedious in the process. Randomness was replaced by predictability.

There is a direct correlation between the calculated placement of hazards and the reduced importance of natural features, often bulldozed or even moved to accommodate such a directed approach. Erasing natural features or re-creating them in different places altered sites to accommodate preconceived design notions rather than reacting to the specific attributes of a site for design cues. The randomness of nature slowly disappeared from the art and the game suffered.

Calculated placement of hazards superseded topographic cues for hazard placement for a good portion of the twentieth century. (Courtesy: Richard Mandell Golf Architecture)

The phrase "a good eye for design" is subconsciously rooted in the utilization of the Elements and Principles of Design. One term that may accurately describe that eye for design is intuition. By definition, intuition relies on one's experience and acquired knowledge over time. It's the basis for many of the decisions we make in our chosen professions and our everyday lives. One specific experience or memory may not lead to this decision-making; it may be a combination of multiple events and the results of each, whether successful or not.

My intuition allows me to apply the Principle of Randomness in order to a) develop variety in my designs by not doing the same thing twice; and b) replicate nature. This happens through instinctual design decisions rather than calculated, repetitive thought processes leading to formulaic design. It's a split-second act based on years of experience, research, etc. Over-analysis quells my intuition and keeps my instincts at bay. The slower I act, the less random and natural are my decisions.

Sand displacement as natural inspiration for green contours. (Courtesy: RMGA)

After an early member commented on how a windmill would look good somewhere at National Golf Links of America, Charles Blair Macdonald had one constructed beside the sixteenth green, only to send the bill to the member. As great a story as that is, I like the story of how he designed some of his greens at National even more. At the suggestion of golfer Horace Hutchinson, he dropped pebbles *"on a miniature space representing a putting-green on a small scale, releasing them, and as they dropped on the diagram,"* placed the undulations according to their fall. By recording the shapes formed by the gravitational force of the pebbles, Macdonald developed a variety of random putting surfaces, the process of which couldn't be repeated no matter how subsequent pebble drops displaced the sand.

I must admit to actually never owning pebbles or a sandbox for this or any other purpose. My "randomness" in greens design comes in me making quick, instinctual design decisions. This randomness occurs by simply letting the first thing that comes to my pencil flow freely onto paper without referencing previous attempts at putting surface design. Ironically, I am *intentionally* trying to make the next green different than the previous green, yet through random acts of design. By somehow controlling my brain to block out any previous efforts, my hope is that every putting surface design can be completely fresh and truly individual. If I search back in my mind for prototypical putting surfaces to complement (or contrast) current work, this and subsequent efforts could be somewhat constrained, forced, and/or repetitive. The ability to act randomly in my design efforts, even after I may have addressed functional needs (such as drainage and tying into existing features), will help keep repetition at bay. It will also hopefully result in successfully replicating nature.

Natural landforms evolve over time based on weathering forces such as wind and water eroding the earth. Because there is so much variation of natural landforms, the erosion process must have some random qualities. Hence, for me, randomness has a place in golf course design. The randomness of nature is what produces the vast palette of landscapes on this planet, whether for golf or other uses.

Randomness as a principle of golf course design is the incorporation of existing or man-made features in an instinctual way leading to unexpected results. For example, I am a huge fan of the lone mound suddenly rising up out of a fairway or approach. The mound establishes a vertical element while breaking up a consistent slope simultaneously. It seems random because it pops up where most may not expect (such as from a nondescript flat landform).

Hole #13, Isla Del Sol Yacht & Country Club in St. Petersburg, Florida. The random appearance of a mound breaks up the horizontal slope of a greenside hollow's face, giving the golfer pause to consider short-game club selection. (Courtesy: Richard Mandell Golf Architecture)

From a strategic standpoint, the mound can deflect a golf shot in one of many directions, impeding a golf ball from reaching its intended target by unexpectedly slowing progress along the way. This is mostly realized within landing areas yet is more intriguing within green approaches. The same effect can be achieved with a sand bunker cut into the slope of an existing ridge crossing a fairway at a seemingly random distance. Canadian architect Stanley Thompson almost always cut bunkers into natural slopes regardless of their placement within his routings. As a result, the random pattern of his bunker placement comes into play for a variety of golfers.

Bunkers cut into each slope of Stanley Thompson's 12th hole at St. George's Golf & Country Club, in Etobicoke, Ontario, Canada, create random hazard placement that challenges a cross-section of talent levels. (Courtesy: St. George's Golf & Country Club)

The potential for variety is exactly why one tries to incorporate as many natural features as possible. Following Thompson's lead, random natural features may be located immediately off the tee, others may be in the landing area, and some may be found between a landing area and a green. These features should always remain within the existing landscape to maximize the natural character of the ground, no matter how random they seem. Of course, incorporating these random landforms really isn't all that random; only their existence is random. They were simply unexpectedly found on an otherwise predictable piece of ground. As golf architects, it's our job to actively seek out these features to create strategy.

Strategy is not a black and white decision-making process. In fact, it's the gray area in between which all great golf holes possess. The random incorporation of natural landforms as hazards ensures different options will be presented to different golfers at different times under different conditions. By following one's instincts, one can maximize this randomness to create a golf course that maximizes the ground upon which it sits.

The Principle of Randomness is best utilized in the detailed shaping of features such as mounding, hollows, putting surface contours, or feature slopes. Randomness is achieved by breaking up homogenous slopes with instinctual movements from the dozer blade through the simple act of doing something different, anything different. Randomness is achieved because the detailed slope of a mound or exactly where a bulge may appear just doesn't matter. It just matters that it is different.

One of my more-colorful design terms is the *"mule-fart"* I referenced in the chapter on the Element of Form. It's a nod to the animals that often pulled the wooden drag pans early golf course constructors used to shape features. I often direct my shapers to create a mule-fart to break up slopes simply based on my sense that a slope has a little too much "sameness" (lacking a bump or hump or roll or hollow). The mule-fart is intended to break up that consistency. Yet its location is purely established by instinct.

Hole #5 Keowee Key Golf & Country Club in Salem, South Carolina. Random "mule-farts" create naturally-appearing slope changes. (Courtesy: Richard Mandell Golf Architecture)

Establishing the first mule-fart is the easiest step. Subsequent ones become more difficult because the more mule-farts there are, the more difficult it is to maintain randomness. Restraint becomes important because in these cases less is always more, particularly to conceal any patterns that may emerge from the process.

The grading decisions I make on paper are almost all geared toward random shaping of fairways. I don't like to over-think things in this regard; instead I just let it happen. In other words, I'll grade something out in one spot and let whatever is needed to connect the surrounding elevations happen organically. I will solve the issues at hand first – drainage, tying features into the ground, building off of existing features – but how these details connect happens instinctively in order to develop a sense of randomness without calculating too much or repeating the same landform.

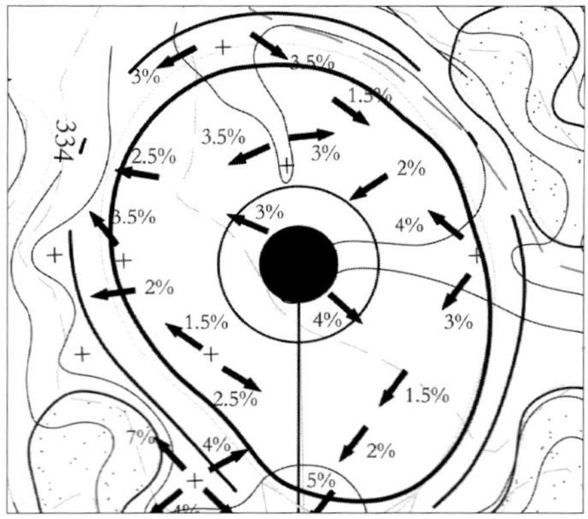

Green plan, Hole #2 White, Army Navy Country Club in Fairfax, Virginia.
(Courtesy: Richard Mandell Golf Architecture)

I take the same approach with interior putting surface contours as well, allowing my shaper to tie in seemingly conflicting details. These include a variety of drainage arrows which may seem to be in conflict, or a series of elevations that may be a bit too aggressive on paper. Yet that's where the art of shaping, coupled with creative design on paper, can create great putting surfaces.

Great golf is about creativity and inventiveness in shotmaking, traits which have become practically non-existent in today's version of the game. Shotmaking skill to gain proper distance, ball trajectory, and direction is helpful to incorporate the Principle of Randomness in course design. A fairway with rolling contours connected by high and low points strewn throughout requires exact placement of the golf ball in a specific spot for the best result. On a flat golf hole, one can be a little less dialed in because the ball will react the same way regardless of where it hits the ground.

Considering golf course conditioning, long, wet golf courses neutralize randomness because balls will stop almost exactly where they land, regardless of the contouring. Over-watering a golf course takes the uncertainty of bounce and roll out of the golfer's equation, allowing one to strictly rely on a yardage book to hit the same mechanical shots necessary to record the lowest possible score. Modern golfers expect consistent turf, receptive landing areas, smooth putting surfaces, etc. With such control locked into a golf course, the golfer can predict outcomes at a very high rate. Gone is the ingenuity that fast and firm links golf first presented, particularly the random bounce and run that made golf such a gift in the first place.

Mowing heights can have a neutralizing effect on the randomness of a golf shot as well. Deep rough will penalize all shots equally, eliminating the gray area of club selection that may come from imperfect conditions. Simply blasting out of the rough with a wedge will suffocate any and all creativity brewing in a golfer's mind.

One fallacy about Donald Ross is that he designed for tightly-mown conditions surrounding putting surfaces such as those at Pinehurst No. 2. This ideal couldn't be further from the truth. Strategically, he preferred manageable rough around greens to allow for short-game recovery. He preferred chipping from random locations determined by the speed of each roll. Sufficient grass height will create enough friction to stop a ball at a variety of spots along a green's slope, but tightly-mown conditions force every golf ball to settle at the same low point. Randomness is erased, eliminating the varying short-game challenges that Ross preferred.

Hole #13, The Water's Edge Country Club in Penhook, Virginia. Fairway cut around this green provides random lies for multiple club choices. (Courtesy: Richard Mandell Golf Architecture)

When golf architects intentionally direct a golfer to play a hole one specific way, they minimize the variety of possible outcomes, effectively eliminating the Principle of Randomness in the process. For instance, a fairway twenty-five yards wide bounded by bunkers on each side will yield few variations on the same tee shot. Either one is in the fairway or one is penalized. A random mound or slope in the fairway will not change that possibility either. But a wider fairway can offer up multiple possibilities of distance and angle to the next target. The more random shaping within that wider fairway, the more those possibilities will increase.

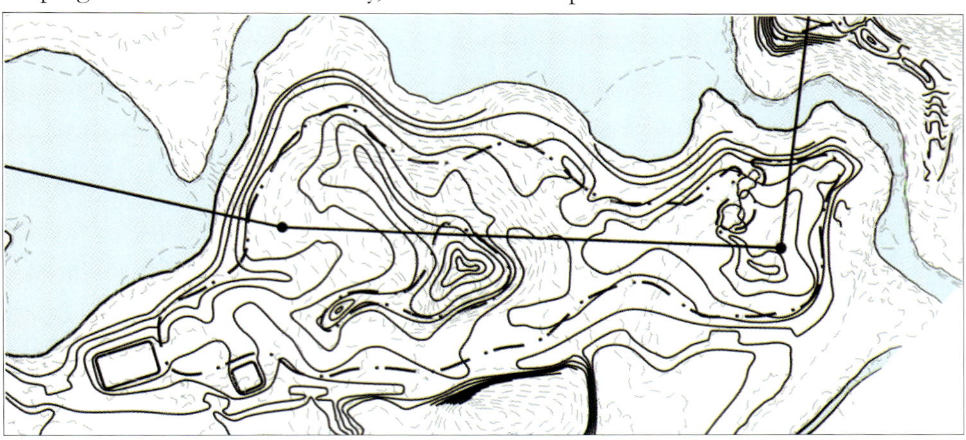

Fairway Grading Plan, Hole #16, Braemar Golf Course in Edina, Minnesota. (Courtesy: Richard Mandell Golf Architecture)

The sixteenth hole at Braemar Golf Course is a good example of how random mounds and other features within a sixty-yard wide fairway can result in a variety of lies and angles all the way to the green. Provided fast and firm conditions exist, random lies are endless from day to day and so are the shot choices.

If randomness is indeed without *"method or conscious decision,"* you might ask, then can one really be random in one's efforts if their intention is to actually be random? Designing to create randomness in golf architecture is a surprisingly intentional process. Pulling off the Principle of Randomness is about design efforts to create both a random appearance when considering aesthetics, and unexpected challenges when considering strategy.

The ripple at the front left of the third green at Macdonald's National Golf Links is a good example of randomness converted to strategic calculation, possibly influenced by natural sand displacement patterns through pebbles in his sand box. (Courtesy: Richard Mandell Golf Architecture)

As random as Macdonald's use of pebbles to conceive of putting surfaces may seem, once those pebbles dropped, the randomness of those results was calculatingly converted into functional design. So, whereas the Principle of Randomness has such a large presence in my design process, it's really fueled by my instincts to implement other principles of design such as Contrast, Emphasis, Unity, and Variety.

In some ways, variety and randomness almost go hand in hand. Randomness counterbalances predictability in design and ensures that both visual and strategic interest vary from shot to shot and hole to hole. Randomness is a safeguard so that similar results will rarely occur, keeping the game exciting, varied, and the golfer engaged.

18 The Principle of Intention

Intention - What one plans to do or bring about.

Almost everything that we undertake in life begins with an intention. Every artist, designer, engineer, and architect utilizes the Principle of Intention as the first step in their efforts to solve problems or create a piece of art or architecture. In golf design, the Principle of Intention is the conceptualization of a plan one will execute, first on paper and then on the ground.

The Principle of Intention for each project varies with site-specific goals. These goals may center on certain landforms one wants to incorporate, such as a creek or a specific saddle point that may make a great green site. An entirely different list of goals evolves when the course architect discusses the project with the owner, typically referred to as "programming." Certain goals include the type of facility they intend to create and the type of golfers they expect will play the course. Other goals may be more operational or for development purposes, such as ensuring the driving range is large enough or the need to include acreage for a hotel.

When I begin to sketch out a routing, the Principle of Intention incorporates many, if not all, of those goals. My intention is to implement as much of the list as possible into a plan through the elements and principles of golf architecture from a very general point of view - as if I was in a plane thirty-thousand feet in the air. The Principle of Intention continues to direct initial decisions as I dial in the details from, say, a three-hundred foot elevation as well. Here I crystallize the size and shape of the elements of the plan through the Principle of Connection, precisely connecting those goals through design.

For example, connecting a hotel with adjacent golf holes occurs at the thirty-thousand-foot viewpoint. Ensuring there is enough distance between the hotel's pool and the fifth fairway happens at three-hundred feet. As I get closer to the ground, such as thirty feet, there are a myriad of goals – with much finer detail – that emerge regarding overall grading and shaping - such as how adjacent fairways will drain into a pond. Finally, during construction, I get to the six-foot-high point of view. Making sure a bunker on the fifth hole intended to protect the line of flight toward the pool has slopes that are varied enough happens at that six-foot level. Each of those points of view begins with the Principle of Intention.

30,000 - Foot View, Bobby Jones Golf Club in Sarasota, Florida: The intention from this point of view focuses on general placement of golf holes in relation to the practice facility, constructed wetland and park, and clubhouse area. (Courtesy: Richard Mandell Golf Architecture)

300 - Foot View, Bobby Jones Golf Club in Sarasota, Florida: From this viewpoint, intent comes into more focus regarding planning spaces for safety, for example, such as a wetland separating the driving range and a path. (Courtesy: Richard Mandell Golf Architecture)

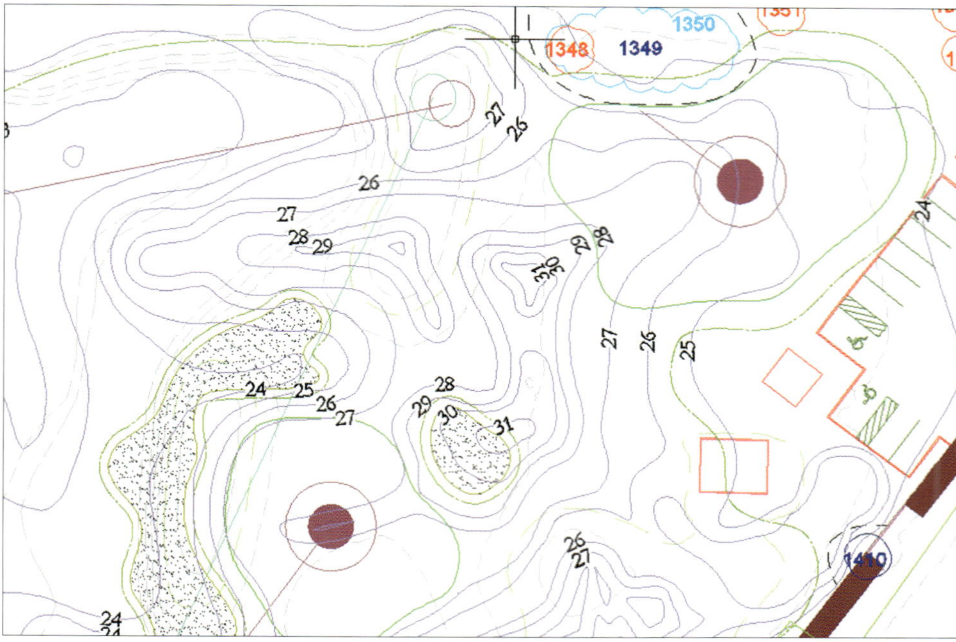

30 - Foot View, Bobby Jones Golf Club in Sarasota, Florida: The design intent of how a mound complex will provide visibility to a bunker and extend from one green into another is considered at this point. (Courtesy: Richard Mandell Golf Architecture)

3 - Foot View, Bacon Park Golf Course in Savannah, Georgia: Design intent at three feet is working to tie different planes together to ensure convex or concave slopes that flow seamlessly in and out of adjacent slopes. (Courtesy: Richard Mandell Golf Architecture)

The Principle of Intention is also a window into a course architect's design philosophy. Included in mine is the intention to make features look natural or ensure a hazard shall challenge and not penalize. Other aspects of my design philosophy are an affinity for central hazards and to develop a golf hole's strategy based on the site's existing landforms. These concepts all start with the Principle of Intention. I intend to create central hazards; I intend to utilize hazards for challenge, not penalty. This is always my methodology regardless of the project. It's what I plan to bring about in my work. However, I also describe myself as a reactionary designer. I intend to react to what the ground provides and make sensible decisions to ensure variety and avoid over-thinking, which can result in repetitiveness and boredom. The Principle of Intention applies to designers who are purely reactionary just as equally as those who are deliberate and analytic in their actions.

A client of mine once bristled that every bunker I placed on a course, which previously had none, was exactly where he hit all his shots. The client had already mapped out the best way to play his course (he designed it himself a decade earlier) in order to play it in the fewest strokes possible. But he knew my bunkers were going to challenge his game plan. To my eyes, it was a job well done and it illustrated my Principle of Intention to ensure hazards challenge but don't penalize the golfer. In fact, it might just be my overall design intent: to challenge each and every golfer's game plan. My Principle of Intention is to allow golfers to forge their own path from tee to green according to their own strengths and abilities.

Course restoration is a different animal which usually begins with, "How do we restore the original architect's intent for this hole?" Was the architect's original intent to utilize a specific land form for a green site and everything else accommodated that decision? Or was the architect's intent to use a high-point-to-high-point-routing for the specific hole? Or was it simply to create a challenging tee shot with hazards flanking both sides of the landing area? Without an understanding of the original architect's design intention, it's easy to misconstrue the original plan.

I cringe each time I hear one talk about how Donald Ross or A. W. Tillinghast "intended" for the golfer to play a hole a certain way. Restoring the design work of the greats is an important endeavor that requires an understanding of their intentions, not someone else's interpretation decades after initial construction. One simply cannot define an architect's design intent based, for example, on a single hazard promoting a single route along a twenty-five yard wide fairway if the original fairway was *twice* as wide. Earlier course architects that repeatedly displayed a design approach of presenting a hole with multiple routes don't become one-dimensional years later (especially since those architects are no longer around).

If a golf architect's original design intent is so easy to interpret, so streamlined and specific from hole to hole, odds are that architect's design ability is limited and their approach was mediocre. On the other hand, a golf architect whose preferred line of play is consistently established is simply dictating a specific game plan for everyone, regardless of ability. One cannot say what Donald Ross intended with certain golf holes or shots. I don't recall seeing any of his notes that called for a player to achieve a strategic goal, such as cutting the corner of a dogleg to gain an advantage.

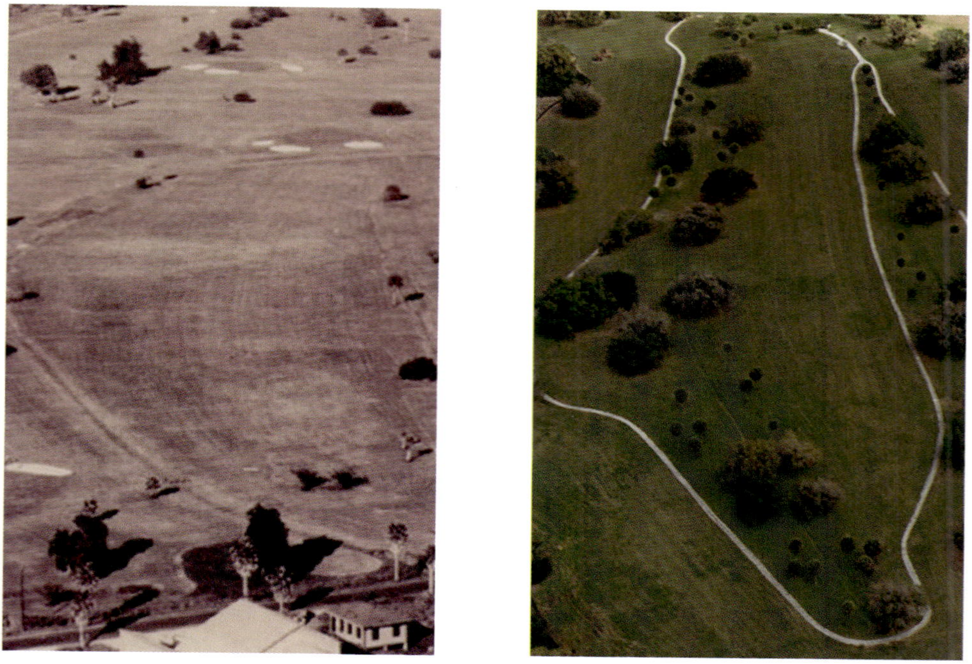

Hole #5, Bobby Jones Golf Club in Sarasota, Florida (Left - 1926; Right - 2022): As trees were planted and the fairway got narrower, a much wider hole evolved into a straight, penal hole that did not reflect the original design. (Courtesy: Richard Mandell Golf Architecture)

One *can* say beyond a shadow of a doubt, though, that Ross intended to place certain hazards in specific locations. That knowledge is clear in his notes regarding the placement of features in specific spots with specific dimensions. Ross's intent was to design specific features. That's what he *"planned to do or bring about."* But his plans never specifically outlined how his features were to influence the golfer's decisions.

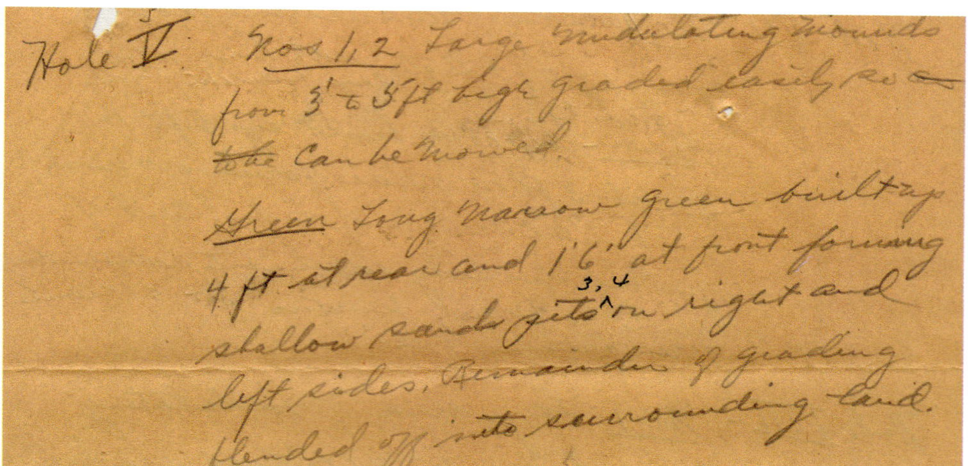

Hole V. Nos 1, 2 Large undulating mounds from 3' to 5 ft high graded easily so ~~that~~ can be mowed.

Green Long narrow green built up 4 ft at rear and 1'6" at front forming shallow sand pits 3, 4 on right and left sides. Remainder of grading blended off into surrounding land.

Hole #5, Bobby Jones Golf Club in Sarasota, Florida (Donald Ross Notes): Ross just specifies directions such as *"undulating mounds from 3' to 5 ft. high"* in his notes as opposed to strategic direction. (Courtesy: Richard Mandell Golf Architecture)

Although we can't know the actual design intent of an architect unless it was written down or spoken about, as long as we have their construction intent, does it matter? Interpretation of an architect's strategic intent is such a subjective process that it may be fruitless to follow that path. But the intention to place a bunker here or there as described graphically on paper or in the field makes the point moot. The architect's intent was to place said hazard in said place. Whether it was for strategic, aesthetic, or even playability concerns, one may never really know.

Yet it's not uncommon for an architect's intent to change from design to construction. Site conditions factor in just as much as free will in that regard. Interpretive mistakes are made in the field and improvements in equipment technology complicate the matter as well. For example, when a previous architect specified a hazard in a particular spot within a fairway, it was expected to collect a ball hit a specific distance. But because the ball travels much further one hundred years later, the bunker may not perform its originally intended function. For these reasons and many others, golf course restoration is such a challenging and controversial endeavor.

The notion of interpreting art or design is the whole reason for the critic's existence. Standing in front of a Pablo Picasso or Alexander Calder work of art absolutely calls for one to interpret the meaning of the presentation: *"What did the artist intend for this work?"* So it goes with golf architecture. This is an understandable approach because it, too, is an art form. Yet golf architects are never engaged to restore a Picasso. Art restoration is a painstaking process that often takes longer to accomplish than the time it took to create the original artwork itself. In art restoration, there is rarely room for interpretation of the artist's intent. It's right there in black and white (or color). A line exists. A certain color is revealed upon careful removal of centuries of residue. When one restores a work of art, it's a scientific process.

Interpreting artwork, however, is simply through viewing of the physical work; Picasso's intent stays on the canvas. But interpreting a golf architect's design intent requires the additional step of transferring drawn plans in two-dimensions (intent) to a canvas in three dimensions in order to be experienced by someone else entirely.

It's almost impossible to design anything without the Principle of Intention. By definition, design is the act of problem-solving. An engineer intends to solve a particular problem, an artist intends to bring enjoyment to their audience or evoke a certain feeling, and a golf architect intends to solve the problem of how to place a course on a piece of property so that it's fun, playable, challenging, maintainable, operational, and profitable. All at the same time.

Hole #6, Country Club of Asheville in Asheville, North Carolina
(Courtesy: Richard Mandell Golf Architecture)

19 The Principle of Chance

Chance - An occasion that provides for a particular outcome in an uncertain situation; an opportunity.

Luck - Success or failure apparently brought by chance rather than through one's own actions.

I love the "member's bounce" - aiming away from my target, hoping the ground will funnel my shot in the right direction from somewhere other than a head-on approach. Getting lucky that my ball didn't get stuck on the slope facing a dead downhill shot. When a local knows how to work the ground to gain an advantage, the uninitiated may see it as simply getting a lucky break. But odds are the golf course architect created a member's bounce through design and course set-up. By developing shots that utilize the ground, the architect gives the golfer the chance to succeed in more ways than one – the essence of strategy.

According to USGA rules, "Rub of the Green" occurs *"when a ball in motion is accidentally deflected or stopped by any outside agency."* My personal interpretation of Rub of the Green creates opportunities for luck to play a part in an uncertain situation through the Principle of Chance. A golfer can't choose to be lucky based on their intent. Instead, luck randomly occurs through chance. Chance only brings luck into play once the golf ball makes contact with the ground.

The consequence of what happens when the ball first lands is always subjective - the result is either good luck or bad luck. We may not even be aware of an occurrence of good luck on the golf course because we expect most shots to work in our favor, oblivious of what turned our fortunes toward success. Those who seem to be luckier than others may just have sought out chance in order to make their own luck. As a golf course architect, I cannot design for luck, but I can create those opportunities for chance by providing the golfer with alternate routes to the same target. An example is incorporating a natural hillside as an alternate approach to a green. By extending a ridge from the hill onto the putting surface, and by encouraging the course superintendent to keep the grass along the hillside short, the golfer now has the choice to play directly at the target or use the hillside to get there. If the entire hillside was covered in thick rough, however, no member's bounces would be had, whether lucky or unlucky.

Playing for a "member's bounce" over the left bunker when the flag is tight to that side may be a better choice than playing directly at the flagstick on the 9th hole of the West Course at Broadmoor Golf Club in Colorado Springs, Colorado. (Courtesy: Richard Mandell Golf Architecture)

Englishman John Low was the first person to write about the principles of golf course architecture in his 1903 book *Concerning Golf*. In summarizing his philosophy, he said *"A course should never pretend to be, nor is it intended to be, an infallible tribunal of skill alone. The element of chance is the very essence of the game, part of legitimate the fun of the game."* H.N. Wethered concurred in 1931 and wrote *"In the old spirit of golf, 'luck' was regarded as part of the legitimate fun of the game, without which as a sport the game would suffer."*

Although luck isn't a by-product of skill, the more skill one possesses the better chance one seemingly has of getting lucky. A skilled golfer has a better chance of hitting a small green completely over water from 180 yards than a lesser-skilled golfer. The better golfer only sees the pin, oblivious to the surrounding hazard. Chances are that golfer will succeed without needing luck. For the lesser-skilled, their reliance on luck is more a matter of survival. Many of the shots they are forced to play are simply out of their skill range - particularly evident at places like Bethpage Black, which is why there is a warning sign on the first tee just for them.

The better golfer's reliance on luck is a by-product of their gambling instincts. Increased skill allows a golfer to gamble more because precision is an element of the shot process. As a golfer's skill increases, they are able to hit a precise shot when required, such as one that goes past a lone mound or off the correct side of it to gain a favorable bounce toward the target. Because they possess more skill, they can take more chances and often appear luckier in the process.

Strategic gray area is a blurring of a line. When that line is distinctly drawn, golfers are either on one side of it or the other and the risk of chance is clearly defined. But when that line blurs, definition is gone and with it the risk of chance increases because an uncertain situation arises.

I utilize the Principle of Chance to coax a player into more gambling positions by offering multiple options without any crystal-clear best choice. The more strategic gray area there is, the more options the gambler has to choose from to be successful

A highly-skilled golfer may be more apt to bounce an approach off the front left mound of the seventh green at Pasatiempo Golf Club in Santa Cruz, California, to get closer to a front-left pin placement than one who lacks such skill. (Courtesy: Richard Mandell Golf Architecture)

(and the more chance for luck to occur as well). That ambiguity of choice simply does not exist in the black and white world of penal design. For example, playing over a bunker surrounded by clump grasses in the corner of a dogleg to gain an advantage is a gambler's paradise; the diagonal line of the hole brings the Principle of Chance into play. Contemplating how to follow that line forces the golfer to consider how much of a chance they take with the shot at hand. The Principle of Randomness provides the variables that increase the chance that a golf ball may not find the intended target. Grass heights differ along the line (fairway or rough), variation in the density of the rough grasses differ, and a bunker crossing diagonally across the chosen line introduces another opportunity for success or failure.

This example illustrates multiple challenges that produce a variety of outcomes in an uncertain situation. Any "bad luck" that results may be based more on the demanding line of flight that was chosen and made due to skill level. Players with less skill have the option to avoid those challenges by not following the diagonal line and their chances of finding bad luck along the longer but safer route is reduced.

The Principle of Chance isn't used in penal design because it's simply more predictable. Penal design creates a more controlled environment with limited choices resulting in fewer gambling chances from tee to green. A straight hole with rough on all sides is a clear strategic situation – players have the opportunity to drive it as far down the hole as they can. If they hit a poor shot, they will be in the rough. Chance plays no role in that. Skill (or a lack thereof) was the factor that led to that result.

The gray area of strategy isn't the only way an architect introduces the Principle of Chance. A well-defined bunker line expresses that a golfer will either be lucky to be out of the sand or unlucky to be in the sand. But a blurred bunker style where the sand and grass connection is not so well delineated can raise the degree of penalty, thereby bringing more risk. Not only can a golfer be in sand, they can be somewhere in between sand and grass – a situation that could be worse than the sand itself.

The Principle of Chance is illustrated by the opportunity a golfer may take to cut the corner of the seventh hole at Pinehurst No. 2. The variation in lies will influence the golfer's line of flight and the amount of "bad luck" one may encounter. (Courtesy: Coore and Crenshaw)

The same can be said for areas of rough consisting of random clump grasses of various size and density, and ground that runs the spectrum from hardpan soil to sugar sand. Chances are the variation in lies will increase one's perception of luck. For example, there may be a chance of catching a lucky break and finding one's ball sitting on hardpan without a clump of grass between it and the club needed to play the next shot. But a well-defined fairway line with four inches of rough next to it leaves the golfer with a very high risk for failure. The grassing strategy for such a hole does not incorporate the Principle of Chance because, frankly, many golfers won't take the risk; a poor shot will only find deep rough, so why take such a chance?

Another way a golf architect utilizes the Principle of Chance is by re-introducing the Golden Age device of surrounding contours that collect running shots into a bunker. Much more excitement and interest can be generated by incorporating bunkers that collect rolling shots in addition to those that may land directly within their confines by an aerial route. Demanding more precision to control the bounce and roll of a shot requires more skill; a bad result may be considered an unlucky break.

The Principle of Chance is simply not incorporated into strategically black or white golf holes. These holes will play exactly the same way day in and day out because there is no option to attack them differently. Shots cannot be deemed lucky one day and unfair the next because the penal features don't change. Granted, for those who focus strictly on score each day, the lack of chance is a welcomed opportunity. But for others, boredom may set in very quickly.

At National Golf Links of America, Macdonald expanded the influence of his bunkers by shaping the surrounds to funnel stray shots toward the hazard. (Courtesy: Richard Mandell Golf Architecture)

When one designs for a single, pre-determined route from tee to green with complete visibility and perfect conditions, there is only one way to play the hole. Therefore, luck will never be a factor other than by covering up the golfer's flaws from shot to shot.

Chance is not a factor on shots with only one choice, such as this particular straight tee shot at Desert Forest Golf Club in Carefree, Arizona. Yet luck does come into play. Bouncing off a desert plant and back into the fairway would be good luck. (Courtesy: Richard Mandell Golf Architecture)

Hole #14, Skydoor Golf Club in Zhangjiajie, Hunan, China. With the green set on a high point around the corner to the left, the Principle of Chance entices the gambler to take the most aggressive line of instinct in that direction. Safer options abound for those adverse to risk.
(Courtesy: Richard Mandell Golf Architecture)

I prefer not to design with such a straightforward approach. I prefer to implement the Principle of Chance by bringing those elements into play that are specific to the site that I am charged to work with, and allow uncertain situations to unfold based on those site-specific components. My goal as a golf architect is to give golfers a chance to succeed and enjoy the game through the provision of strategic options. The Principle of Chance provides the lesser-skilled golfer more opportunity for success through options and the better player a chance to indulge their gambling instincts based on skill. Blurring the lines of strategy creates the chance both golfers crave.

Hole #8 Blue, Army Navy Country Club in Arlington, Virginia.
(Courtesy: Richard Mandell Golf Architecture)

20 The Principle of Par

Par - The score a scratch player would expect to achieve on a hole under normal course and weather conditions, allowing for two strokes on the green.

There are actually two definitions for par in the USGA Rules of Golf. The above is from its Rules of Handicapping section. It's universally understood by all golfers and is a target of sorts for all skill levels. The variable that identifies the different par types (3, 4, 5, and even 6) is yardage.

Before the twentieth century, "bogey" was used to identify the target score for recreational golfers and "par" became the ideal score on a given hole for more serious players. In 1911, par was officially introduced by the USGA as the score to beat and golf holes were distinguished in the following manner:

- Par 3 for men up to 225.
- Par 4 for men 225 - 425 yards.
- Par 5 for men: 426 - 600.
- Par 6: 601 yards or more.

These numbers were slightly revised in 1917 and re-defined in 1956 when the longer distance for each hole type was increased and yardages for women were established. In 2020, hole distances were updated once again:

- Par 3 for men up to 260 yards; women: 220 yards.
- Par 4 for men 240 - 490 yards; women: 200 – 420 yards.
- Par 5 for men: 450 - 710; women: 370 – 600 yards.
- Par 6: 670 yards +; women: 570 yards or more.

The definition in the *"General Playing Rules"* of the USGA simultaneously addresses both par and bogey without actually defining either. Rather, the USGA refers to how a player scores in comparison to a "fixed target score" set by the committee in a competition. The fact that it's specifically defined as it relates to handicapping but not specifically defined in the General Playing Rules is the tell-tale sign that par can be somewhat of an arbitrary goal for golfers; one that changes on a personal level.

For a golf course architect, par designations mean that for every par-three hole that's designed, one only needs to find a teeing ground and a green site. A par-four hole necessitates a teeing ground as well as one landing area and a green. A par-five hole necessitates two landing areas in addition to a teeing ground and green site. The Principle of Par challenges the golf architect to consider the basic needs of each type of hole within an overall golf course routing and how those requirements are applied to the ground.

In the day-to-day playing of the game, though, the number assigned on a scorecard to a hole's par is somewhat irrelevant to the playing of the hole. The knowledge that a hole may be a par four or a par five doesn't technically help us swing the club any differently when faced with a 470-yard-long hole. It shouldn't change one's strategy either. But it does. Par designation does not change one physical element of a particular hole, yet take a stroke off the scorecard and it becomes that much more difficult to many golfers.

Hole #8, Bacon Park Golf Course in Savannah, Georgia. Knowing the hole plays as a par five despite measuring only 470 yards from the "Ross" tees provides a sense of security more so than if the scorecard showed par as 4. (Courtesy: Richard Mandell Golf Architecture)

I remember playing a junior tournament at Tamarack Country Club in Greenwich, Connecticut, in 1985. Two of the first four holes were par fours of 446 and 463 yards. Looking at the scorecard, prospects did not look good for me (I wasn't very long but always down the middle). My little blue Ram driver just didn't have it and I didn't have another club to reach either hole in regulation. So I played them as par fives and made four on both holes, doubling down on my focus when confronted with fewer shots designated on the scorecard. I played within myself to ensure that I could take advantage of my short game and was successful getting up and down each time.

I then made bogey on the 491-yard par-five thirteenth hole. Although I had a whole extra stroke to get in the hole, I still made a six. Not only did I let my guard

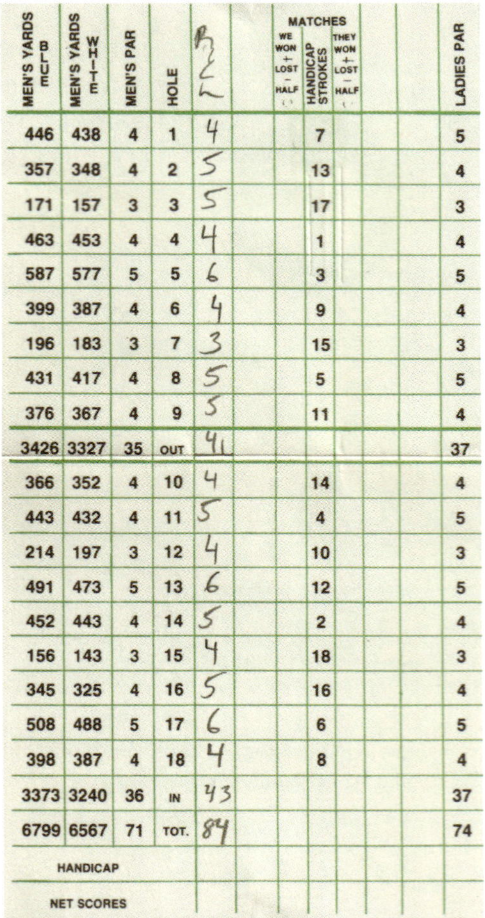

MEN'S YARDS BLUE	MEN'S YARDS WHITE	MEN'S PAR	HOLE	[illegible]		MATCHES: WE WON + LOST − HALF ( )	HANDICAP STROKES	THEY WON + LOST − HALF ( )			LADIES PAR
446	438	4	1	4			7				5
357	348	4	2	5			13				4
171	157	3	3	5			17				3
463	453	4	4	4			1				4
587	577	5	5	6			3				5
399	387	4	6	4			9				4
196	183	3	7	3			15				3
431	417	4	8	5			5				5
376	367	4	9	5			11				4
3426	3327	35	OUT	41							37
366	352	4	10	4			14				4
443	432	4	11	5			4				5
214	197	3	12	4			10				3
491	473	5	13	6			12				5
452	443	4	14	5			2				4
156	143	3	15	4			18				3
345	325	4	16	5			16				4
508	488	5	17	6			6				5
398	387	4	18	4			8				4
3373	3240	36	IN	43							37
6799	6567	71	TOT.	84							74
HANDICAP											
NET SCORES											

Author's scorecard from a 1985 round at Tamarack Country Club: The printed par on a scorecard is secondary to the actual shots played. (Courtesy: Richard Mandell Golf Architecture)

down, I was much more aggressive, lulled into the false perception I had an extra shot to play with. The reality was that I didn't because my final score was the accumulation of eighteen holes worth of shots being compared to the other golfers in the field.

Yet the par assigned to each hole changed my thinking. Other than the number on the scorecard and a few more yards, those three holes couldn't have been more similar. None of them had water and all of them had openings in front of the green. Regardless, the prospect of a number on the scorecard greatly affected my strategy, focus, and subsequent results. Although par threes, fours, and fives are clearly defined by distance, the anguish the Principle of Par brings to the golfer is what makes the game so vexing.

There are basically three ways one can look at their own score after they hole out: the actual number of strokes; whether one's effort resulted in being under, even, or over par; and by comparing scores with the people you were playing with or against. In that case, the number of strokes does not matter. All that matters is if you won or lost the hole.

That third approach – widely known as "match play" – is one way to minimize the influence of par on the scorecard. The difference between match play and stroke play (also known as "medal play") is that the golf course is solely the playing field in match play. Therefore it has absolutely no bearing on a one–on-one match-up. A golfer's score is only being compared to their opponent's score, not to multiple golfers playing that day or even the course.

Match play frees our mind of the clutter involved in posting a number on a scorecard after every hole. Whether a 275-yard hole is a par three or a par four is irrelevant. In fact, these "half-par" holes can accommodate a variety of skill sets much like a boxing match between two fighters with contrasting attributes. Will the one who can drive such a hole come out on top or will the one who can take dead aim with a wedge be victorious?

Freedom from the shackles of par has another liberating effect through match play: Whatever gamble the golfer takes will only affect them on that specific hole. One won't carry the weight of their decision for the remainder of the match. In stroke play, the burden of par grows heavy when the prospect of making up for a quadruple bogey on the previous hole is forefront in one's mind. Yet in match play the cost was just one hole. The golfer's focus can move directly to the next hole with the possibility of gaining back the previously lost one.

Hole #10, Keller Golf Course in Maplewood, Minnesota (previously above/today below). A willingness to vary total par for each nine provided the design flexibility to find the best holes on the property. (Courtesy: Richard Mandell Golf Architecture)

When the idea that a "championship course" must be 7,000 yards long gained a foothold in the golf course development world, so did the matching standard par of 72 strokes, typically divided between each nine. The Principle of Par took a turn for the worse when architects ensured their design work met those thresholds, regardless of site characteristics. To this day, that standard is strong in the minds of developers, architects, and golfers.

When I re-designed Keller Golf Course in Maplewood, Minnesota, and swapped par for the ninth and tenth holes, the move caused initial heartburn for the pro shop staff. For many years, Keller had two nines of 36. But when we converted the ninth to a par four and the tenth to a par five, the nines became 35-37. Despite the overall par remaining at 72, this change brought about much debate, centered solely on the fact that the golfers who only played nine-hole rounds would feel slighted if the front nine didn't play to a par of 36. Management felt that if the par was less, they couldn't charge as much for green fees. Eventually, common sense overcame emotion and flawed economics. Not only was safety improved by spreading out the ninth and eighteenth greens (by shortening the ninth), the architectural value of each hole was strengthened as well by converting a very short par five into a par four and transforming a boring par four into a risk-reward par five.

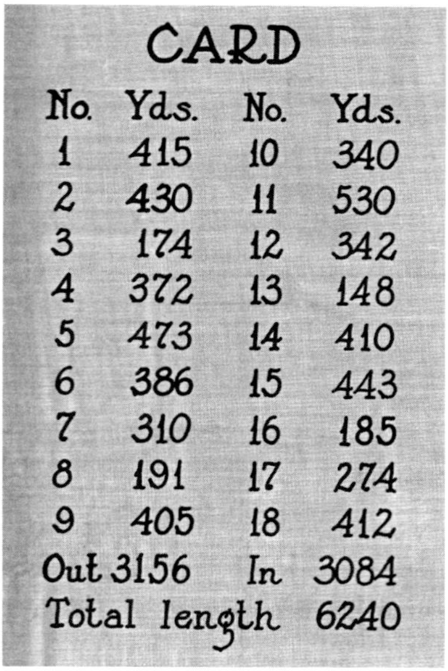
CARD

No.	Yds.	No.	Yds.
1	415	10	340
2	430	11	530
3	174	12	342
4	372	13	148
5	473	14	410
6	386	15	443
7	310	16	185
8	191	17	274
9	405	18	412
Out	3156	In	3084
Total length			6240

1925 scorecard for "Municipal Golf Course and Recreation Grounds" (today's Bobby Jones Golf Club), Sarasota, Florida. (Courtesy: Tufts Archives)

Donald Ross almost never assigned par to any of the holes he designed. From Ross's earliest layouts, such as his 1915 routing of Oconomowoc Golf Club in Wisconsin to one of his very last projects, Raleigh Country Club in North Carolina in 1948, only the hole number and yardage were denoted on Ross's plans. His separate golf hole drawings showed a number followed by "yards" with a period at the end. To this day that period seems to say, "don't worry yourself over the required number of strokes. Just play." He was very cognizant of the need to find the best features and lay out the best holes without mucking things up with distance classifications.

Ross would probably be appalled at judgments rendered about a hole's quality based on its distance. He might just argue that a short par four should never be judged any less of a hole than a par four that measures one-hundred yards longer. The shorter hole could be chock full of a variety of challenges based on natural features found along the way and its distance may not hinder any number of golfers from trying numerous shots in the spirit of the Principle of Challenge. The longer hole, though, may be a bore and a trudge from start to finish, avoiding those same natural features because they may not tie into the "championship" distance. The Principle of Difficulty is in full wearisome bloom when length overrules nature.

Simply put, the Principle of Par should never be in the forefront of an architect's mind. First of all, when routing a course it takes more space and earthwork to create additional landing areas. In addition, if one is conditioned to create a "standardized" par 72 course or to evenly distribute strokes between each nine, natural landforms may be bypassed for more manufactured features. For example, adding fifty yards to a 450-

yard par four to create an additional par five may require the substitution of a great natural green location with a less-than-stellar one, bringing the overall experience down a notch in the process. Without focusing on such a standardization, the architect is free to seek out the best natural attributes for the most memorable golf features.

The USGA's rules of golf define par only as it relates to handicapping and doesn't mention the word by name when discussing competitions. That should scream loudly to the golfer that par isn't intended to affect the everyday playing of the sport. Therefore architects should not focus on the Principle of Par as a design tool nor should golfers look upon it as a goal to grind over (obviously easier said than done).

Hole #9 Red, Army Navy Country Club in Arlington, Virginia. This drivable par four (291 yards) is much more intriguing because of its proximity to Fort Richardson, a Civil War fort whose parapets and ditches remain to the left of the green. The par on the scorecard is secondary to the memory of its challenge and setting. (Courtesy: Richard Mandell Golf Architecture)

Although a golf course should be a single unit held together through the Elements of Design, individual shots are what we remember most. We forever recall the one shot that keeps us coming back and when we recount that shot in our mind, the score for the hole is often secondary. What is prime in our mind is the lie, the yardage, the club in our hand, contact with the ball, and its path until it stops, concluding with our own self-declared brilliance in orchestrating it all.

Golf architects should always find the best holes possible to create the most interesting and fun shots, without a pre-conceived scorecard driving design decisions. Stringing multiple shots together makes the journey that much more enjoyable and the story-telling that much more vivid. I believe the quirks and challenges of golf course architecture can be more freely appreciated by highlighting the land instead of emphasizing the importance of numbers on a scorecard.

21 The Principle of Visibility

Visibility - Capability of affording an unobstructed view.

The Silver Scot, golfer Tommy Armour, once said *"A blind hole is only blind if a golfer wants,"* meaning only once is a golf hole blind, providing a golfer has any recall at all. Armour attributed blind shots to emotions that affect a golfer's game, enhancing the mental aspect and effectively relegating visibility as secondary to the enjoyment of the game.

When it comes to the Principle of Visibility, golf architects fall into two camps: Those who strive for full visibility and those who don't concern themselves with visibility on a conscious, design-driven basis. Generally speaking, each camp is inherently tied to historical preferences. Those who follow the tenets of Golden Age design don't value visibility in their design process so much and don't shy away from a blind situation or two. Those who were trained by architects from the mid-twentieth century are typically inclined to provide full visibility in their work. The latter philosophy ties the introduction of large-scale, heavy machinery to the business at that time, which allowed architects to manipulate the ground to the point where topography wasn't a limiting factor. For the first time, the freedom to move dirt allowed designers full reign to eliminate landforms they perceived as in the way. Aesthetics over strategy was of paramount importance and what better way to show off one's eye candy than by providing unobstructed views of those features from tee to green.

A merciless cut through a ridge opens up the view of the fifteenth green at Interlachen Country Club in Edina, Minnesota. (Courtesy: Richard Mandell Golf Architecture)

Those more recent designers may have assumed that blind landing areas, greens, and even hazards were only blind because the Old Tom Morrises of the world didn't have the machinery to eliminate these features in the first place. If Old Tom on the eastern side of the Atlantic and many Golden Age designers on the western side had the means, then surely they would have eliminated these annoyances, right?

Imagine if heavy machinery were indeed available at the turn of the twentieth century. Would so many quirky features and blind targets have been erased from the start? If so, the sport of golf may very well have not survived. Those elements were among others that made a round of golf that much more engaging, allowing the game to gain a foothold in American culture. Yet, to an extent, even Alister MacKenzie had a less than enthusiastic opinion of blind holes: *"The greater the experience the writer has of designing golf courses, the more certain he is that blindness of all kinds should be avoided. The only form of blindness that should ever be permitted is the full shot up to a green whose position is accurately located by surrounding sandhills. Even in a hole of this kind, it is not the blindness that is interesting, but the visibility of the surrounding sandhills."*

"Visibility of the surrounding sandhills" guides the second shot of the par-five seventh at Royal St. George's Golf Club in Sandwich, Kent, England. (Courtesy: Richard Mandell Golf Architecture)

I fall in a slightly smaller category: Those who may intentionally conceal the whole view to create visual interest, even a bit of mystery. That said, I am surely in the minority because it seems the business of golf has only grown since the advent of heavy machinery.

Admittedly, I tie the introduction of heavy machinery used to improve visibility to a mid-century shift from match play toward medal play, promoting the lowest score possible. Many of today's golf professionals would just as soon demolish anything that comes between themselves and the shot at hand. Armed with detailed yardage books, they prefer to see every inch of a golf course in order to make the best decisions toward achieving the lowest number. The unadulterated ability to move dirt has made visibility on a golf course the expected norm, and maybe not for the best.

So what is full visibility in golf course design? I would define it as simply laying everything out for the golfer to see from tee to green, no questions needed. The entire fairway awaits with zero surprises. Every hazard is well-defined and fully discernible without any question as to the shape, length, width, or depth of each. As for greens, they would be canted from back to front so the entire surface was visible.

Full visibility is often an element of penal design which, by definition, clearly establishes a black or white decision-making process. When everything is visually presented on a hole with only one strategic option, redundancy and boredom can set in. Not only is there just one choice to be made, the road map is being spoon-fed as well. Yet concealing just a bit of the map can introduce a little doubt in the golfer.

Despite being in the minority when it comes to full visibility, I do believe that hazards should be partially visible from at least one angle when on a tee or in a landing area. The golfer doesn't need to know the full extent of the trouble, but they shouldn't be completely in the dark, either. That said, I don't necessarily believe all targets need to be visible. In other words, golfers don't need to see all of what they are aiming at but should see at least a part of what they are trying to avoid.

Fairway bunkers past the first landing area of the par-five thirteenth hole at the Minikhada Club in Minneapolis, Minnesota, obscure the green and a crossing creek in the second landing area. (Courtesy: Richard Mandell Golf Architecture)

However, I also feel that greenside hazards on a reachable par-five don't necessarily need to be visible for those going for the green in two shots. Nor do greenside hazards need to be seen on a drivable par four. Any attempt to reach either putting surface with fewer shots than par requires is, to me, technically a gamble, and therefore does not qualify for a *"visibility discount,"* so to speak. The lack of visibility of those hazards should be a factor in the hole's strategy and associated risk.

For many, the full visibility route is an approach to golf course strategy unto itself, albeit not one that instills too much excitement. Rather, it's a basic formula geared toward achieving the lowest possible score and nothing else. I call that boring golf course architecture. The pro would likely expect it: Nothing standing between their skill-set and a low score.

Golf should be approached like a game of chess and a glimpse of a hole can influence the golfer to plan ahead. Providing views of the next target to determine the next move is much different than displaying the entire hole from the start as a mechanism toward just one option. Of course, on a completely wooded site, that may be impossible to accomplish.

Golf architects can certainly utilize the Principle of Visibility as strategic incentive for taking a specific route, though. For instance, if one is on the left edge of a fairway facing a hazard that isn't visible from that side, it may be a hint that the next shot is best attacked from another spot. I utilized this technique in two different ways at Braemar Golf Course. The fourteenth hole is a dogleg-left par four with a ridge cutting into the fairway at the turning point from that side. A trio of bunkers is cut into the ridge, challenging the golfer who takes that shorter route off the tee. Those who decide to take the longer, safer route to the right concede visibility of the green the farther right they play.

This idea holds true on the twelfth hole as well but in reverse. On this dogleg-right par four, visibility improves the farther away one plays from the corner of the dogleg. This device increases the safety buffer from the adjacent eighteenth hole (a dogleg-right par four as well) where the play closer to the corner of the dogleg is rewarded. Once golfers realize the better angle into the green on twelve is the left side, and the better the angle into the green on eighteen is the right side, fewer will test the area separating the holes, resulting in fewer stray shots in adjacent fairways as well.

Holes #12 & #18, Braemar Golf Course in Edina, Minnesota.
(Courtesy: Richard Mandell Golf Architecture)

From an aesthetic standpoint, many debate the preference for isolated golf holes. Marketing gurus sell the prospect of eighteen individual environments as a benefit to playing a particular golf course isolated from everyone else. Others prefer a more open environment similar to links courses. The popularity of playing in an isolated environment rests in what is known as the "Prospect – Refuge" concept, in which people prefer environments whose surroundings can quickly be surveyed for suitability. Environments with both prospect and refuge elements are perceived as safe places to explore and dwell, and consequently are considered more aesthetic than environments without these elements. The comfort sought through the Prospect – Refuge concept mirrors the comfort golfers find in a black/white strategic scenario rather than a gray area. A more open environment, such as a links course, without clearly defined strategic options, creates an uneasiness many would rather avoid.

Hole #5, The Water's Edge Country Club in Penhook, Virginia.
(Courtesy: Richard Mandell Golf Architecture)

Whereas I have had some memorable moments of isolation on some golf courses - rounds at Cypress Point and Swinley Forest first come to mind – I also recall fondly those days playing high school golf matches communicating with my teammates across more open holes with updates about our matches.

Granted, these memories aren't a by-product of the architecture of the golf course, they are an experiential component of the architecture. The question, from a design standpoint, is should this be something architects strive for in their routing efforts? If I am handed an absolutely wooded site, then my decisions are made for me: I will have a mostly wooded golf course. But even though I see the emotional benefits of a series of wooded golf holes, I still bend to the Principle of Variety, preferring to route holes through both wooded and open landscapes.

The Author's junior days at Rye Golf Club, in Rye, New York, included many high school matches exchanging results with teammates on adjacent holes (#4 above is flanked by #5 to the left and #6 to the right). (Courtesy: Richard Mandell Golf Architecture)

In a wooded setting, I'll still create open corridors from hole to hole to maximize specific side-to-side views. Personally, my favorite view is standing on one fairway looking past the green to see how the next hole may unfold. The anticipation of what is coming next excites my senses. Strategically, this simple design device can distract the golfer just enough to create even more challenge for the task at hand.

Holes #17 & #18 at Hamilton Farms Golf Club (Highlands Course) in Gladstone, New Jersey. (Courtesy: Richard Mandell Golf Architecture)

Another mental battle the architect can create is keeping the elevation of each tee box as low as possible, concealing how much of the fairway is visible. In a round of golf, the desire to see one's ball physically land is strictly a means of comfort so by taking that away, the architect has ramped up the mental challenge, creating just enough discomfort to distract.

A perceived need to make fairways visible has created a standard of artificiality - tee boxes raised at least three or four feet above grade. This is, in some ways, the very definition of the Principle of Visibility in golf architecture: providing the golfer unobstructed views to witness the ball make contact with the ground. The result is a group of monolithic landforms which are hardly natural and require some challenge to maintain an accessible slope for golfers and equipment alike. Low-profile tee boxes, just high enough to shed rainfall and provide just enough definition, are more natural-appearing. Lowering one's line of sight those few feet provides just enough mental anguish to make the golfer ramp up their focus. This is a simple form of strategic "hazard" because it requires increased concentration, something both low and high handicappers are capable of and should rely on more than they probably do on a shot-by-shot basis.

Hole #2, Tanglewood Championship Course in Clemmons, North Carolina. Converging lines for two fairway bunkers (inset) creates the appearance of four bunkers. (Courtesy: Richard Mandell Golf Architecture)

I love to create varying sand bunker lines that don't completely reveal the shape of a bunker until one is standing over it. I particularly prefer to make single bunkers appear as multiple bunkers from the most common line of play. For these aesthetic advantages, I prefer to flash sand rather than create grass faces. Being mindful of maintenance and the ever-present challenge of keeping sand on bunker faces, I don't have one consistent specification as to how much sand to flash up the face of a bunker. That's entirely determined by the player's view. Bunkers placed uphill from the shot will have a good amount of sand flashed for visibility. Bunkers downhill from the intended shot may have minimal flashing, just to keep balls from getting stuck under the grass face and promote positive drainage.

Although the amount of flashing varies from situation to situation, the minimum sand-flashing must stay in proportion within the feature itself as well as the overall composition. There must be a visual balance of sand and grass to avoid scale issues. I only know of one way to explain these preferences to my construction team and that's in terms of pasta. I will never accept a flash of sand that's as thin as a strand of angel hair when viewed from where the next shot is to be played. It's just simply too thin to contribute to the aesthetic and all it takes is a few days removed from regular mowing before the sand is screened from view. In that vein, I am not much of a spaghetti or linguine guy, either. In fact, I will accept fettuccine at a minimum yet my preference runs somewhere between pappardelle and lasagna, nothing less.

That said, if constructing a visible hazard comes at such a cost to build and/or maintain, it's better left hidden. One spot where I was forced to leave a hazard concealed was the ninth hole at Keller Golf Course, one of the last holes we built there. Up to that point in the construction process, I was able to flash enough sand for all of the bunkers with little difficulty. But as we began constructing a fairway bunker to the left of the fairway, visibility from the tees became a challenge. The hole starts in a low area and quickly rises to the start of the fairway before gradually adjusting to a rise of five percent or so the rest of the way to the green.

Once my shaper completed the rough grading of the mound complex that would frame the sand, I began the process of painting the sand line, walking back and forth from the tee to see how much could be seen and adjusting the line after each trip. The last line that I painted brought tears to the superintendent's eyes. It was at that point I had to sacrifice my personal preferences for maintenance purposes. A blind bunker won't be as vilified over time as one that can't hold sand on such a steep slope. I surrendered, knowing that at least the top of the mounding gives some clue as to the bunker's presence.

Hole #9, Keller Golf Course in Maplewood, Minnesota. The bunker in question above. Get a good look, because you won't see it from the tee.
(Courtesy: David Parker Photography)

One golf course feature that should never be visible are cart paths. To me, there's nothing worse than a cart path that runs past tee boxes only to methodically cross to the other side of the fairway (surpassed only by a cart path that cuts between a fairway and a bunker). This design laziness is of epidemic proportions. Sadly, many

This combination of cart path front and center coupled with an over-the-top waterfall to the left and condos beyond is the Principle of Chaos in full regalia. (Courtesy: Richard Mandell Golf Architecture)

well-known golf courses have finishing holes (among many others) that absolutely clutter up the view with such an abomination.

Even sadder, I've lost many a cart path debate when "pace of play" and convenience won out. At one particular par four, I ran the path directly to the following tee instead of the green, which required golfers to walk the thirty yards to the green when the hole restricted carts to the path (a rare occasion on sandy soils). After just one season, claims of slow play motivated the General Manager to authorize construction of a cart path spur and turn-around just fifteen paces from the putting surface edge. The extension, it was claimed, saved everyone five minutes a round.

I'm very particular about keeping cart paths out of the golfer's cone of vision (the extent of one's normal area of view) and work diligently to conceal them. As early as the routing stage, I work to direct the cart path in such a way that it doesn't cross a golf hole. In addition to working out the cart path routing before construction begins, I ask my shapers to cut the path into the ground as they shape the golf course features simultaneously. That way, it's easy to screen it from view in a naturally-appearing way. If one waits until the golf course is completely shaped and irrigation is already installed to route the cart path, options will be severely limited.

In cases where it's impossible to avoid crossing a hole, concealment through elevation change can still do the trick. Simply dropping the path a foot or so as it crosses the fairway will be enough to conceal the path from the tee. In these cases, planting no-mow areas of native grasses does a great job of cart path concealment in addition to reducing manicured turf. Pitching the path away from the golfer is another way to conceal the path.

Adjusting the alignment of the path just a few degrees can greatly reduce the exposure to one's cone of vision as well. Sometimes, construction of a simple ridge can hide it from view all the way to the green. Other cases may necessitate a few mounds, which can be a risky proposition. No matter how well intentioned this approach may be, some path always seems to peek through the moguls. Often times, the mounds themselves will attract attention to the path.

One cannot discount the safety issues that make the Principle of Visibility such an important aspect of the profession. Most golf architects shy away from creating blind holes due to the risks involved. Although golfers take on a certain element of liability every time they step on a course, not adhering to safety standards, such as how far apart features must be spaced, can be considered negligence on the architect's part. Because land is at such a premium and historical precedent has created many tight situations, it's hard to pin down specific distances for guidance. Regardless, the golf architect should lean on the side of caution.

Beyond implementing safety distances between golf course features, devices such as mounding or trees (used sparingly) can create a buffer. Whereas mounding is a better alternative, either option can provide a false sense of security from both sides of the buffer. I have removed numerous hedgerows between greens and tees that were mere yards apart to provide visibility both ways. If no barrier exists, one (hopefully) knows to yell fore and others will quickly see where the danger is coming from. This full visibility approach is paradoxically effective.

In addition to safety, another benefit to the Principle of Visibility is pace of play. Although a blind shot may only be blind once, finding one's ball can last a lifetime. This is probably what MacKenzie was referring to when lamenting blind holes. Those surrounding sandhills are crucial in determining the path of a ball and subsequent reconnaissance. When balancing the Principle of Visibility and concealment of certain features, the golf architect must try to integrate as many details on the ground as possible to help golfers locate their line of flight to find their ball.

Inspiring golf course strategy is all about that gray area of indecision and conquering uncertain situations rather than making clear black or white choices. If one can see everything that's laid out in front of them there are no surprises, there are no questions, and there is no gray area. Again, fine for some, but I don't subscribe to that as a means to an end. I'd rather incorporate the Principle of Visibility just enough to make the golfer consider the best decision to make. It can make a powerful statement if one properly balances enough visual comfort to recognize potential danger while concealing enough strategic gray area to leave the golfer wanting more.

Hole #13, Bacon Park Golf Course in Savannah, Georgia. The view of the swale in front of the green is concealed from the left but the view of the putting surface from the right is concealed by the oak. (Courtesy: Richard Mandell Golf Architecture)

22 The Principle of Playability

PLAYABILITY – THE DEGREE TO WHICH A PIECE OF GROUND USED FOR SPORTS IS IN ACCEPTABLE CONDITION AND SUITABLE FOR PLAYING ON.

Many people confuse the idea of playability with how difficult a course is. Golfers may say a course is unplayable when they really mean that it's difficult to shoot a low number on or even enjoy the experience. Those who primarily seek out a low score on a difficult layout complain about playability more than those who don't worry about score and are only interested in it for the experience, taking things as presented.

The way I see it, if the components of the golf course exist and the journey from the first tee to the eighteenth green does not injure or kill someone, then it's playable. Those basic components are a teeing ground (only one is necessary), a fairway, and a green with a cup somewhere within its perimeter. One really doesn't need hazards such as water or sand to have a playable golf course by definition. While it's true that a course without such hazards may be boring or too easy, it doesn't affect it's playability. Nor does a course technically need rough. No matter how one classifies certain areas such as rough, those areas are the void surrounding the basic components of a playable golf course.

This chapter would be over by now if I simply dissected the technical definition of playable (suitable for playing on). Most courses, from those with million-dollar-plus maintenance budgets to those with a shoestring allowance and a skeleton crew are technically considered playable. The difference is the degree to which it's in "acceptable condition."

Golf architects must consider the Principle of Playability simply as a means to accommodate many different talent levels playing on many different sites. A designer that only provides the minimum "acceptable condition" wouldn't have much of a career and it's doubtful their courses would be very interesting.

Whereas the Penal School of Design is typically associated with a difficult golf course, it's still a playable layout unless there are extreme conditions such as fairways that require everyone to walk single file. Yet those conditions don't exist in anything but novelty posters. A narrow fairway with sand down both sides is still playable simply because it has grass to play off and sand to play out of. Extremely difficult? Yes. Unplayable? No.

When it comes to implementing Playability, though, its confusion with how difficult a course is muddies the water. The perception of a difficult condition

The third hole at The Ocean Course in Kiawah Island, South Carolina, becomes more playable as a golfer becomes more skilled enough to carry the water.
(Courtesy: Richard Mandell Golf Architecture)

varies from one golfer to the next. It can even change for the same golfer over time. Golf holes that I found difficult when I first played them as a youth became much easier after just a few years of practice and improvement. As equipment technology expanded, I was able to hit the ball farther and that made longer, more difficult holes more manageable.

Yet the courses from my junior golf days were always technically "playable," even those with plastic tees protruding from the bottom of actual door mats to begin every hole at Saxon Woods or Maple Moor in Westchester County, New York. But over time my definition of "playable" changed. When I was content shooting 100 most of the time, I had a wider berth for acceptable playing conditions. But as I (and most others) strove to get better, those courses were less "playable" to me based on my desire for more gratification. Yes, they were technically playable, but they weren't enough for me to continue enjoying the game.

I remember conducting a course walk-through for a project with a woman who played golf for more than twenty-five years but whose handicap was still north of 30. Ironically, she fought me on the idea of forward tees, certain that few women would ever use them. She also mentioned that she disliked her irons. The deep-rooted reason for her disdain, it turned out, was that she rarely got a chance to hit them. It took some time for her to realize it, but because the golf course from the teeing ground she used was so long she mostly hit woods, hence her high comfort level with those clubs. What caused her resistance to forward tees was the scary possibility of learning how to actually hit her irons. I would also venture to say she thought her home course was eminently playable because she never strove for improvement (most likely because she never thought it was an option). The components of golf were there so she seemed not to be too worried about ever getting her handicap under 30 or reaching a green in regulation.

So let's consider an expanded definition of playability and what the golf architect's responsibilities are to provide a playable golf course beyond simply "acceptable condition." Much of what encompasses the Principle of Playability (beyond the textbook definition) is associated with conditioning and maintenance rather than design.

Creating playable conditions for golfers of all talents is easier than creating equity for all (if that was the golf architect's goal). In other words, it would take extreme conditions to create a course or single hole that's unplayable for all. Playability specifically keys in on the "piece of ground used for sports" (in this case, golf).

In terms of actual playability, forced carries are really the only element of golf course design that can render golf shots unplayable, being impossible to hit for some talent levels. Severely undulating greens with no flat areas for pin placements (there actually aren't any rules for this, the USGA only suggests a two-foot radius surrounding the cup) can be considered physically unplayable as well. But beyond that, from a design perspective, all things are a go if the designer so chooses.

Alister MacKenzie's twelfth green at Sitwell Park Golf Club in Rotherham, England, was one of three controversial greens deemed unplayable by the members and subsequently demolished. He argued that an element of luck was a factor in playing the greens and *"if you succeeded in eliminating it, you would only succeed in making both cricket and golf uninteresting."* (Courtesy: Simpkin, Marshall, Hamilton, Kent, and Co. Publishers)

Yet similar to the Principle of Fairness, using the Principle of Playability to ensure the enjoyment of the game will result in a more successful product. From a literal standpoint, as in *"the degree to which a piece of ground used for sports is an acceptable condition and suitable for playing on,"* golf course features don't allow for playability.

Simply their existence, covered with an acceptable amount of grass on those features and sand (in any form) in the bunkers, is enough.

The point to be made is, with such a short and blunt list of "playable" features, the art of golf architecture has few, if any, restrictions on design. Placing the Principle of Playability at the forefront of one's design philosophy is a pretext for making things easier and eventually renders a golf course less interesting as well.

Yet from a design standpoint, the profession has taken a lot of the bite out of our hazards (in the name of playability) as a reaction to complaining golfers who put more value on their score than they do the overall experience. I have no problem utilizing the Principle of Playability to ensure the game's success for future generations but not to fix perceived difficulty or unfairness.

Nonetheless, contemplating the Principle of Playability can open up numerous opportunities for designers who choose to elevate their art beyond the basics of just making things "easy." One can't help falling into strategic design when making wide fairways. Fairway width allows a designer to consider different playing angles to different pin placements from multiple locations. A narrow fairway, albeit sufficient to be considered playable in its most basic form, limits the use of angles for strategic purposes. It's a difficult design challenge to vary one's angle of approach with a mere twenty-five paces or so to work with. A wider fairway not only opens up strategic possibilities, it allows for an easier tee shot to the fairway for the majority of golfers.

The Principle of Playability should never be the leading arbiter in the design or renovation of a golf course because it could lead to boredom and uninspired golf holes. If I was forced to design a golf course strictly for playability it wouldn't have designated tee boxes, allowing golfers to determine their own starting point on each hole. There wouldn't be water or sand anywhere and every fairway would funnel from the sides to collect golf balls to the middle, where lift, clean and place (on an artificial mat) would be in effect for one to hit their approaches to greens that direct everything to the center. Only a fantasy golf course with those characteristics can truly be considered playable by all.

Instead, I prefer following the basic definition of a golf course being in *"acceptable condition and suitable for playing on."* Beyond tees that don't minimize forced carries, a few out-of-scale bunkers, and greens with zero flat areas, there is almost nothing we can design that couldn't technically be considered playable.

The high bar of golf architecture knows the Principle of Playability is a great use of strategic form following function. The form of many features not only creates strategic challenge but makes the game more playable for those just starting out. If we provide those playing fields for beginners, they will soon graduate to aficionados who appreciate the challenge that strategy brings. The creative architect knows the use of width, angles, options, and choices fit the Principle of Playability like a comfortable glove. The formula for success is that more strategic options automatically create more playable conditions.

23 The Principle of Difficulty

Difficulty – Something that is hard to accomplish, deal with, or understand.

Difficult – Needing much effort or skill to achieve.

The literal definition of the Principle of Playability (suitable for playing on) leaves scant room for debate. Yet lengthy deliberation often occurs when regarding the figurative meaning of playability: Difficulty. The definition of difficulty is *"Something that is hard to accomplish, deal with, or understand,"* which differs from playability because the "something" (the golf course) may be designed in such a way as to make it hard to "accomplish" a low score or have an enjoyable experience. The course is still playable, but it requires extra effort or skill to achieve success.

Design features that can make a course difficult are bunkers that are too deep, greens with few flat spots, and forced carries. Design tools that can alleviate that difficulty comprise a short but powerful list as well: Additional tees to assure "Tee Shot Distance Equity," wide fairways, manageable carries, and putting surfaces that have at least some square footage for manageable cup locations.

Oakmont Country Club outside Pittsburgh, Pennsylvania, is considered one of the most difficult courses on the planet - even by professionals - characterized by numerous bunkers as well as deep rough. Shown is the 18th hole at the 2016 U.S. Open. (Courtesy: Wirestock Dreamstime.com)

Because playability is more akin to conditioning and course setup, many golfers confuse the terms playability and difficulty. Decisions made about deepening rough, narrowing fairways, and speeding up greens can cross the line from difficult to unplayable regardless of design intent. I prefer that features themselves derive difficulty for the golfer rather than maintenance adjustments, which are often made independent of a feature's design and usually without input from the course architect.

Putting surface design is one area where a golf architect can go over the line of difficulty with just a few inches of elevation change, especially if a club's membership is left to its own devices to chase green speed. That said, the design of greens complexes is a focal point where the golf architect can introduce the Principle of Difficulty without creating the perception of being unplayable. Detailed shaping of features that require a raised level of concentration will create that difficulty. With added details, the architect increases the level of difficulty for shots by asking the golfer to hit to specific spots along the target line.

Merely creating a continuous uphill slope from the front of a putting surface to the back allows golfers to chip or putt along that slope with little concern other than how much force to put into the shot. It requires some level of skill, but not as much as there would be if a mound was coming out of the slope between the golfer and the target. For example, one may have to land the ball on the opposite side of the mound for any chance to get on the green. Without the mound, the golfer only has to determine how much of a stroke should be made to get the ball rolling. The Principle of Difficulty incorporates the golfer's need to aim at a specific spot and correlate that aiming point with the proper amount of stroke.

One reason I am fond of creating tiers in putting surfaces, and why I think Donald Ross put such a premium on the same, was to place value on the short game to increase the golfer's concentration. It's much more challenging to chip, pitch, or putt to a specific quadrant on a green than it is to one with a continuously facing slope. It requires more focus from the golfer to successfully execute the shot.

Hole #12, Country Club of Asheville in Asheville, North Carolina. Without any original Donald Ross drawings to reference, we adapted a four-quadrant green from a similar Ross hole for this 321-yard, uphill par-four. (Courtesy: Richard Mandell Golf Architecture)

Utilizing the Principle of Difficulty around greens doesn't require fast putting speeds or adjusting grass heights. Deep rough will simply quell any detailed roll of the ground and minimize club selection as well, forcing only black or white decisions. Rather, the strategic gray area of a hole is a fulcrum for the Principle of Difficulty, creating just enough doubt in the golfer's mind as to the best shot choice. A narrow fairway with deep rough and sand down both sides has absolutely no gray area for consideration. A black and white strategic choice such as this leans toward penal, pulling the golfer to the wrong end of the difficulty fulcrum and away from strategic.

Par fives are my favorite hole to design because of the complexities of stringing three shots in a row. I particularly enjoy placing value on the second shot so there is some consideration beyond simply advancing the ball. For instance, placing a mound in the second landing area can be enough to create consideration for failing to hit the mark. My goal isn't to over penalize but to increase concentration and demand beyond just a gratuitous whack at the ball with few ramifications for lack of execution.

One par five with such an incentive is the fourth hole on the Red Nine at Army Navy Country Club's Arlington, Virginia course. Because I added what I call a "lingering hazard" short of the green (in this case a bunker), most golfers need to note the yardage and play accordingly. They can't just let loose in an attempt to get as close to the green as possible. Both full shots or lay-ups on this downhill hole may equally find that lingering hazard on the right side. The penalty for a lack of homework and/or focus will be one of the tougher shots in golf: a sand shot from fifty yards.

Hole #4 Red, Army Navy Country Club in Arlington, Virginia. The bunker set fifty yards short and right of the green complex lingers in the golfer's mind just enough to demand a precise second shot. (Courtesy: Richard Mandell Golf Architecture)

There are many courses that have built their reputation on the Principle of Difficulty. Oakmont Country Club in Pennsylvania and Muirfield in Scotland come to mind. These courses, and a good number of others, are considered extremely difficult to play for even the best golfers in the world. The memberships at both facilities (as well as many others) espouse this notoriety as their identity. Other clubs identify themselves as a major championship venue and constantly re-invent it for the next one. Congressional Country Club in Washington, D.C., Merion Golf Club in Pennsylvania, Oakland Hills Country Club in Michigan, and countless others have consistently added yardage to keep up with the pros at the expense of their lesser-skilled members.

The Black Course at Bethpage State Park on Long Island hosted its first major championship in 2002. Owned by the State of New York, it was completely revamped by Rees Jones in preparation for its first foray onto the major stage. Prior to that, the Black had undergone very few changes since A. W. Tillinghast's 1936 effort. One of my favorite courses of all time, it's also one of the most difficult. Even so, its topography is so good that as a youth in the 1980's I was willing to leave my house on countless summer Monday mornings, sit in bumper-to-bumper traffic for three hours, linger for another three hours before teeing off, and then spend an additional six hours losing ten balls and shooting ten shots over my average. Yet I enjoyed every minute of the experience. By the time we crossed Round Swamp Road heading for the last four holes, we morphed into a seven- or eight-some to, ironically, speed up play.

For me, the extreme difficulty of Bethpage Black was secondary to the tremendous routing of its holes. For others it was the cost to play. Regardless, as course architect George Thomas once remarked, we were all *"astounded by the fury of the battle."* Since its inception as an Open venue, however, Bethpage's mission has been to replicate the conditions of a major. Along with that shift came extreme green fees and extreme conditions as well. Gone are the wide fairways draped over the great rolls of the property, replaced with 25-yard-wide ribbons disconnected from the very topography that attracted golfers there in the first place. The artfully restored bunkering is disconnected from the ground, buried deep in the rough. The shame of

The disconnect between the bunkers and fairways of the 10th and 11th holes on the Black course at Bethpage State Park in New York. (Courtesy: Google Earth)

the modern Bethpage is that the State of New York has banked its marketability on the Principle of Difficulty rather than its great routing. The strategic charm of the layout gets lost among the narrow fairways and persistent length. And yet, it's harder than ever to get a tee time. The danger of embracing the Principle of Difficulty at Bethpage is what those who play there may take away from the experience – that difficulty may be the barometer for greatness.

The USGA's interpretation of difficulty can be inferred through its Course Rating and Slope Rating, two calculations developed to help establish golfer handicaps. A USGA Course Rating *"represents the score a scratch player, with a Handicap Index of 0.0, should achieve on a golf course under normal course and weather conditions."* For example, when a scratch plays a layout with a Course Rating of 73.0 they would expect to shoot a 73 under normal conditions. A Course Rating is established from each set of tees taking into account how roll, wind, elevation change, altitude, severity of dog-legs (which can impact the effective yardage of a hole), and forced carries impact the length of each hole.

To determine the Course Rating, the USGA utilizes ten specific "obstacle factors" to evaluate every hole for both the scratch (zero handicap) and bogey player (classified as a 20 handicap for men and 24 for women). These are *"topography, fairway, green target, recoverability and rough, bunkers, crossing obstacles, lateral obstacles, trees, green surface, and psychology."* An assessment of these factors from the bogey player's viewpoint determines an intermediate value called the "Bogey Rating." The numerical difference between the Bogey Rating and the Course Rating becomes a course's Slope Rating, which provides a variable handicap based on each course's difficulty instead of using the same handicap everywhere.

Considering Course Rating is mostly derived from the yardage quotient of a golf course, the USGA clearly considers length a major factor in a course's difficulty for the scratch golfer. I tend to agree because, for instance, it's more difficult to hit a green from 190 yards than it is from 140 yards. The USGA's Slope Rating, though, places much more value on their "obstacle factors" for the bogey golfer (by a factor of 2.5 times compared to Course Rating).

In other words, the USGA recognizes that many more challenges besides length affect the lesser-skilled golfers. Topography, fairway width, green size, the ability to recover from rough, number and depth of sand bunkers, forced carries (crossing obstacles), hazards along fairway edges (lateral obstacles), trees, putting surface contours, and the psychological ability to keep it all together from tee to green are much more challenging for the bogey golfer.

Because length is a common attribute of better players, their attraction to long courses is what drives much of their perception of what makes a golf course great. Usually blessed with more accuracy as well, most better players believe that long, narrow golf holes are the winning formula for great golf courses, squarely equating difficulty with quality. Add the aesthetic sizzle from hazards bordering each hole and there is little wonder what type of golf course dominates the mind and attention of the better golfers. As a result, new golf course development and a lot of renovation work - often led by golfers who are more scratch than bogey - almost always trends toward difficult more so than enjoyment. It's fair to say that better golfers are not as affected by rolling contours, target width and size, hazards, trees, and extreme green surfaces as much as the bogey golfer. Therefore, they forget about the genuine difficulty of the game that the lesser-skilled experience.

So it should come as no surprise that golf courses designed by professional golfers are inherently more difficult than those designed by professional golf architects. Quite often those courses are then marketed to the masses as a quality "golf" experience. Whether the clientele is physically capable of enjoying these "must-play" venues is another matter – a matter of consequence when so many players turn away from the game as a result.

The Principle of Difficulty should be sparingly utilized because of the exponential increase in difficulty from the scratch player's perspective to the bogey player's viewpoint. Courses should specifically mitigate difficulty by ensuring that length is not the sole basis behind strategic intent. Design sense is what divides the lines between enjoyable, difficult, and unplayable. By integrating Difficulty with other principles of design, such as Playability and Challenge, the golf course architect can effectively balance those lines.

Holes #6 (foreground) & #3, The Easton Club in Easton, Maryland. Balancing playability and difficulty can be accomplished by offsetting surrounding water features with large putting surfaces and manageable slopes. (Courtesy: Richard Mandell Golf Architecture)

24 The Principle of Fairness

FAIRNESS - THE QUALITY OF BEING REASONABLE AND JUST WITHOUT FAVORITISM OR DISCRIMINATION.

> *"Equity has nothing to do with golf. If founded on eternal justice the game would be deadly dull to watch or play. The essence of the game is inequality. Take your medicine where you find it and don't cry."* – Charles Blair Macdonald

Fairness is almost considered a dirty word to golf course architects, especially when uttered by golfers. Rarely, though, is a golf architect allowed to turn a blind eye to the Principle of Fairness, free to design without practical considerations. No matter how much a golf architect may want to sidestep the discussion, it's hard to avoid.

Whenever I engage a membership about its golf course the notion of fairness comes up almost immediately and by a cross-section of talent levels. As one breaks down their concerns, the *"fairness"* issue reveals itself as a matter of *"I don't like that because it keeps me from my low score, which I deserve and am entitled to."*

Lesser-skilled golfers often cite unfairness because they lack the ability to achieve a desired score. Many better-skilled golfers have much higher expectations but are the first to complain when they aren't met – often blaming just about everything but their own shortcomings. Some even cry foul when they witness the lesser-skilled *"getting away"* with a poor shot when it ends up equaling the results of their own *"much better"* shot.

Most games of skill are such that all elements of the playing field are completely equal. Every tennis court is exactly the same size. The height of the net is the same for everyone, the ball is the same size and made of the same material for everyone. The service court is in the same place and the out of bounds lines are the same every time. Only when the playing field is the same for everyone can a player's skill be fairly judged against an opponent.

The folly in trying to make golf courses fair for everyone is due to the fact that they're so varied. There are no common dimensions other than the diameter of the cups on the greens. This lack of consistency is why golf is better described as a sport played within and against a *natural setting* rather than a game of skill played on a dimensioned court or field versus an opponent.

Many golfers mistakenly confuse "fair" and "playable" when it comes to golf course architecture. Fair (defined as *"in accordance with the rules or standards"*) refers to the way a task should be undertaken. When the issue of fair comes up among many golfers, though, the target of their frequent attacks is usually the golf course itself or features therein. But in reality, the argument is actually about golf course preparation and conditioning (how the task of maintenance should or shouldn't be undertaken). The act of undertaking something may be fair or unfair (making a green too fast for existing contours) but an inanimate object (the green itself) cannot be deemed fair or unfair. It just exists.

The definition of playable (suitable for playing on) applies strictly to the appropriateness of a playing field. A course that has the necessary features to play the game such as a tee, landing area, and green (including the hole itself) are the basic parameters of playable. Whatever the composition of those features is (or what exists between those features) is irrelevant if one follows the strict interpretation of the definition. Even if there are hard-to-see sand bunkers strewn across a fairway from tee to green, technically the hole is playable, although likely considered unfair by many.

"Being particularly anxious that we should have one perfect hole on our new course, we canvassed separately the opinions of six of our leading links architects as to the construction. Their ideas we adapted 'in toto,' and feel that now we have at least one ideal hole!" (Courtesy: W. H. Smith & Son)

Many complaints about fairness have to do with green speed and quality of bunker sand (operations). Secondary issues such as a narrow fairway due to trees on both sides are also a by-product of course operations. The bottom line is, when one breaks down the definition of fairness on a golf course and eliminates any maintenance considerations, there are very few architectural features that can be construed as unfair. One such feature might be a shallow green fronted by a hazard that requires a certain club to reach it but a different trajectory to hold it. In other words, if the right club to carry the hazard is with a three-iron but the trajectory needed to keep the ball on the green is that of a pitching wedge, the putting surface is too shallow. If no hazard existed, at least the golfer could call on a variety of possible approach shots to handle such a shallow target.

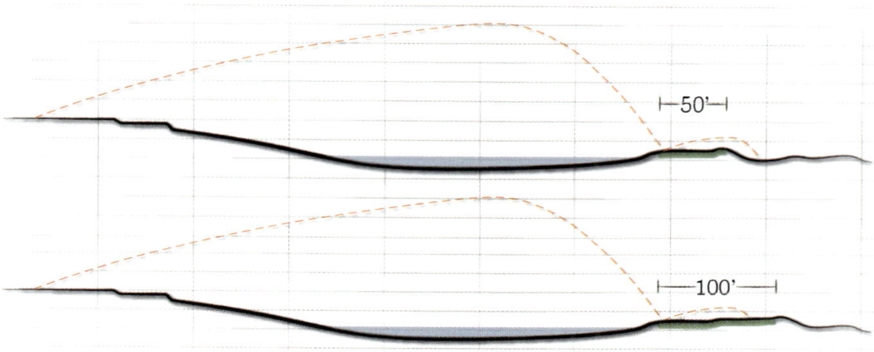

A forced carry to a shallow green with a long-iron has little chance to stay on the putting surface for most golfers (top) compared to a green that has more depth (bottom). (Courtesy: Patrick Gainer)

Another case is much more rare but happens enough that a golf architect must consider it: Creating a sand bunker that's so small that even the best golfers in the world have no ability to take a swing without hitting one side of the hazard with their swing. Due penalty for being in a bunker is an acceptable half-shot to a full shot, provided a swing can be made. Yet those who insist on fairness believe that every time golfers encounter sand, they should have the same success rate they have from the fairway. That's just not the case, because a bunker is a hazard and it should extract penalty for those who find one.

By 2012, the bunker to the right of the eighth green at Maidstone Club in East Hampton, New York, became too narrow to make a swing. Within months, the Coore-Crenshaw team restored it closer to its original width. (Courtesy: Richard Mandell Golf Architecture)

A difficult putt that must be perfectly struck isn't unfair; it's just difficult. Rarely, if ever, should the contours of a green be considered unfair because its speed can always be adjusted to match those contours. Unfortunately, that rarely happens because the modern golfer insists on speed over substance, eschewing fun and interesting highs and lows, ridges, swales, tiers and platforms for glass-like conditions with two-percent slopes everywhere. Daily pin placements are often considered unfair, even though they, too, are tied directly to green speed. Perhaps the only deviation is when pins are cut too close to the edge of a putting surface. Otherwise, cups cut anywhere else on the putting surface are well within the rules.

Even golf holes routed along severe side slopes that make it hard for a ball to stay in the fairway run a fine line between playable and unfair. Although many golfers zero in on the side slope as being the impetus for the unfairness, the fairway cut itself is often the culprit. Most of the time, adjustments to mowing height can compensate for the slope.

Hole #15, Oconomowoc Golf Club in Oconomowoc, Wisconsin. A severe cross-slope gives the impression that this fairway is unfair. Instead of a massive regrade, our solution to widen it to the left will keep tee shots in the fairway instead of always rolling into the right rough. (Courtesy: Richard Mandell Golf Architecture)

A frequent criticism that I hear from golfers of all abilities is the lack of flat lies in the fairways of many courses. I am always taken aback by these complaints because some of the greatest golf courses in the world have rolling fairways as a result of the natural topography on which they lay. This characteristic is one of the many reasons why golf and golf architecture are so compelling to so many. When golfers cry foul over a lack of flat fairways, I believe they are missing a joyous aspect of golf.

On the other hand, rarely do I hear that narrow fairways are unfair. It's as though golfers accept this condition as a critical tenet of the sport of golf. Originally only a course setup issue, it has crept into the design side as well. Thankfully, a renewed focus on strategic design and firm and fast conditions have re-introduced wider fairways. Unfortunately, the better golfers dislike wide fairways, feeling they "dumb-down" the golf course and minimize skill. Upon closer inspection, though, they might realize that wide fairways can be more treacherous to the higher-skilled than a narrow, runway-type fairway. A wider fairway can demand more ball control from better players because their usually longer tee shots can garner much more bounce and roll and balls can run farther off line. If the fairways are narrow, those same tee shots likely wouldn't find much trouble beyond rough. The lesser-skilled, on the other hand, gain a larger target for their frequent less-than-straight tee shots.

The first hole at Lake Forest Country Club (Hudson, Ohio) is a good example of how a wider fairway can be more challenging than a narrow one. Once we widened the fairway, a ridge was revealed that had previously been covered by deep rough. A line of White Pines blocked a creek at the bottom of the ridge further left. After widening the fairway and removing the trees and surrounding brush, the hole took on a brand new character because that ridge in the landing area now demanded much more precision off the tee. Any shots hit too far left can carom off the bulge

Hole #1, Lake Forest Country Club in Hudson, Ohio: Before clearing (above), rough and trees kept balls from straying too far off target. Once trees were removed (below), a natural crown deflected tee shots closer to a creek farther to the left. (Courtesy: Richard Mandell Golf Architecture)

down the hill toward the creek. Yet short hitters or the lesser-skilled simply gain a big catcher's mitt short of the ridge without the worry of hitting too far.

If fairness is indeed *"the quality of being reasonable,"* then a lack of tee box choices is unfair. Forcing the lesser-skilled to fall by the wayside because they lack the ability to reach a green in regulation from the only tees available is not a good formula for the business of golf.

Truthfully, much of the tee unfairness argument stems from the fact that most golfers play from the wrong tees based on their own unreasonable expectations. If a golfer playing from a certain set of tees is hitting it into water or bunkers on nearly every hole, that doesn't necessarily mean the golf course is unfair. Most likely it means they are playing from a teeing ground that may not match their skill set. The Principle of Fairness does not apply for those too stubborn to move up a tee or two.

Even though I never let fairness guide my creativity, I do utilize the Principle of Fairness so that more than one skill level can experience golf course strategy. As one who loves the central hazard, I prefer my tee boxes equitable so golfers can wade into the gray area of how that feature may affect one's decision-making. If lesser-skilled golfers were forced to play from tee boxes that are too far back for their game, they would never encounter a central hazard. They would always be hitting short of it off the tee and over it on their next shot. Creating multiple tee boxes to promote strategy for a variety of talent levels is a much more sensible use of the Principle of Fairness than removing interesting features elsewhere to eliminate *"unfairness."*

Of course, the central hazard is an easy target for those seeking out fairness in their golf games. The argument is always "How can you put a bunker in the middle of the fairway where everyone aims?" My usual response is an explanation of centerline golf, emphasizing the fact that the center of the fairway, although it may indeed be the middle, may not always be the best line of flight from tee to green. In

Hole #16, Myers Park Country Club in Charlotte, North Carolina. The central bunkers were built the year before the club constructed a new tee complex, which allowed everyone to challenge the hazards as designed. Lesson learned: Make sure the corresponding tees are built at the same time. (Courtesy: Richard Mandell Golf Architecture)

many cases, the proper line may be to the left or right. Ironically, it's also "more fair" to have multiple routes to choose from rather than just one.

The Principle of Randomness versus the Principle of Fairness would be a true heavyweight bout for the ages. If the primary reason to develop randomness is to create variety, uncertainty, contrast, and more, it would be impossible to develop fairness at the same time. By definition, fairness aims to create equal conditions or parameters for all players, which isn't the intent of the Principle of Randomness.

This conflict goes back to the thought that golf is not really a game of comparative skill between two opponents, and therefore does not need to provide comparable conditions for each. Golfers never technically fight for possession of a common object. A round of golf does not consist of one player on the offensive side trying to accomplish something specific and an opponent taking the defensive side trying to keep the offensive person from succeeding (although that would be fun to watch). Rather, competitive golf is between two people (or teams) comparing scores on a hole-by-hole basis (match play) or a group of people (or teams) comparing scores on a stroke-by-stroke basis (medal or stroke play) over a series of golf holes based on how each performed against nature (the course) in whatever condition the course may be in. Tennis, by contrast, pits two people of varying abilities on a court of exactly the same dimensions for both, an equally fair venture from both sides of the net and a game that ramps fairness up further by making players switch sides at equal intervals.

The Principles of Fairness and Visibility would certainly make great doubles partners. Visibility is a clear crutch for many, particularly those who strive for fairness in golf. The primary benefit of the Principle of Visibility is to let golfers see everything in front of them. That's certainly a fair approach, so to speak. As long as every golfer can see everything, there wouldn't be any hidden features or surprises that one might use to gain an advantage. I say the advantage goes to the team of Randomness and Chance, serving for the match over the teams of Visibility and Fairness. Home-course knowledge and the member's bounce tip the scales for me.

Unlike strategic and heroic design, penal design does not provide multiple options and often involves a carry that some golfers may not be able to pull off. That doesn't necessarily make penal design unfair, though. For starters, if teeing grounds are provided to achieve Tee Shot Distance Equity, any forced carries should be manageable provided the golfer has chosen the appropriate tees for their corresponding ability. Secondly, the width of a particular penal fairway is the same for all players regardless of which tees they are playing from. Hazard locations (which may line both sides) on a fairway are also the same for all. Granted, playability may come into question but fairness cannot. For example (theoretically), if one player were forced to play a narrow penal golf hole as their eleventh, and their opponent gets to play a wider, more open, and even shorter hole as their eleventh then that's certainly unfair. Yet playing the same exact hole cannot be considered unfair for one and not the other. Less playable, yes, but less fair, no.

A golfer cannot claim unfairness citing a lack of ability either; that's why the handicap system exists. Handicapping is a way to create equity among golfers of varying abilities, specifically because golf's playing fields differ so much. In fact, that is the exact reason every golf course has its own Course Rating and Course Slope for every teeing ground. Tennis does not need a handicap system because the court's dimensions are exactly the same for everyone.

"Rub of the Green" has been part of golf since its origins. The "Road Hole" starts with a tee ball over the Old Course Hotel. A shot off the wall is an *"accidental deflection"* with no sympathy for where the next shot may come from. (Courtesy: William Fullerton | Dreamstime.com)

The "Rub of the Green" concept defines how we should all consider the Principle of Fairness. It was originally explained in the Rules of Golf as an accidental deflection which has no bearing on its result; the golfer was to play the ball as it lay. Despite its removal from the rules in 2019, it still means there's no room for unfairness in golf. An accidental outcome in the path or lie of a ball is a deeply-rooted element of the sport. Therefore, if one's ball gets stuck under the lip of a bunker, and one's opponent's ball rolls to the bottom of the same bunker, as Mr. Macdonald advises, don't cry about it.

So what does all this mean when we consider the Principle of Fairness? Simply put, a golf course architect has very little responsibility in making a golf course "fair." Yet there is some benefit to architects who strive to make their work playable for as many golfers as possible. The trick is to design such a course where playability is achieved for all while providing challenges commensurate with each talent level without sacrificing strategic or visual interest. This is how the best designers apply the Principle of Fairness through the other principles of golf architecture.

What makes golf different from sports such as tennis or baseball is the diversity of its playing fields. By virtue of this diversity, golf is not a game meant to be fair. As soon as we give up on this diversity in order to balance the skill levels of the participants, we may as well give up on the sport of golf altogether. A game that's played outdoors and often in a variety of weather conditions cannot possibly worry itself about fairness.

"The only unfair hole is one on which a cup has not been cut." - Forrest Richardson

25 THE PRINCIPLE OF PENALTY

PENALTY - DISADVANTAGE, LOSS, OR HARDSHIP DUE TO SOME ACTION.

PENAL – HAVING A HARMFUL EFFECT; CAUSING DISADVANTAGE.

By definition, penalty implies that the *"disadvantage, loss, or hardship"* comes about based on a person's actions. In golf, as opposed to a penalty given to a player for breaking a rule, that particular action is a shot taken that did not go as planned. The person swinging the club is indeed the one who took action but the result of that action, where the ball ended up, is what results in penalty.

The most common topic of conversation in golf course design almost always comes down to strategy. Nearly every book on the subject references the "holy trinity" of golf course strategy: Penal, Strategic, and Heroic, and each one of these schools of thought centers around one common concept: Penalty.

The Principle of Penalty goes hand in hand with strategy. Without penalty to influence decisions, there is little need to strategize; whatever one chooses to do, there won't be ramifications. The variable among each strategic school, and what helps to differentiate each, is how often one faces potential penalty. Simply put, fewer strategic options increase the chance of penalty but the more options a hole offers, the less one may be penalized. As for what that penalty might be and how severe and in what form it comes, that's up to the designer.

Hole #10, Long Bay Club, Longs, South Carolina. (Courtesy: Long Bay Club)

The Penal School of Design centers on the concept that a hole can only be played one way. If a golfer doesn't play it that way, the golfer will be penalized. Any straight hole with a forced carry is undeniably from the Penal School of Design. A straight hole with hazards that run the length of each side is clearly penal as well. There is only one way to approach each example: Avoid the hazards. When there is a turn or bend in a hole, options are revealed through the Strategic School of Design, starting with cutting the corner of the dogleg to take a shorter route to the target. Expanding a narrow, straight fairway and varying its path around hazards allows a golfer to choose an option by introducing angles as well (at the very least, there are two routes). Even with sand down both sides of a turning fairway, a hole is strategic because of the different angles of approach.

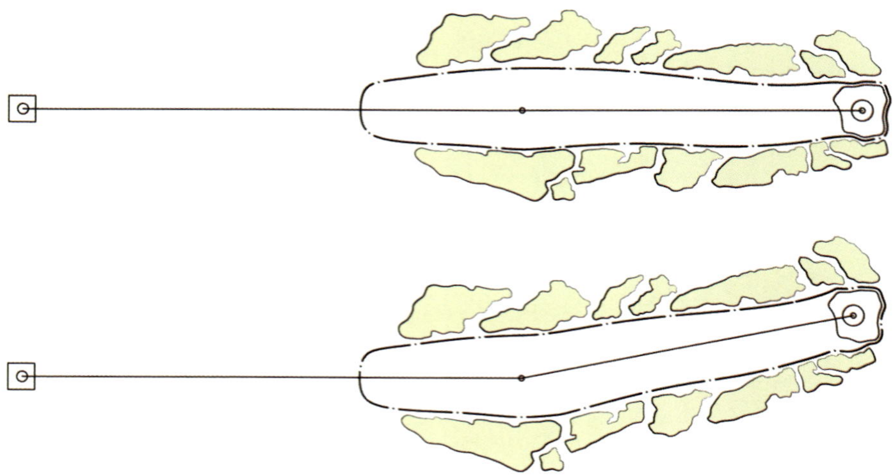

A penal hole (above) becomes strategic when just enough turn to the landing area is added (below). (Courtesy: Patrick Gainer)

I would venture to say that there are really only two overarching categories of course design strategy: The Strategic School and the Penal School. The Heroic School is a subset of the Strategic School for the simple reason that Heroic is a strategic approach to providing the golfer options. Placing a target on a diagonal to the line of play to entice one to "cut off as much as one can chew" to gain an advantage is the entire premise behind heroic design. The original approach of this type may well be Charles Blair Macdonald's "Cape" hole design with a target on the edge of a hazard set on a diagonal from the teeing ground or approach, egging the player on to carry as much danger as possible for a shorter second shot, or play to a safer point *away* from the hazard. By choosing the latter, the player is accepting the extra distance needed for the next shot as a penance for taking less risk. Macdonald's par-four fifth hole at The Mid Ocean Club in Bermuda always comes to mind, the risk clearly evident from its elevated tee.

Hole #5, The Mid Ocean Club, St. George's, Bermuda. (Courtesy: The Mid Ocean Club)

Robert Trent Jones, Sr., made the concept his own by deliberately creating hazards to carry off the tee that asked the golfer to take more risk with the promise of more reward, even naming it "Heroic." Originally utilizing sand as the primary hazard, he eventually incorporated water as his heroic hazard.

The Heroic subset of the Strategic School of Design can be utilized in less obvious ways as well. For instance, my use of central hazards has a bit of heroic design when there is just a hint of a turn to a golf hole. In reality, carrying the far corner of a central bunker to cut the dogleg is a form of heroic design.

This differs from the more traditional strategic approach utilized by Jones' golden age forefathers, even dating back to the heathlands-style course designers of the British Isles. Jones early contemporaries such as Ross and Tillinghast often approached strategy in a more subtle way based on the day's course set-up. For instance, a bunker on one side of the fairway may come into play based on where the cup is located that day. If it was placed on the left side of a green, the golfer's better angle to attack the flag was from the right side of the fairway. The golfer would have to position their tee shot as close as possible to a bunker on that side in order to have the best angle to the green. If the hazard was close enough off the tee, the golfer could also try to play over it.

Often times, golden age architects would place bunkers on both sides of the fairway to allow for different lengths of tee shots to be played. On days when the pin was on the right side of the green, the right-side bunker would not factor into play. Instead, the left-side fairway bunker would become the focal point of the day's strategy, and if it was the shorter of the two off the tee, it could be carried. This really is Strategy 101, the most basic approach to the Strategic School of Design. Yet, along with the fundamental concept of the Heroic School, there are numerous variations to strategy. The one common denominator is that the golfer always has two or more ways to play a certain hole. If the golfer chooses one way and fails, appropriate penalty will be administered.

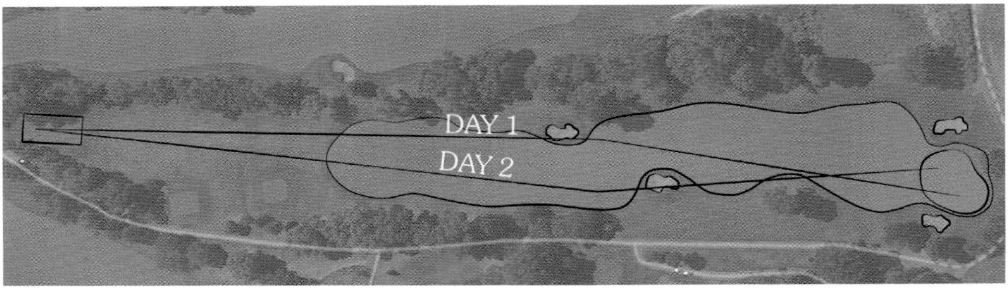

Hole #8, Keller Golf Course in Maplewood, Minnesota. Fairway bunkers are juxtaposed to create challenges based on the day's hole locations. (Courtesy: Richard Mandell Golf Architecture)

The codependency of strategy and penalty is either a cup half-full or cup half-empty scenario. Over the past century or so, American golf architecture has leaned more toward the idea that penalty is the focal point of strategic design. In other words, one will design a specific hole to ensure the golfer will be penalized for failing to perform a shot. If one is looking to penalize failure, what better way is there than to add yet another bunker to the side of a fairway or the corner of a dogleg? Multiple bunkers in the corner of doglegs are the ultimate expression of penal design.

British golf designer Tom Simpson reveals a more positive, half-full approach that rewards the golfer for accomplishment rather than penalizes the golfer for failure. *"Broadly speaking, in the 'penal' school you are directly punished by the fact of your bad shot being trapped in a hazard. For ourselves, who adopt the 'strategic' principle, we would never countenance the placing of fairway bunkers to catch a bad shot. To play a hole as it is intended by this* [strategic] *method means that certain positions are laid down for opening up the play to a green, and if the player fails to reach them he is faced with certain disagreeable consequences."* This approach also limits the need for multiple hazards right out of the gate because if one wants to reward specific play, only one hazard is needed.

In course architecture, there is a great distinction between the words penal and penalty. Penal indeed has a *harmful effect* on one's score and *causes disadvantage* in trying to shoot a low number. The penalty itself (actual *disadvantage, loss, or hardship due to some action*) can be doled out regardless of a golf hole's strategic intent. For example, hitting into a fairway bunker off the tee will result in penalty by the sheer fact that it wasn't intended and is literally a detour from the golfer's plan. It will take more effort to extricate oneself from that bunker and back onto the road to par than from the fairway.

The Principle of Penalty's effectiveness varies based on how much a penalty actually detours one's plan and is measured in added strokes to one's score. Did the hazard not affect the golfer at all in the pursuit of par? Will it take one stroke or more to get back on track? Generally speaking, the more strokes it takes to get back on track, the more penal that particular hazard is, which is entirely subjective based on who is playing. Better golfers may only incur a half-stroke penalty whereas others may place more than a full-stroke penalty in the same hazard based on their own personal skill level. After all, the effort a 30-handicapper undertakes to get out of a bunker will always be more than a tour professional.

Obviously, there is no such thing as a half-stroke penalty in golf. No one ever shot a 79.5. What a half-stroke penalty means is that for every two times a golfer hits a shot into a particular hazard, that golfer gets "up and down" for their intended score only one of those times. When one refers to a hazard with a stroke penalty value to it, the accepted result is understood to be one stroke more for the hole than if one *did not* hit into the hazard. It must be noted that the "penalty" of a half-stroke or more in the discussion of hazards is purely figurative. It's a measurement of how many more strokes one may take to recover from a hazard.

A hazard's difficulty is mostly defined by the golfer's ability to extricate the golf ball from the hazard. In the case of a sand bunker, the factors that affect its difficulty are depth of sand, whether the sand is firm or soft, and how large the bunker is. In other words, do the conditions of the bunker allow one to take a reasonable swing at the ball? The deeper and smaller the bunker is, the more penalty that bunker may impart. A shallow waste bunker, by contrast, may pose no more difficulty for the majority of golfers than playing a shot from the fairway. An attempt from a ten-foot-deep bunker, however, may impart more than a one-stroke penalty - especially if one can't even make a proper swing in it.

Water, on the other hand, will always impart the same stroke penalty. It doesn't matter how deep or small the hazard, golf balls will sink to the bottom every time. But the most penal hazard in golf is marked by white stakes, denoting areas that are out of bounds with a stroke and distance penalty applied, meaning not only is a stroke added to the score, one has to return to the spot where the shot was played from and hit again.

On the opposite end of the spectrum, rough has varying degrees of penalty. Shallow rough may be considered a quarter-shot penalty. Two-inch-deep rough is typically considered a half-stroke penalty. When rough gets deep enough (around three inches) to be a one-stroke penalty golfers begin to take notice and consider some sort of insurrection when it gets any longer. Rough any deeper than a one-stroke penalty is usually reserved for U. S. Opens and other such challenges.

The Principle of Penalty as it relates to hazard placement should reflect the topography. For the architect who considers the ground itself a hazard, few additional hazards are needed, allowing the land to determine strategy and suitable penalty. When one is blessed with dramatic features such as the coastline of an ocean, one also accepts more penalties for wayward shots than for those on featureless property. Typically, more artificial hazards are found on land that lacks natural inspiration. For some reason, many golf architects pre-determine penalty as a viable substitute for the lack of natural features. That inherent urge to create penalty when the ground is not so interesting ties directly to applying the Principle of Penalty for penalty's sake.

Golf holes that appear penal and hazards that are penal are not necessarily conjoined. Hardpan sand surrounding a hole may not be any more difficult to play from than playing off a tight grass lie. On the other hand, the pair of bunkers that were added to the middle of the fourth fairway of Woking Golf Club, in Woking, England, by John Low and Stuart Paton in 1893, were *strategically* located yet are very *penal* hazards. The bunker closest to the tee measures barely twenty feet by eighteen feet and the farther pot measures just eighteen feet in diameter. Modeled after the famous "Principal's Nose" bunker complex found in a similarly-central spot on the Old Course's sixteenth fairway in St. Andrews, they were pivotal in forming Tom Simpson's design philosophy: *"I realised for the first time, as soon as I saw this much-maligned hazard, that the true line to the hole should not always be the centre of the fairway, and the placing of a bunker had a far more serious and useful purpose than merely the punishing of a bad shot. This led me to see the importance of golf architecture as an art as well as a science."*

Hole #4, Woking Club, Woking, England. (Courtesy: Richard Mandell Golf Architecture)

For most golfers, the center of the fairway is the presumptive best route to take, which is probably why so many golfers deride central hazards as being penal by nature. But unless they cross the fairway entirely with no alternative route, they shouldn't be considered an element of penal design. In fact, they are the antithesis of penal design because they inherently offer the golfer at least four options of attack: playing short of the hazard, playing long, or to the left or right. The central hazard forces golfers to reconsider the notion that hazards shall only be limited to the edges of a target.

Many golf course designers throughout history have made penal design their trademark. The question is whether they did so as a by-product of aesthetics or under the auspices of strategy. Such a question is ripe for debate and has been since golf courses were first designed. For William Fownes, co-founder of Oakmont Country Club outside Pittsburgh, there was no question as to his architectural intent: *"A shot poorly played should be a shot irrevocably lost."* Hundreds of sand bunkers later, he had indeed created a monster that has rarely been matched. Fownes chose not to pursue design beyond the confines of Oakmont.

The author in a "penal" bunker on the "strategic" seventeenth hole at Pete Dye's Honors Course in Ooltewah, Tennessee. (Courtesy: Richard Mandell Golf Architecture)

Many other designers have shared Fownes' appreciation for penal design over the years but I have trouble bringing them to mind, likely because their approach led to short careers. A designer such as Pete Dye, though, often considered someone who penalizes golfers repeatedly, isn't necessarily a penal golf architect. In fact, his approach to golf architecture was to create a gray area of strategy to challenge the better golfers. Essential to his approach are many avenues to achieve a low score. The lesser-skilled just get caught up in a vortex of penal hazards along the way, making it seem as though Dye is indeed the godfather of the Penal School of Design.

How much penalty is too much? In most justice systems, the bigger the crime, the bigger the penalty. But following this line of reasoning in golf design penalizes the very people who can't handle such penalty: the lesser-skilled. Although their actions produce a specific result, those actions are rarely intentional. Yet most hazards are structured so that the further offline one's shot is the costlier the penalty. Even Donald Ross specifically made the portion of some his bunker faces furthest from the line of play the highest, referencing his work on the fifth hole at Brae Burn Country Club in West Newton, Massachusetts, as a prototype, *"Raised faces should be asymmetrical. The farther off line a shot is, the higher the bank over which one must play."*

This late-1930's view from the fifth fairway of Pinehurst No. 2 shows both fairway bunkers and greenside bunkers with higher faces farther off-center. (Courtesy: Tufts Archives)

Yet penalty administered for shots that are simply mishits only slow down the pace of play, discouraging the lesser-skilled in the process. Applying the Principle of Penalty for the most wayward shots to the least-equipped is especially excessive because it rarely penalizes the better players in the same way. Better players intentionally try precarious shots, understand the risks they're taking, and usually have the skill to pull off those shots. Therefore, a hazard that challenges the golfer to take the most risk should be more penal than those that are put in place simply to collect poor shots. For example, a fairway bunker that's a challenge to the golfer that goes for a reachable par five in two should be a penal one – possibly costing the player, if unsuccessful, more than a one-stroke penalty. On the other hand, bunkers that guard both sides of a green but have no real effect on gaining an advantage shouldn't be as penal.

> *"Hazards should only be calculated to catch and punish a player who, after playing a bad or faulty stroke, deserves to meet such a fate."* – J. H. Taylor, five-time Open Championship winner (before World War I).

It always seems to me that better players have the half-empty attitude regarding strategy mentioned earlier in this chapter. Personally, I'm just not a fan of penalty for penalty's sake; siding with Simpson more so than Taylor (and the many professional golfers that followed Taylor). Unfortunately, to this day, those better players are also the most influential. Their design approach of "Penalty is King," exclusively using hazards to curb success, flies in the face of fun and enjoyment. Whichever approach toward penalty that architects adopt usually reveals their penchant to promote challenge or penalize failure. The variety in both approaches makes the art of golf architecture so diverse, once again hammering home the idea that there are no rules in golf course design.

I often frustrate golfers who ask me to describe my intentions for a particular hole. My usual response is that I don't have a specific, mapped-out strategic intent. I know how *I* may play the hole but I deliberately don't dictate the way others should play a particular hole from start to finish. If I wanted to do that, I would just design penal golf holes, forcing all players to follow the same route.

I do, however, contemplate the possibilities as I design. In the end, I prefer to simply present a hole to golfers and let them determine their best path and attack it in whichever way they choose. My job as a golf architect is to provide starting and ending points for a golf hole that fit as naturally into its environs as possible, presenting a variety of thought-provoking elements in between. Those features solely exist to challenge the golfer to finish in as few strokes as possible. The choices made are by their own volition and as long as I provide options, their final score is their own as well. The Principle of Penalty is never one I intentionally pursue in this process. I am a "half-full" designer and my mantra will always be that the placement of a hazard is to challenge, not penalize.

26 The Principle of Challenge

CHALLENGE – A STIMULATING TASK OR PROBLEM THAT TESTS A PERSON'S ABILITY; A CALL OR SUMMONS TO ENGAGE IN BATTLE, CONTEST, SPECIAL EFFORT, ETC.

In golf, the Principle of Challenge is often mistaken for the Principle of Difficulty. The terms are practically interchangeable because better golfers consider a difficult shot or hole challenging when their physical ability offers them an opportunity to succeed. The lesser skilled, on the other hand, see difficulty as a bit less desirable.

Just as the level of managing difficulty expands with an increase in proficiency, the same is true for challenge as well. The simple challenge of not topping the ball is plenty for beginning golfers. Yet as their skill increases, the challenge of carrying a water feature from a particular tee, making birdie on a particular hole or breaking one-hundred, ninety, eighty, etc. replaces the challenge of keeping one's head down.

The fundamental difference between the Principle of Challenge and the Principle of Difficulty is also the fundamental difference between the Strategic and Penal Schools of Design. Penal Design requires all golfers to overcome the same obstacle(s) one specific way regardless of ability. If one lacks the skills to overcome the obstacle, any attempt to do so is pure difficulty. It does not stimulate one's mind to solve a task or problem, especially if one is buried in a pot bunker five feet below the surface of a fairway and lacks the skill to get out.

The sixteenth at the Cypress Point Club is a difficult challenge, even when played as a par four from the front tees, as viewed from above. (Courtesy: Richard Mandell Golf Architecture)

The Strategic School, by contrast, is more thought-provoking, allowing golfers of varying skill sets to overcome the same obstacle through alternative routes. The Principle of Challenge involves the testing of not just one's physical ability but intellectual prowess as well. Designers who try to ensure that the majority of golfers have options based on varying abilities structure their whole strategic approach around the Principle of Challenge. It's called upon when the architect's motivation is to provide reward for a good choice rather than simply surviving to the next shot. That's just difficulty.

Challenge is a vital principle for golf architects who seek out opportunities for gain rather than roadblocks to success. Looking at a split fairway, wondering if one should go left, right, short, or long, is a challenge to embrace. "Which is my best route to take to get to the green in the least number of strokes?" is always more stimulating than "I don't have a shot for that."

Hole #6 White, Army Navy Country Club in Arlington, Virginia. Fairway bunkers offer a choice of playing an approach from either side of the fairway, hitting driver as close to the green as possible, or laying back from the trouble for a full short iron. (Courtesy: Richard Mandell Golf Architecture)

The very definition of strategy is to challenge the golfer and one way to do that is to provide options for a choice that may or may not work that day. If the golfer chooses an option that *doesn't* work, the chances are good they will choose a different option the next time. One may not realize it in the moment, but if the desire to choose *another* option is equally strong, the course architect may have succeeded in incorporating the Principle of Challenge. Without it, golfers lack options to choose from and have no reason to return to that particular golf course. As designers, that's what we want from the golfer, the realization that there was more than one solution and the desire to try again.

The architect's placement of hazards through penal or strategic design will directly affect that desire one way or another. If success or failure is only based on physical ability (penal design), there isn't an opportunity to play a course differently and there is no desire to return. Yet if the test is multiple choice (strategic options), the golfer can choose a different answer on subsequent visits, learning the subtleties of the site along the way. A golf course that repeatedly applies the Principle of Difficulty through only one skill set, such as length, will attract only one type of golfer and minimize repeat play. Even those that have the requisite ability will often find such a layout redundant if the Principle of Challenge does not address any other elements of their golf games.

What complicates matters is when strategy is lost on the player who routinely hits driver/wedge on holes where most golfers will be hitting approach shots with four-irons to seven-irons. At some point, all the strategic options in the world cease to challenge the longest hitters. A hole with a wide fairway, for example, whose strategy favors one side off the tee to avoid a bunker protecting the green, will not affect the bombers. For players that routinely drive it so long and precise, strategic angles don't matter. The bomber's skill set allows them to hit a shot as high as they want, knowing they can drop it over a bunker to a tight pin and stop it quickly. Whereas the lesser-skilled may be content with avoiding the sand and reaching the green in regulation, a more appropriate challenge for the longer players may be to hit their approach within a five-foot circle of the flagstick.

Hole #16, Monroe Country Club in Monroe, North Carolina. The less skilled golfer may be content by simply avoiding the front bunker. The better golfer will find it challenging to drop an approach over the bunker to a front pin placement. (Courtesy: Richard Mandell Golf Architecture)

Rather than completely change a hole to combat length (adversely affecting everyone else in the process), golf architects should focus on general hazard placement for the majority and turn to the little details of design to challenge those who regularly hit driver/wedge within a five-foot circle. A smart architect will utilize the Principle of Challenge to place a mound or a ridge in a particular location or create a swale running through the green to make it more challenging to get a ball inside that circle.

The Principle of *Difficulty*, on the other hand, does not always apply to brute strength. Golf courses with eighteen roller-coaster greens are difficult for everyone other than the expert putter. Placing such a premium on putting not only neutralizes the long hitter, it minimizes the effectiveness of golfers who hit expert approach shots as well. That's because it doesn't matter how good one's iron game is or how smartly one can decipher strategy if one doesn't ever have a reasonable putt. On a course where every green should have a windmill, playing approaches from whichever side of a fairway doesn't mean much.

A challenge is *"something that by its nature or character serves as a call to battle, contest, or special effort."* The best golf architects embrace this call to incorporate the Principle of Challenge every chance they get, whether it's from tee to green or simply from the front edge of a putting surface to a back pin placement. The architect transforms the ground and its landforms into tools (hazards) to summon players to engage in a battle of wits between the course and themselves.

Hole #15, Isla Del Sol Yacht & Country Club in St. Petersburg, Florida. The Principle of Challenge can simply be found in a chip or pitch over a grass hollow to a back pin placement. (Courtesy: Richard Mandell Golf Architecture)

For the Principle of Challenge to be most effective, there must be some assessment of risk. Standing on a tee box with the opportunity to swing out of my shoes happens only when I lack any fear of reprisal. If there are never any ramifications for one's shot choice, there's no skin in the game. Golfers must be willing to live with the consequences of their actions to truly be challenged.

The Principle of Difficulty demands the question: "Will I be able to overcome this physical test?" But the Principle of Challenge asks a more thoughtful question: "What options do I have to overcome this test?" Challenge allows golfers to assess their own abilities and determine their own risk from shot to shot, a process that allows different skill-sets to overcome the same obstacle. All of the great courses of the world - from the Old Course to Pebble Beach - incorporate challenge in this way.

27 The Principle of Quirk

Quirk - Something that is strange and unexpected; a sudden twist, turn, or curve.

The primary definition of Quirk is *"something that is strange and unexpected."* The discovery and appreciation of that something makes the Principle of Quirk an intriguing, almost ethereal, aspect of golf architecture. Quirk's effect ranges from emphatic on the natural side to subtle on the manufactured end.

A more specific definition of Quirk, *"a sudden twist, turn, or curve,"* connotes a change that creates an opposite, or contrasting, quality. The common thread in both definitions is the element of surprise (defined as *"a completely unexpected occurrence, appearance, or statement."*) Golf architects can utilize the Principle of Quirk by incorporating a natural feature into a hole, or deliberately creating a sudden twist, turn, or curve within the structure of a manufactured feature. If done well, the strange and unexpected result will be a surprise, and hopefully a pleasant one.

Being surprised at how good something may be is not the same as discovering something that is strange or unexpected. One does not utilize the "Principle of Surprise" to coax a reaction from the end user. Genuine surprise on a golf course comes from the discovery of something unanticipated. Because surprise is a feeling that doesn't *physically exist*, it's wholly dependent on a vehicle like the Principle of Quirk for that reaction.

A fine line exists between what is considered a quirky feature compared to one that's simply thought-provoking. If a random mound's appearance is a pleasant result of a site constraint, quirk is achieved. If the appearance isn't pleasing, though, that doesn't necessarily mean it's a bad idea. It may just mean it isn't quirky.

To me, quirk only works if it's actually appreciated, making it a subjective ambition. Designers who set out to deliberately create "quirky" golf course features often cross the line toward poor design. When quirk is done poorly, and lacks appreciation from the end user, pleasant surprise is replaced by disdain, exposing the Principle of Gimmick. By definition, Gimmick is *"a trick or device intended to attract attention, publicity, or business."* The Principle of Gimmick is expected to garner a surprise from the golfer just like the Principle of Quirk. But the result is fleeting at best, especially once surprise subsides and the reality of an impossible shot stares the golfer down.

When quirk fails, one is left with gimmicks running the gamut from artificial rock formations to angular golf course features to manufacturing building ruins as strategic challenges. Randomly dropping a stone wall within a hole is pure gimmick. Replicating holes which are more famous for their actual setting than their architectural quality falls into the gimmick category as well.

Although a designer may want to manufacture quirk in golf architecture, to me, *genuine* quirk is revealed when an irresistible force runs into an immovable object. When a golf hole (the irresistible force) must be routed around a topographical feature (immovable object) because that topographical feature can't be altered, the form the hole takes becomes quirky. Quirky golf course features are simply anomalies of the landscape that can't be avoided.

One such anomaly that falls into the realm of quirk is the lone drumlin that anchors the property of Braemar Golf Course in Edina, Minnesota. Its presence is surprising because it's the only feature of its kind rising out of a rolling piece of ground. Granted its scale can hardly capture anyone by surprise, but its existence is such a contrast to the surrounding property that it's simply unexpected. It's also unavoidable, given its close proximity to the clubhouse area. Although someone suggested bulldozing it flat, it was an immovable object that wasn't going anywhere. My job was to apply some irresistible force to that object. That force became the much appreciated teeing ground for the par-three thirteenth hole, its green spread out eighty-five feet below. Although there are other downhill shots at Braemar, none unfold so dramatically within such a short distance. My placement of the tees can hardly be considered a surprise or even unexpected, though. In fact, I felt compelled to go as far uphill as I possibly could to take advantage of this landform. Whereas the landform may be quirky, the hole itself is not a quirk at all.

Hole #13, Braemar Golf Course in Edina, Minnesota: Looking back from behind the thirteenth green gives the best perspective of the height of the central drumlin, which dwarfs the rest of the rolling property. (Courtesy: Richard Mandell Golf Architecture)

My perception of the Principle of Quirk requires authenticity, meaning that quirky golf holes evolve out of naturally quirky landforms. An example is the Dell hole, the 154-yard par-three fifth hole at Lahinch Golf Club in County Clare, Ireland. Its shallow and hidden green sits within a collection of large mounds. I would say the green site was chosen by designer Old Tom Morris *because* of its position within those dunes. Being an Irish links site, few, if any, features there would be considered quirky because they are typical of the landscape in that corner of the world.

Old Tom could have placed that particular green anywhere else on that piece of ground. The fact that he chose the greensite that he did – nestled inside a trio of natural dunes - does not make it a quirky hole. On a links site, it's not a surprising or unexpected green location. It's the opposite: Almost an *expected* location for a green within the realm of great links design on such a property. Its location is a testament to the talent of Old Tom Morris. There are other greens in Ireland chosen by Old Tom Morris that simply aren't as memorable.

The "Dell Hole" at Lahinch Golf Club, County Clare, Ireland (circa 1900)
(Courtesy: Lahinch Golf Club)

The Dell hole is not a result of the Principle of Quirk. Rather it's simply a result of great design. Fast forward a few hundred years and let's place that green somewhere within the interior of the United States. If I saw it in the sandhills of Nebraska, I still wouldn't credit the Principle of Quirk because that landscape is dominated by similar natural features. On the other hand, place it within a series of hills on a relatively flat landscape on the outskirts of Mobile, Alabama, and it would probably be looked upon as strange and unexpected. In that case, the Principle of Quirk would have had as much to do with its location as anything else.

Extreme elevation change is always a surprising revelation for golfers. For modern designers, it's a product of Shock Scale (*can be either smaller or larger than a human, but in such a dramatic way that it literally takes our breath away*). Pete Dye relied on such vertical change by utilizing other principles of design (such as Contrast and Emphasis) with such regularity that there is little unexpected surprise from the golfer. His features are extremely dramatic, but not necessarily quirky.

Yet Golden Age architects that implemented the same approach are credited with successful utilization of the Principle of Quirk, partly because their work has been in place for so long. Their earthwork limitations and apparent restraint in replicating these features from hole to hole bring the Principle of Quirk to the forefront as well. Such vertical exaggeration is the irresistible force based on the immovable-object limitations of a site.

Architects such as C. B. Macdonald and the team of William Langford and Theodore Moreau utilized extreme vertical exaggeration simply as a device to create grade change. Their work, more than many of their contemporaries, stands out to this day for contrasting reasons. Macdonald's was performed for some of the most exclusive golf clubs in America which, thankfully, had the foresight not to allow changes over time. Thus his features are well-preserved. Langford and Moreau's design work resided more in the public domain and, fortunately for history's sake, there was no opportunity to change their work. The seemingly quirky appearance of many of their bunker-less greens is due to cost-cutting bunker removal as much as anything.

A green without a bunker is often seen as a quirk yet is most likely the result of an initial design decision by the architect or as a maintenance decision as described above. I will often create at least one bunker-less green per project just to demonstrate that sand should never be a requisite for good design. As quirky as that philosophy may seem, it isn't necessarily a product of the Principle of Quirk.

Hole #15, Isla Del Sol Yacht & Country Club in St. Petersburg, Florida: This bunkerless green is one of my favorite designs because it offers more short-game options than if it were surrounded by bunkers. (Courtesy: Richard Mandell Golf Architecture)

Many course features which are considered quirky today were most likely viewed as part of the design lexicon of the past. Immovable objects that were focal points of many holes were considered the price of doing business. It's usually not an issue today because those same types of objects are no longer considered immovable.

Design features from the past that still exist today, such as blind and square-shaped greens or the occasional "chocolate drop" mound, are considered quirks because they stand out in form and shape compared to modern features. The same is true of many punchbowl greens, which were once immovable objects because of earthmoving limitations. In other cases, they were intentionally placed in hollows to take advantage of natural irrigation. Today, they are accepted as quirky design staples from another era. Specifically, they are quirky because it's rare to encounter putting edges that rise up rather than roll downward.

A completely blind green that's a result of the inability to move dirt is the embodiment of the Principle of Quirk, yet blindness is not the only requisite for a quirky green. Odd-shaped greens that seem gimmicky at first may be a response to the ground through the Principle of Quirk. A basic example is a putting surface that's wider than it's deep. Any putting surface which is forced into its location based on the immovable character of a particular site can be classified as a quirk.

Many greens at White Bear Yacht Club in Dellwood, Minnesota, are fitted in and around dramatic topographic features, taking on unexpected shapes based on their settings. For example, the third hole is balanced on a narrow neck running along the southernmost edge of the property. Early architect Willie Watson utilized this corner of White Bear for a 133-yard par three with a green of less than four-thousand square feet. Not only is the setting of the hole a quirk, the sharply-pointed mounds that border the hole stand in contrast to the rest of the course, incorporating the Principle of Quirk in a different way. Their sharpness comes from the inability to tie them into grade because the opposite slope falls away so abruptly. These are the only features with such character on the course.

Hole #3, White Bear Yacht Club, Dellwood, Minnesota (Courtesy: Brian Ross)

White Bear's thirteenth green sits on another neck of ground at the end of a long par five. Dramatic drop-offs on both sides of the putting surface not only create a unique green shape, they eliminate the need for sand and the incorporation of the landform is a pleasant surprise. No other feature at White Bear resembles this green; it's an excellent utilization of the Principle of Quirk.

An entire golf course may be considered quirky if the majority of the greens are blind due to constraints within the original site. Among the many uphill and downhill holes of my home course of Rye Golf Club in New York, only three greens there I would classify as truly blind. A result of early 1920's architecture, they would certainly be classified as quirky. Although many of the other greens require some effort to see them, I would not classify the course itself as quirky.

Blind greens that are designed solely for effect may seem quirky at first, but are in fact gimmicks. One shaped like a U. S. state is clearly a gimmick, as is a bunker shaped like Mickey Mouse (even if it *is* at Disney World). The Principle of Gimmick also takes over when shapes are so extreme that one must putt *off* the green in order to access another part of the green. An icon such as the seventeenth green at Pebble Beach struggles to maintain its quirk for this reason. Originally much larger and wider in the middle than it is today, its site was constrained by the ocean setting on three sides. But as the middle narrowed over the years, golfers that miss this green are often forced to putt through the fringe, placing it on the brink of gimmick.

Hole #6, Pebble Beach Golf Links, Monterey, California. (Courtesy: Photogolfer | Dreamstime.com)

My favorite hole at Pebble Beach happens to be the par-five sixth hole, which has such a sharp rise between landing areas that the fairway is interrupted by rough. The hole is a product of the Principle of Quirk because of the forced abruptness necessary to take full advantage of the peninsula it occupies along the ocean. Six is a throwback to golden-age architecture when bulldozers or dynamite weren't reflexively called upon to erase nature's essence.

Pebble's sixth served as the inspiration for the eleventh hole at Skydoor Golf Club in Zhangjiajie, China. Although the ground was an immovable object, the client's resistance to moving dirt was even more immovable. I believed we needed to move a bit more in order to create a continuous fairway to the green but was forced to adapt. Fortunately, the client's push allowed me to break open the Principle of Quirk to build one of my favorite holes.

Hole #11, Skydoor Golf Club in Zhangjiajie, Hunan, China. The transition from the fairway to the green surrounds is steep yet still mowable. (Courtesy: Richard Mandell Golf Architecture)

I utilized the Principle of Quirk to build the thumbprint ninth green at Asheville. It was partly to restore the recollections of the long-time pro there, but also based on the existing topography. Shoehorned into a natural plateau with a road directly behind, the only alternative was a two-level putting surface for visibility. The horseshoe upper level is separated from the bottom by a steep slope to ensure as much pinnable space as possible on both levels. This solution for the green, originally placed in an awkward setting, made a short hole (345 yards) more challenging as well.

Hole #9, Country Club of Asheville in Asheville, North Carolina. This thumbprint green has cup locations above and below the slope. (Courtesy: Richard Mandell Golf Architecture)

The use of internal contours in the form of a thumbprint green to accommodate vertical transition is one of many ways the Principle of Quirk can provide form and function. The iconic doughnut-hole bunker in the center of Riviera Country Club's sixth green in Pacific Palisades, California serves the same purpose. Although its existence can hardly be considered an irresistible force encountering an immovable object, George Thomas's idea of quirk succeeds as a functional vertical transition from one level to another.

Although the road behind Asheville's ninth green limited my options for renovation, it doesn't have an effect on the play of the hole on a daily basis. The Road Hole at the Old Course is another story because its setting adjacent to the Old Course Hotel definitely qualifies as quirky. From the tee, players are required to drive a ball *over* a portion of the building that juts out at the back. Granted, that challenge started out years ago as a bunch of sheds which, at the time, may have been considered immovable objects. Nonetheless, seventeen is an excellent example of the Principle of Quirk because of the inherent strategic challenges that the hotel, the road hole bunker in front of the green, and Old Station Road behind the green all provide.

At the farthest point from the clubhouse, where the Old Course makes a sharp, hook-like turn, two of the holes cross each other. The seventh crosses the eleventh and the eleventh crosses the seventh. This device would be considered an element of the Principle of Gimmick today but centuries ago it was standard practice and probably not thought of as quirky at all. With the River Eden and what must have been off-limits property to the north effectively capping the Old Course routing at the time, these holes remain largely unchanged and certainly qualify as quirk architecture. In more modern times, creating crossing holes would hardly pass the Gimmick test, regardless of how architecturally intriguing they may be.

Many older courses originally ran into immovable stone walls that delineated property lines and some eventually became internal features through land acquisition. They also often determined the length and subsequent strategy of golf holes, providing both authenticity and design precedent. The waist-high wall crossing in front of the thirteenth green at North Berwick's West Links in Scotland is considered a quirk because it was most likely an immovable object when the hole was first created. Preserving such old walls today incorporates the Principle of Quirk. Not because they are immovable objects, but because they are strange and unexpectedly out of context with modern design.

In addition to a few stone walls, other memorable features from my home course at Rye Golf Club are the numerous rock formations that rise up out of the ground. Their presence affected the placement of multiple golf course features because they were the epitome of immovable objects at the time. The eighth hole, for example, has tee boxes set on top of rock with similar outcroppings obscuring the view to the fairway. The hole plays 333 yards from the back tee and it encourages the most aggressive play along a completely blind line. Adding variety among the other blind shots at Rye, the hole is a great quirk because it requires an unexpected turn off the tee. I always found it a pleasant surprise when my tee shot split the middle of the fairway even though it seemed I had aimed way out over Milton Harbor.

The "Pit " Hole (#13) at North Berwick West Links, looking back to the fairway left of the wall. (Courtesy: A. C. Hutchison)

Although something intentionally designed for effect may not be a result of the Principle of Quirk, golf architects can still utilize the principle by deliberately and simply creating a sudden twist, turn, or curve within a particular feature or one that independently comes out of the ground. As long as it's a pleasant, unexpected surprise, it qualifies as quirk. One particular quirk we built was a mound in the approach of the uphill 291-yard ninth hole of the Red nine at Army Navy Country Club's Arlington campus. It unexpectedly extends out of a flat rise in order to challenge the big hitters off the tee. This feature is a point of emphasis visually but also a quirk because the primary intent is to strategically surprise the golfer. It works because it's not encountered elsewhere within the round.

Hole #9 Red, Army Navy Country Club in Arlington, Virginia. The mound coming out of the ground about fifty yards from the green on this 291-yard par four challenges the longest of tee shots to stay on line once it hits the ground. (Courtesy: Richard Mandell Golf Architecture)

If features that share common elements such as form or shape are repeatedly encountered throughout a golf course, a subsequent feature that shares those same characteristics, yet at a more dramatic scale, should not be viewed as a quirk. At whatever point in the routing repeated features are encountered, they are no longer *"strange and unexpected."* Retrospectively, that initial quirk will subconsciously leave the golfer's memory as similar features are encountered later in the round.

Architects know that a potentially great golf course starts with the ultimate site. A quirky golf course is very hard to create because once we locate that perfect site we actively seek out all those great features we are conditioned to seek out. We then expect to tie them into a cohesive routing of eighteen holes because that's always our goal.

Sand Hills Golf Club in Mullen, Nebraska, designed by Bill Coore and Ben Crenshaw, is an example of a property with wonderful topography that resulted in wonderful holes. According to both of them, it was just a matter of finding the right eighteen among a thousand possibilities. Because the entire site was full of great topographical landforms, it was hardly unexpected when they incorporated them into ideal features for golf. To me, none of the holes or features at Sand Hills qualify as quirky because few people would be shocked at their existence. Impressed? Absolutely. But extracting a surprising reaction out of the golfer probably wouldn't happen.

If an entire golf course is full of natural quirky features, it can only be considered "quirky" if the surrounding landscape doesn't share those same attributes. In other words, a truly quirky golf course site must singularly stand out as strange and unexpected among adjacent properties. As quirky as some may consider White Bear Yacht Club, I wouldn't classify it as a result of the Principle of Quirk. The features that makes this course my favorite - the roller-coaster fairways - are a result of the topography of the region, not an anomaly. A similar White Bear site found in Myrtle Beach in the South Carolina low country or an Irish links landscape outside Mobile, Alabama, would qualify as quirky golf course sites.

The Principle of Quirk checks many boxes when it comes to the character of a golf course, which creates memorability in terms of aesthetics and strategy. Yet of all the principles of golf architecture, Quirk is the most intriguing because it requires such restraint to develop. Authentic quirk happens when that immovable object meets that irresistible force. When golf architects realize they're literally stuck between a rock and a hard place – no design alternatives exist – it's acceptable to invoke the Principle of Quirk.

As the game of golf became more and more results-oriented rather than experience-driven, golf architecture took on a more manipulative approach rather than in response to the land. Immovable objects from past eras are simply erased today by the convenience of heavy machinery. Preservation of features that weren't so quirky a century ago is the best way one can sustain the Principle of Quirk today.

28 The Principle of Mystery

MYSTERY - THAT WHICH PRESENTS FEATURES OR QUALITIES OF SUCH PROFOUND, INEXPLICABLE, OR SECRETIVE CHARACTER AS TO AROUSE CURIOSITY OR SPECULATION.

In many cases, golf holes with everything spread out in front of the player are not very intriguing. Yet uncertain routes often garner attention. The mystery of what may be around the corner, strategically or aesthetically, will often entice golfers to delve deeper.

The genesis for this book was in the fall of 1992. On a crisp, blue-sky day that October, I had the privilege of walking two of the best courses in the U. S. and the world: Shinnecock Hills Golf Club and The National Golf Links of America, adjacent layouts on the eastern end of New York's Long Island. Among all of the great golf holes at Shinnecock I explored that day, I found myself fascinated by the

In 1992, the Principle of Mystery came to light for the Author exploring the path from the fourteenth green to the fifteenth tee at Shinnecock Hills Golf Club in Southampton, New York. (Courtesy: Richard Mandell Golf Architecture)

sight of a path to the right of the fourteenth green. I was immediately obsessed with what the path would lead me to as it snaked uphill before disappearing out of site. Trees and shrubs blanketing that side of the green hung over the path like a pergola, adding even more mystery to its disappearance. Since this was my first time at Shinnecock, I had no idea of where the path led or what I would see if I followed it. But the mystery of what was at the end of the path was too much to ignore.

Excitedly walking up the gravelly path - broken up by stray tufts of grass between parallel ruts - I followed it to the left and continued to climb. The path burst open above the tree tops, revealing the dogleg par-four fifteenth hole as it tumbled downhill to my left. From one of the highest points of the property I could spy National's clubhouse and windmill in the distance. It was a breathtaking sight.

The path was simply a way to get from the fourteenth green to the next tee. I'm sure it wasn't intentionally designed by anyone in particular. Rather it evolved over time as the means to an end. The enclosed space at the beginning of the path and its movement out of sight called me to see what was around that corner. The payoff was the top of a wooded expanse of eastern Long Island framing some of the most rolling links land the western side of the Atlantic Ocean has to offer. From that moment on, I began to seek out curious golf course elements everywhere I went. From fairways dipping downward out of view, to stark ridges cutting in front of greens, to bunkers that appear differently from a variety of angles, the Principle of Mystery is one that I fell in love with and strive to incorporate in my design work to this day.

The reward for following that path was an expansive view (as seen that day in 1992) all the way to National Golf Links in the distance. (Courtesy: Richard Mandell Golf Architecture)

Mystery is best defined as *"That which presents features or qualities of such profound, inexplicable, or secretive character as to arouse curiosity or speculation."* A golf architect can incorporate the Principle of Mystery through a variety of tactics. The most common approach is concealing a golf course feature with a landform such as a mound, ridge, or other rolling contour.

When the golfer encounters a hole that's entirely visible and well-defined by rough or a series of bunkers, almost everything is a black or white decision. The Principle of Mystery transforms the black or white strategy of a hole to a gray area by utilizing elements that arouse curiosity. Concealing targets and preferred landing areas is how one creates golfer curiosity when it comes to that gray area, forming uncertainty in the golfer's mind. Visible hazards such as sand or mounds can be used to conceal those preferred areas. From the golfer's point of view, they will question the best route to take when a certain area is just "around the corner," especially when it's along the line of instinct. Seeing just a portion of a target not only increases excitement, it keeps one's interest longer than a full reveal.

Utilizing converging lines is the best way to conceal features when developing mystery. This is accomplished by layering features in front of each other, incorporating the lines that make up one feature to obscure the lines of another feature. Objects in the foreground and mid-ground can create an instant sense of mystery in the background. The foreground can be the area between the tee and fairway, the mid-ground may be between the landing area and green, and the green complex is the background. Because one's perspective changes as one moves through the golf course, the designer must adjust the layering from as many perspectives as possible. Incorporating converging lines, such as a mound partially concealing a portion of the fairway, can be very effective in stoking strategic speculation.

Hole #14, Braemar Golf Course in Edina, Minnesota. The line of bunkers converging from the left and the green profile line converging from the right conceal fairway in between. (Courtesy: Richard Mandell Golf Architecture)

Utilizing a natural landform to conceal a target can provide a level of authenticity to one's use of the Principle of Mystery. That translates to golf by utilizing existing hills, ridges, mounds, and other features to partially block a view of the landing area or a portion of the putting surface. Designing with this approach will invite the golfer to explore areas that aren't that clearly outlined. For instance, the Principle of Mystery may conceal a large dip along the line of instinct between the fairway and the putting surface that can pull a shot off target, such as what often happens with the "Valley of Sin" on the eighteenth hole at the Old Course in St. Andrews.

Another example is a feature I incorporated at Creekside Golf & Country Club in Hiram, Georgia. The seventh hole is a 318-yard par-four that doglegs left around a pot bunker cut into a lone mound placed along the direct line from the tee. That mound conceals a deep swale that fronts the green much like the Valley of Sin. What often happens when a big hitter tries to drive the green is that swale will kick a tee shot well left of target about forty feet below the putting surface. The safer play off the tee is the vast fairway to the right, which offers a shallow target for the approach as the strategic trade-off. The line of instinct over the mound provides the best angle to a green that's much deeper than it is wide, yet the mound also conceals the danger that lurks just beyond it. The Principle of Mystery combined with the golfer's desire to hit driver make the swale in front of the green a very effective hazard.

Hole #7, Creekside Golf & Country Club in Hiram, Georgia. A drive that's too aggressive may find the swale protecting the front of this green hidden by a mound along the hole's centerline. (Courtesy: Richard Mandell Golf Architecture)

Another way to introduce the Principle of Mystery in course design is through the Principle of Deception. Deception is *"an act which misleads as an illusion, hides the truth, or promotes a belief, concept, or idea that is not true."* Architects use deception as a trick to try and convince the golfer that something isn't exactly as it appears. The golfer's reaction to the deception can either be curiosity or speculation.

Many greens of the early twentieth century were built up for drainage and visibility. Because technology limited how high and far the ball could travel, most shots stayed low to the ground, relying on roll to reach the target. Therefore, designers positioned bunkers and other hazards twenty to fifty yards in front of targets to catch balls as they first hit the ground. The Principle of Deception was used by early designers to build these bunker complexes at the same elevation as the greens they guarded, which effectively concealed the thirty-odd yards of approach in between. The visual result was bunkers that appeared to be built into the green's base.

I observed this trick by studying how Australian golf architect, Walter Travis, elevated fairway bunkers twenty yards in front of his greens back in 1901 on the original Plantation nine at Sea Island Golf Club on the coast of Georgia. It was there during my college years that I first came to appreciate the art of concealment. What Travis was doing, it seemed to me, was causing golfers to question the distance to the target. The Principle of Mystery pushes one's mind to explain why the green looks so much closer than it actually is because the intervening ground is completely blocked from view.

The Element of Scale can also create deception by varying the size of a course's features. Increasing the size of greenside bunkers, for example, alters the composition to make a target appear closer than the actual distance. Reversing the trend can make the green seem farther away. These concepts can be implemented from both the tee *and* the fairway.

Visual fairway line manipulation can be done on a vertical scale by lowering the height of tee boxes. For decades, the tendency was to build them up in order to completely see the target. This full visibility approach can leave the back tees five to ten feet above grade in order to see over the most forward tees. An elevation change of such magnitude will provide relatively sweeping views of the fairway lines, removing any Mystery as to where to hit the ball (or know where it landed).

Artificially raising tee areas is yet another example of moving away from the sport's links roots. Golf's first teeing grounds were simply areas that were roughly two club lengths from the previous hole in the ground. Maybe they were flat, maybe they weren't. Low-profile teeing grounds built just high enough to promote positive drainage can drastically change a golfer's visual perspective of fairway lines. The lower viewpoint will not only arouse curiosity but create uneasiness in the golfer, which will translate to indecision. Such a simple design adjustment can bring mystery to the forefront by challenging the golfer's psyche.

The Principle of Mystery can also be implemented through bunker design. A cape-and-bay bunker style is most effective because converging lines of capes can effectively conceal portions of the corresponding bays. Converging lines created by fingers and noses in the foreground help conceal sand lines in the background as well. The mystery of what the bunker actually looks like is magnified when viewed from multiple angles.

One of my favorite approaches to bunker design is to create the appearance of multiple bunkers with just one. Sufficient elevation of mounds, fingers, and noses along the leading-edge is necessary to conceal sand lines coming off the bunker face on the opposite side. The vertical dimension bleeds into the grass portions on that other side, creating isolated pockets of sand that are seen as individual bunkers.

To keep the mystery going as a golfer's viewpoint changes requires the architect to patiently adjust bunker lines during construction. The architect must move

Hole #8, Tanglewood Championship Course in Clemmons, North Carolina (above and below. Converging cape-and-bay lines create a wide range of views, all based on the golfer's perspective. (Courtesy: Richard Mandell Golf Architecture)

back and forth between painting bunker lines and observing the resulting appearance, much like the way an artist will step back from the canvas to get different views and an overall feel for the painting. Views of a bunker from different perspectives require slight adjustments to the details to ensure that converging lines actually conceal sand, if that's the intention. The architect must also create enough vertical movement by directing the paint gun up and down at the correct points rather than strictly making horizontal movements while painting the sand lines.

The Principle of Mystery through converging lines can be used when detailing a green as well. A modest rise of a foot-high mound, coupled with a drop of six inches of the putting surface directly behind, can conceal a good portion of a green floor. Such a design can cause excitement in golfers as they make their way from the fairway, straining to see how close their ball may be to the hole.

The one golden-age architect that wrote about and practiced camouflage on the golf course more than anyone else was Alister MacKenzie. His philosophy regarding golf construction was almost identical to his philosophy on camouflage: *"If a defensive position is indistinguishable from the natural objects or particularly the natural undulations of the landscape, it will escape the disagreeable attention of the enemy."* Yet despite his teachings and results, he was never a fan of fully blind shots: *"There may be a certain amount of pleasurable excitement in running up to the top of a hillock in the hope of seeing your ball near the flag, but this kind of thing one gets tired of as one grows older."*

Complete concealment impedes the Principle of Visibility and effectively negates any influence the Principle of Mystery may have had. If one were to completely hide a feature, the golfer may not even be aware of its existence, oblivious to any attempts to create mystery. The Principle of Mystery is simply not as effective when applied in that regard. For it to be effective there must be some tease created by the architect to garner at least some curiosity. By showing just enough of the target, the golfer's interest will be heightened.

A dune crossing the sixteenth fairway at the Bandon Dunes course in Oregon incorporates the Principle of Mystery by concealing not only just enough of the landing area directly behind as a tease, but the green to the far right as well, peeking out from the highest point of the dune. (Courtesy: Richard Mandell Golf Architecture)

To me, hazards should never be concealed. I believe a hidden hazard is not a virtuous element of the Principle of Mystery. I'm guessing there hasn't been a golfer in history who was happy to have found a blind hazard. Their curiosity wasn't ever satisfied as they bounded over a ridge to find their ball stuck under the lip of a bunker.

By 2001, maybe ten trees remained to the right of Shinnecock's fourteenth green. Three years later, the number was down to about six. Three were still there in 2010. By 2013, a single shrub stood alone, leaving an unobstructed view of fifteen tee from anywhere on the fourteenth green. The path itself was gone the following season. One could still take a right off the green and walk up the hill through native grasses but the only designated path was from the left side, rounding the back of the green that ended in a cul de sac at the fifteenth tee. The opportunity to burst out into the open with a surprising gaze across the horizon was gone. Of course, the views are even better now with the trees gone. There's just no mystery to it anymore.

A few years after my initial visit to Shinnecock I returned to watch the 1995 U.S. Open. The uphill eighteenth hole is a dogleg left following a ridge to the green tucked around a corner formed by the ridge itself. The more visible approach is from the right side yet the green is partially concealed from that lower portion of the fairway as well. On the final day of the Open, leader Corey Pavin hit a 226-yard four-wood from that right side. Upon making contact, he sprinted around the corner, chasing his Titleist to see if his dream of a major championship was solidified. The anticipation of his fate was a direct result of the Principle of Mystery. Five feet from the pin, nestled comfortably on the putting surface, was that Titleist, owned by a soon-to-be major champion.

Blind golf holes are the epitome of Mystery for the obvious reason that you can't completely see where to go. The mystery of the unseen raises one's senses as one stands over a golf shot with no sure knowledge of the result without chasing after it. Unlike MacKenzie, I have never once tired of running up a hillock to see where my ball came to rest and I still never get tired of running around hills to see where my ball has landed. I'm sure Corey Pavin doesn't get tired of it either.

In Arnold Haultain's book The *Mystery of Golf*, published in 1908, he writes about how the game plays havoc with the golfer's mind. To him, only focused minds can overcome such havoc to execute the shot at hand. The Principle of Mystery is a tool in the golf architect's box to wrap the golfer's psyche in curiosity. Because mystery kindles such speculation about what is around that corner, golfers often return to a course to explore even more corners. The height of design is when a golf architect adds mysterious charm to the line of instinct, ensuring that route will be the one that garners the most curiosity.

Hole #18, Country Club of Asheville in Asheville, North Carolina from behind green.
(Courtesy: Richard Mandell Golf Architecture)

29 THE PRINCIPLE OF ANGLES

ANGLE- A SPECIAL APPROACH, POINT OF ATTACK, OR TECHNIQUE FOR ACCOMPLISHING AN OBJECTIVE

Golf architecture purists wax poetically about angles. The inference is that golf holes should have angles (*special approaches or points of attack*) that create multiple strategic options for golfers to play. These angles are formed by the space between converging lines that define the outer edges of a fairway and where they meet at a green's center. The larger the angle formed, the wider the fairway. The Principle of Angles is dependent upon such width to provide these optional lines of play.

For example, the angle formed by the lines of convergence for a 45-yard wide-fairway of a 400-yard hole at 150 yards from the green is seventeen degrees. The angle formed by converging lines of a 25-yard-wide fairway at the same distance is ten degrees. Simply put, a larger angle creates a wider fairway with more spots to play the next shot from. If one were to pace off five-yard increments from across that 45-yard-wide fairway, there are eight spots from which one can play an approach. Within a twenty-five yard wide fairway there are only *four* spots to play one's approach to the target. The difference in the angle of play between one side of a 25-yard-wide fairway and the other is so small there is little effective difference in playing from either side. Yet moving twenty paces from the middle of a 45-yard-wide fairway dramatically changes the angle of approach on such a hole.

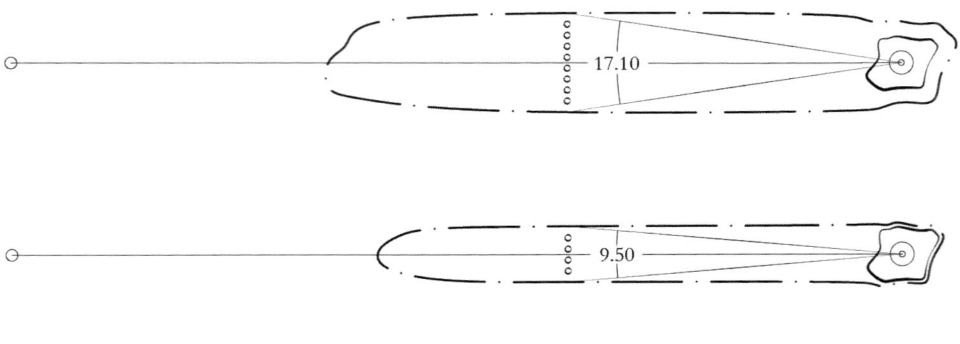

A 45-yard-wide fairway (top) has more spots to play an approach from than a 25-yard-wide fairway (bottom), creating more variation in the angle of approach (17° versus 9.5°).
(Courtesy: Patrick Gainer)

The Principle of Angles illustrates the contrast between the Principle of Challenge and the Principle of Penalty. Those designers who consider angles in their work inherently create targets that are wide enough to allow golfers different options for the next shot (challenge). Those who focus on penalty inherently consider the narrowest route as the only option of play through the smallest of angles: two lines that figuratively close upon themselves, leaving just one line to follow. Those who are apt to place hazards on one side of a green or the other typically are more prone to invite strategic options through the Principle of Angles. Those who tend to place hazards consistently on *each* side of a green eschew the Principle of Angles in favor of the Principle of Penalty. In this case, strategy yields to penalty regardless of how wide a fairway is or what side may be chosen to approach the green from.

Golf architects who endeavor to incorporate the Principle of Angles will often vary the shape and size of a green to promote play from one particular side of a fairway or the other. By orienting a green so the primary axis forms a large angle off the centerline, the larger the golfer's target becomes from that particular side. A smaller angle leads to a smaller target with less room for error. When the golf architect designs in such a way, they are utilizing the Principle of Angles.

Golf architects who front the primary axis of a putting surface with a hazard incorporates risk and reward into the Principle of Angles by forcing the golfer to make choices based on consequences. The strategy in this particular sense is to take full advantage of a wider target (the better angle into the green), requiring play over the hazard as a form of payment. The alternative is to avoid the hazard altogether by playing toward a narrower target from the opposite side, the payment being a lesser angle into the green.

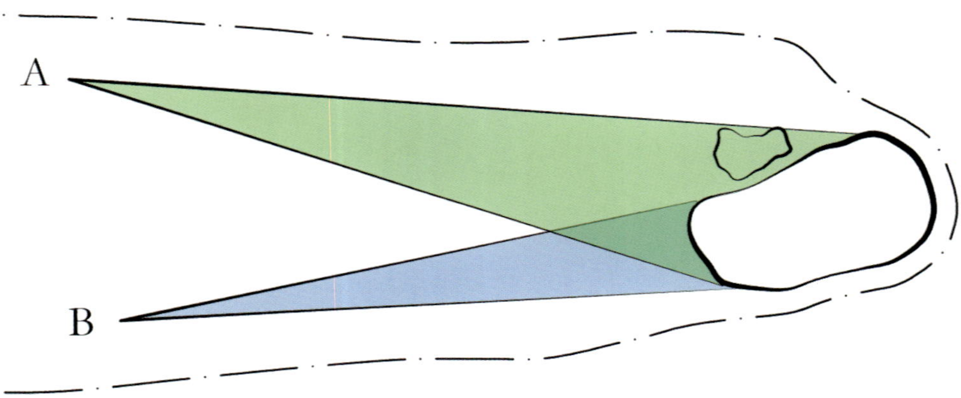

A larger angle into the green above from one side (A) provides a wider target to aim at versus a smaller angle and narrower target from the opposite side. The risk of playing over a hazard from side (A) may be worth the reward of a wider target. The reward of bypassing a hazard from the opposite side (B) may be worth the risk of a narrower target. (Courtesy: Patrick Gainer)

Course setup can have a wide-ranging impact on the preferred angle into a green as well. If a golfer is confronted with a right-side pin placement, they may choose to play their approach from the left side of the fairway, opening up the best point of attack at the hole location. On days when the flagstick is on the left side of the hole, they may choose to play their approach from the right side of the landing area. Width is again a crucial component of this equation because the wider the landing area, the wider the green entrance from that side will be, providing the golfer more surface area to play to from that side.

The Principle of Angles applies to the design of a green's inner contours also. By shaping a green's contours to be perpendicular to a particular angle of approach, the green may be more receptive to the shot from that side and stop closer to the target as a result. But if the inner contours run parallel to the chosen line of play, odds are a ball may continue to follow that slope and roll further away from the target.

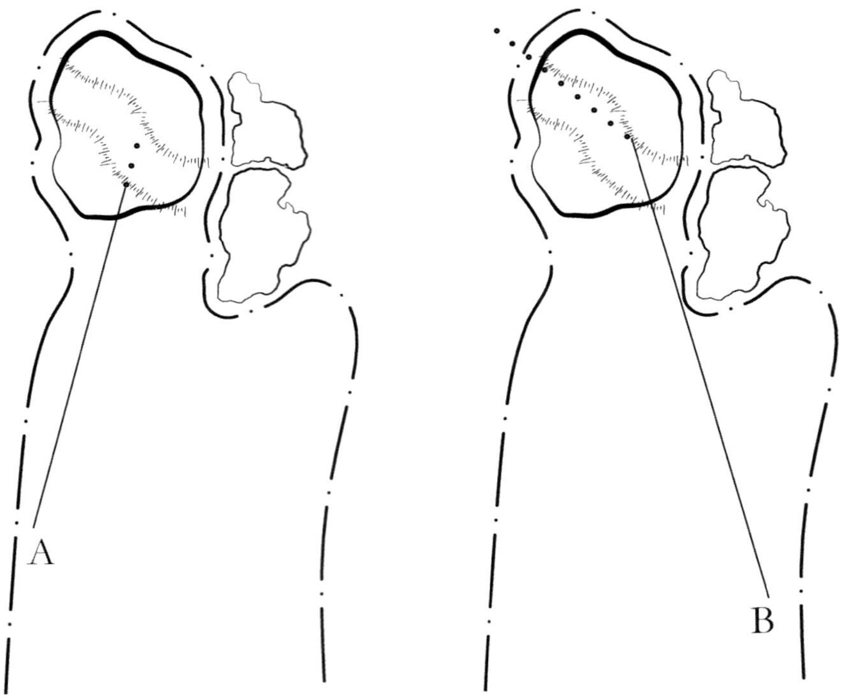

An approach from the left side (A) will find a more receptive green because the slope of the putting surface is perpendicular to the shot. An approach from the right side (B) has a greater possibility of rolling off the green because the putting surface slope is parallel to the shot from that angle. (Courtesy: Patrick Gainer)

The Principle of Angles is practically a synonym for strategy. The illustrative definition of an angle as *lines forming the outer edges of a fairway that converge at a target*, applies when considering different options from tee to green. Angle size is directly proportional to the width of the target and the number of options laid out by the architect. That's the essence of why the Principle of Angles is so important to the strategy of a golf hole. Its figurative definition as *"a special approach, point of attack, or technique"* for playing a golf hole is a major reason why golf architecture exists in the first place. The fact that both definitions are so different yet inherently intertwined may be why the concept of strategic angles is such a poetic element of golf course design. The question is, how will the architect utilize angles to create such poetry?

Hole #10, Erie Golf Club in Erie, Pennsylvania. The above view from the left side of the fairway brings a bunker into play in order to take advantage of an angle into the green that's unobstructed by sand. The below view from the right side has no sand in the landing area but guards the angle of play into the green from that side with bunkers. (Courtesy: Richard Mandell Golf Architecture)

30 The Principle of Direction

Direction - The general line that someone or something is moving or pointing in.

The Principle of Direction is crucial to developing variety in a golf course routing. Yet with constraints taking precedence - such as topography, vegetation, and property shape - direction should never impede the architect's search to match the best holes to the ground. That's why the most appropriate piece of property to augment the Principle of Direction is a square site with no contours - hardly inspirational - but without topographic or property line limitations to keep a golf architect from maximizing direction. One can freely integrate as many right-turning holes, left-turning holes, and straight holes as desired on a site with few, if any, attributes.

Sun orientation is a primary element of the Principle of Direction, particularly when it comes to hole layout. The best orientation for a site is a north-south alignment rather than east-west because north-south holes can sidestep most sun glare issues. An architect should avoid routing the first few holes of each nine to the east to avoid glare in the morning. The opposite should be done with the last few holes of a nine to the west so the golfer won't encounter sun glare when finishing a round.

But the direction of the sun on a daily basis shouldn't be the tail that wags the dog. If a great finish happens to be toward the setting sun, it's almost always worth it. Some of the best closing holes in the world face westward, including Pebble Beach in California, National Golf Links of America on Long Island, Pinehurst No. 2 in North Carolina, and Royal Dornoch in Scotland. Only the harshest critics would bemoan a great layout that finishes into the setting sun, but all critics will castigate a finish that doesn't live up to the ground it sits on.

The sun only affects play for an hour or so at the beginning or end of each day so to place such importance on its orientation is somewhat foolhardy. That said, when I face a fresh piece of ground and begin my site studies, I always take note of the four points of the compass. My initial impulse is indeed to direct my first holes away from an easterly direction and consider how the final holes can avoid a westerly orientation. Yet if the topography just doesn't allow for it, the study begins anew.

When it comes to wind direction, it's very much to one's advantage to consider routing holes with as much variety within the four compass points as possible. Whereas I may not sacrifice design to avoid the sun, I do make the effort to have as many holes face as many directions as possible to take advantage of changing winds.

Like sun orientation, I don't pay too much attention to prevailing winds because other site constraints will take design precedence. As long as I plan for holes going in as many directions as possible, I will have the wind factor dialed into the routing with as much variety as possible. I prefer to allow the wind's effect to be more organic because no matter the direction, wind will always make its presence felt. It really doesn't matter to me if it runs parallel to a hole, perpendicular to a hole, or at an angle. There is no need to force the impact of wind on a golf course, especially if it means compromising topography and strategy in the process. It's not that wind isn't an influence on the game of golf because it absolutely is. Links golf, especially, is dependent on the wind.

Old Tom Morris was the first designer that we know of to intentionally route par-three golf holes in as many directions as possible. It's easier to dictate the direction of a par-three hole without compromising other site virtues. Whereas dogleg par-fours and par-fives may run in multiple directions, one can easily focus on varying wind direction with a series of par threes because the hole only goes in one direction.

Laid out by Old Tom Morris, Royal Dornoch Golf Links in Scotland has a typical front-nine-out and back-nine-in routing but with the par threes playing in three different directions. (Courtesy: Richard Mandell Golf Architecture)

Links courses are typically out and back linear routings. Most usually run inland from the coast in one direction and make the turn directly *along* the coast. Because links courses are linear, wind plays a more consistent role than if the holes ran in multiple directions. When the golf course plays in only two directions, wind will be more noticeable, especially on links land that has no windbreaks of any sort other than dunes. One could play the front nine into a strong wind and then ride that same wind all the way home on the back nine, making for very different experiences. Although variety may be lacking, the influence of the wind in such an environment takes on much more meaning than in other golf course settings.

But the game did not originate because the first golfers walked outside in a hurricane one day and decided to see how a stone hit by a stick will go in one direction rather than another. The challenge of wind is a by-product of the links experience, not the reason why the links environment exists.

One of the most recognized holes in golf is Alister MacKenzie's twelfth at Augusta National, similar in many respects to the Eden hole (11th) at the Old Course. Like the Eden, twelve at Augusta is located at the furthest point from the clubhouse and a prevailing left-to-right wind plays a major role in its strategy. Because the right half of the green is angled further away from the tee than the left half, the left-to-right wind can turn a well-played shot into an unexpected splash into Rae's Creek in front. In effect, the club selected to reach the center of the hole may not be the correct club to a right-side pin if the wind pushes it right of target. The wind is a crucial element in the playing of the hole, yet there is no documentation from MacKenzie that it played such a role in his design. His own description of the hole, written for the program of the first Masters, only references the green setting on an angle for both the *"bold player"* and the *"less ambitious"* player. It also makes mention of *"a steep sandy bank covered with beautiful trees beyond the green,"* but makes no mention of wind.

Hole #12 ("Golden Bell") at Augusta National Golf Club in Georgia, plays over Rae's Creek. The prevailing left-to-right wind can push tee shots played to the right side of the green into the water.
(Courtesy: Richard Mandell Golf Architecture)

As great a hole as twelve is, and as great an influence the wind has on its playing, MacKenzie may not have planned the hole around the wind. Rather, he utilized the entire property to find the best eighteen holes and by convenience, the wind became a leading role in the hole's fame.

Whereas the wind at Augusta National may seem to have been derived by the Principle of Direction, the reality is that the direction of this particular hole is purely based on site features, namely Rae's Creek. That said, MacKenzie did route all four of the par threes in different directions within the overall routing.

The most basic application of the Principle of Direction is the routing of dogleg and elbow holes. A. W. Tillinghast specifically defined a dogleg as a hole *"which provides some pronounced obstruction which forms a corner in a twisted fairway from either side."* A dogleg hole required the golfer to play around a particular hazard that can't be carried at the turn in order to access the target. Yet he also utilized an elbow hole, one that turns to the left or right with a hazard at its bend that could physically be carried in order to gain an advantage. Tillinghast's strategic philosophy described it as *"a similar obstruction carried by a courageous shot, which is rewarded by a very distinct advantage."* Unlike a dogleg, it was very possible, even expected, to carry the obstruction at the turn of an elbow hole. Unfortunately, somewhere within the annals of golf architecture, the term "elbow" was discarded and "dogleg" encompassed all holes with any turn in direction, regardless of strategic intent.

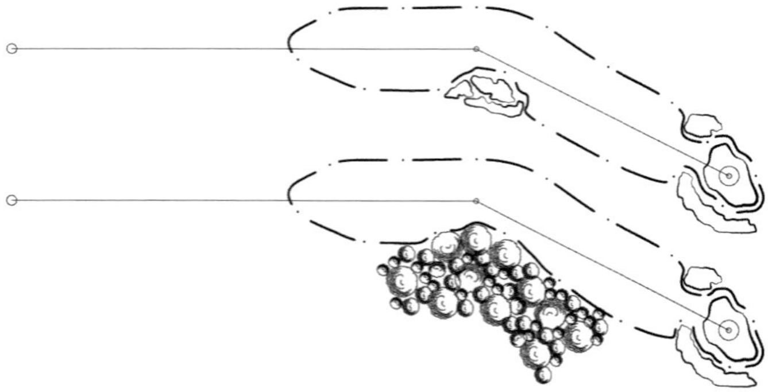

A. W. Tillinghast's elbow hole promoted carrying a hazard to gain an advantage (above). His dogleg hole required playing completely past a hazard in order to play the next shot (below). (Courtesy: Patrick Gainer)

All golf architects inherently utilize direction in their work. I personally take inventory of the number of doglegs–left, doglegs-right, and straight holes and then adjust my routing to ensure as much directional variety as possible (as well as a pleasing rhythm to the sequence of holes). Yet hole direction never supersedes what the topography provides. Ten times out of ten, if the hole isn't as good topographically-speaking, I won't settle just to take advantage of an additional compass point.

Successful golf architects apply the Principle of Direction as a tool to maximize the Principles of Rhythm and Variety more than anything else. Yet, as always, the site shall determine the best golf holes first. It's just not advisable to alter the character of the land just to advance the Principle of Direction for rhythm or variety's sake.

31 The Principle of Definition

DEFINITION - THE DEGREE TO WHICH AN OUTLINE OR DETAIL OF AN OBJECT CAN BE DISTINCTLY SEEN OR UNDERSTOOD.

The history of golf architecture can be categorized by eras as continued responses to design and technological advances. The Principle of Definition was born out of an era from the late nineteen-thirties to the nineteen-sixties that I call the Large-Scale Period. Rather than adapting the *golf course* to the land, the Large-Scale Period differentiated itself by architects and builders adapting the *land* to the golf course. Heavy equipment opened the door for such a change.

This monumental shift saw less use of principles such as Quirk and Mystery. Large bulldozers, track hoes, and earth scrapers re-formed the landscape with ease. There was no need to "endure" blind holes, no reason to play around rock outcroppings, and no motivation to practice the art of golf course routing, because big machines could make a golf hole work almost anywhere. The Large-Scale Period focused on the visual component of golf more than anything else and the Principle of Definition partnered up with the Principle of Visibility to give golfers a complete picture from tee to green. For the first time, architects were able to carve holes

Mission Hills in Shenzhen, China. (Courtesy: Richard Mandell Golf Architecture)

through valleys, eliminate ridges that previously blocked views, and move enough dirt to accommodate manufactured, fully visible green sites. The more definition that was created, the less mystery remained to arouse the golfer's curiosity.

This change also brought about a transformation of maintenance practices. Just as large machines were able to build things differently, they could maintain things differently as well. The form of golf course features evolved with softer slopes and broader surface area to accommodate the function of machine work over hand work. The Large-Scale Period dominated golf construction and maintenance for decades. The change was sweeping and a whole new generation of golfers embraced the movement, particularly the professional golfers who appreciated full visibility in order to shoot the lowest possible scores. The Principle of Definition became entrenched in the golfing public's consciousness.

Robert Trent Jones, Sr. was the most successful golf architect of this era and he fully adopted this new approach. Jones's early work reflected that of his mentor Stanley Thompson and other golden-age architects such as Ross and Tillinghast, who espoused more human-scale features. But Jones soon learned golf courses could be built faster and more efficiently with heavy machinery and was willing to make changes in his work to take advantage of this new technology.

In time, as more and more designers were able to literally bulldoze their way from tee to green, definition became a vital design component for everyone. Yet this new-found creativity was misplaced, inadvertently nudging golf architecture closer to penal design by lining each hole with hazards, automatically defining just a single path from tee to green. The black and white of definition and strategy became one and the same: Penal.

A penal path is often the result of creating too much definition from tee to green.
(Courtesy: Marchello74 | Dreamstime.com)

Definition is best defined as *"The degree to which an outline or detail of an object can be distinctly seen or understood."* Architects incorporate the Principle of Contrast to most effectively define a fairway or frame a golf scene. Elements like Color and Texture are used to achieve that contrast, particularly for a potential television audience. Hazards such as white-sand bunkers, long green grass, and blue water provide the necessary definition for course designers who choose to line holes with sand, rough and lakes. The result is a well-defined target, but often trouble for those who miss it.

A golfscape based on definition (and visibility) can check all the boxes when it comes to the Elements of Design. It can incorporate other principles such as Balance, Rhythm, and Emphasis just as a golfscape with blurred edges or concealed features can. But the difference between the well-defined golfscape and one that may be rougher around the edges is how those elements and principles are applied. For instance, the Element of Line will take on more importance than the Element of Texture for those who lean on the Principle of Definition. Lines may be much sharper and clearly delineate one feature from another. Those same lines may be jagged or broken up by converging lines when the golf architect isn't focused on definition or if mystery is preferred.

One can use the Principle of Definition to reveal the line of charm by wrapping fairway around bunkers to reward golfers who challenge the sand. The contrast of the sand makes the line easier to define, whereas non-contrasting features such as mounds, hollows, or other landforms require more study to determine the best line of play. Yet often the fairway is defined by a straight line. Those same hazards are surrounded by rough in such a way that there isn't a clear benefit to engage them strategically. Fairway wrapping around bunkers defines strategic choices, but a straight-line fairway defines only a single penal option.

Hole #2, The Reserve at Pawleys Island in Pawleys Island, South Carolina. The fairway line wrapping around a bunker defines a strategic opportunity for the golfer. (Courtesy: Richard Mandell Golf Architecture)

One should be careful not to confuse definition with direction, though. Whereas definition is *"the degree to which something can be clearly seen or understood,"* direction is a *"general line that someone or something is moving or pointing in."* Definition can help with direction, but direction may not assist with definition.

The eleventh hole at Creekside Golf & Country Club outside Atlanta is a downhill dogleg-right par five with trees along the right side that conceal the green from the tee. I placed a pair of bunkers along the outside of the second landing area and another bunker on that same side in front of the putting surface with the intent of directing the golfer to the green as the ground dropped in elevation closer to the green. All four bunkers provide definition to a fairway surrounded by mounds and wetlands. This is an example of the Principle of Definition being effective in guiding the golfer from tee to green through the Principle of Direction.

Links courses on the other side of the Atlantic never seem to show well on television or in photographs like American courses yet they are inherently more strategic, specifically because definition is not a guiding design principle. In fact, it's virtually non-existent. Such lack of definition obviously never kept the game from flourishing. Links are the epitome of gray-area strategy, a blend of wide rumpled fairways bordered by contrasting grasses with multiple angles of play. It's up to the golfer to determine the best route possible. Whereas the parameters may be well-defined (choices are clearly seen as fairway or "other"), the gray area still exists as to the best spot to play a shot to or from. Links courses are a window into why a golf course's success isn't dependent on definition.

Hole #11, Creekside Golf & Country Club in Hiram, Georgia.
(Courtesy: Richard Mandell Golf Architecture)

Only in "modern" golf architecture is definition a primary design principle. Because, over time, more and more flat sites were utilized for golf courses (which are much different than the "flat" sites of links golf) and they required definition when there were no visual clues as to hole direction (such as rumpled fairways). This is where the Principle of Definition is necessary, returning to the Golden Age adage that if the ground lacks any particular character, one must develop that character.

Definition and Mystery are two principles which, by nature, contradict each other. For the Principle of Mystery to arouse curiosity, something must be partially hidden for the golfer to question what's around that corner. Yet as soon as one element is partially concealed, the Principle of Definition is compromised, preventing a clear delineation of the path at hand.

Framing is to the Principle of Definition as concealment is to the Principle of Mystery. Framing principles are somewhat basic, creating a focal point while simultaneously blocking out any excesses. Just as mounds can create converging lines along the line of instinct, if they are positioned away from the line of instinct, mounds can screen unwanted views and direct the eye to a specific target.

The rumpled fairways of the Old Course at St. Andrews in Scotland.
(Courtesy: Brandon Tucker | Dreamstime.com)

Yet relying on mounds for definition requires extra work on the designer's part to make these features visually pleasing. A line of mounds is more apt to be repetitive because the designer must cover a significant distance with similar features. Tying a bunker into those mounds (which inherently have a great amount of mass) makes things even more challenging. The only way one can properly scale both features is to span the sand a lengthy distance along the line of mounds. The result may be visually stimulating, but it will be penal as well.

Bunker framing is the extent of my intentional use of the Principle of Definition. The origins of sand bunkers are the places where long-ago animals burrowed into the base of grass-covered dunes to avoid harsh winds, which exposed the sand beneath. So by definition, sand bunkers should always have a grass frame around them, which is my rationale for surrounding bunkers with framing grass. I am adamant about framing grass that equals at least thirty percent of the height of flashed sand, measured from the bunker line to the peak of the mound.

Hole #13 Keowee Key Golf & Country Club in Salem, South Carolina. Bunkers framed by grass maintains historical precedence. (Courtesy: Richard Mandell Golf Architecture)

A large percentage of golfers prefer to see definition as they play. This preference may be simply compared to art lovers who prefer realism in their paintings versus those who prefer impressionism, which bleeds the lines and forms within a composition. Translated to golf, there are those who want to see everything in front of them and others who don't need such rigid lines for guidance. Those who are seek out order in their lives, who may fancy more realism, welcome definition.

It's natural for a proponent of the Principle of Mystery, like myself, to place less importance on the Principle of Definition. Truth be told, I am just not much of a fan of laying everything out in front of the golfer from tee to green. Framing just to create visual eye candy is not worth such rearrangement of dirt, particularly when the site does not require such movement to begin with. Definition should be a natural by-product of the routing process, especially if the site has great topography. Utilizing the right landforms for the task at hand should provide natural framing and visibility. When a site lacks the best ground, the Principle of Definition should be incorporated with a light touch. In my opinion, the need to border every fairway from tee to green to move one's attention away from the edges and toward the center is a flawed concept. Rather, the golf architect should create such memorable landforms - as part of the hole itself - that the golfer is oblivious to the margins of the property.

32 The Principle of Connection

Connection - The act of joining or being joined to something else, usually by something intervening.

Unity is achieved through the Principle of Connection: All parts of a composition are joined by specific commonalities. In golf architecture, the Principle of Connection ties holes to the site and golf course features to landforms. The tools for this connection are the construction equipment that makes physical contact with the ground. Whether it was the dragpan of the Golden Age, the bulldozers and trackhoes of modern design, or the rotovator of today that prepares the ground for grass seed in real minimalist fashion, a course is connected to the ground through these machines.

Golf course shaping is the connector that joins course features to the landscape, either through modification of existing landforms or construction of wholly-manufactured landforms. How the Principle of Connection is applied through this process distinguishes between an aesthetically-pleasing composition and one that's completely disconnected from the ground on which it sits.

Hole #13, Country Club of Asheville in Asheville, North Carolina. Restoration efforts included lowering the green and tying into the hillside. (Courtesy: Richard Mandell Golf Architecture)

The same hole before our restoration, rebuilt in the 1960's, is an example of how imported material creates a poor transition to grade, resulting in a lack of connection to the natural ground. (Courtesy: Richard Mandell Golf Architecture)

Excessive shaping and imported earthwork are signs of a hole with poor connection to the ground. Bringing dirt onto a site often results in a detached appearance because one is forcably connecting foreign material to existing material. It's literally placing a weight on the landscape. Holes that sit "lightly" on the landscape utilize existing landforms for golf features or utilize material that's already in place to create features. Cutting and filling material already on site does not interrupt the natural balance of the site. The connection is more organic and doesn't require much shaping, providing a naturally low-profile appearance. Low-profile features are more connected to the ground than taller features because there is less vertical connection between original grade and the top of the built feature.

Nowhere is this better illustrated than in the construction of a teeing ground. Gradually over the years, tee areas got higher and higher in the architect's quest for full visibility. The abruptness of this connection to the ground (a more pronounced vertical element of three feet or more) created a disjointed appearance. Tee areas just one or two feet above grade appear more connected to the ground because the vertical transition from the top of the tee to the original grade is less.

Regardless of how much shaping occurs during course construction there is always a point of connection between shaped features and the existing ground. This is known as the "tie-in." There are two rules of thumb when tying in a point of connection. The first is to always find an "anchor point" for each feature. An anchor point is a feature itself or an extension of a feature that connects to an existing landform. Its purpose is to act as the intervening component that connects the golf feature to the ground, strengthening the relationship between the feature and the site.

I first noticed this detail playing the old East Lake Golf Club in Atlanta, Georgia, in the late 1980's, prior to its renaissance the following decade. In particular, I saw how Donald Ross had tied the complex of the fourth green to an extended ridge coming from the green's back left. From that moment on, I realized that many of his green complexes - if not a direct extension of a bench or side slope - were tied to an adjacent feature rather than simply placed on top of the ground, unconnected to any existing landform.

Hole #2, Skydoor Golf Club in Zhangjiajie, Hunan, China. The anchor point for this green is the ridge extended from the right side. (Courtesy: Richard Mandell Golf Architecture)

The second rule of thumb is that the further one extends a tie-in slope into an existing feature, the more natural it appears and the connection between built and existing grades will appear more subtle. This is best described as the Principle of Transition, and it applies to how one connects manufactured features to each other also.

Hole #14, Tanglewood Championship Course in Clemmons, North Carolina. The tie-in from the fairway bunkers extends across the fairway to the left as a ridge, an effective way to connect a hazard to the ground. (Courtesy: Richard Mandell Golf Architecture)

The Principle of Transition is translated as a *"movement, development, or evolution from one form, stage, or style to another."* The best use of the Principle of Transition is when one ties a series of mounds to the ground as well as each other. Rather than a line of individual mounds tying directly to grade, it's better to create one intervening base for the mounds to tie into as a transition to the ground. Accomplishing this begins by not creating individual mounds in one's design. Rather, one should visualize a series of high points *within* a larger landform. The key is to connect each high point with a valley in between that doesn't drop to existing grade. In doing so it avoids "flattening out" at grade before rising to the next high point.

This is the Principle of Transition in its most elementary form. As the leading edge of a golf course mound rolls back down toward existing grade, it shouldn't dead-end as soon as it meets the ground plane. Rather, a curved extension of that edge meets the ground plane at a natural angle, sometimes dipping slightly below grade after the point of connection. This approach should be applied when shaping hollows as well, whether it's a grass hollow (self-draining or not) or a sand bunker.

Hole #8, Lake Forest Country Club in Hudson, Ohio. The mounds that frame this fairway bunker are built as multiple high points from a single base and the lows between high points are broader than the high points, mimicking the troughs of ocean waves. (Courtesy: Richard Mandell Golf Architecture)

The Golden Age of golf architecture first introduced both the intervening feature and an anchor to golf course shaping. "Chocolate drops" and "dragon's teeth" (pointy-tipped mounds found in sand bunkers) of earlier eras lacked such a connection to the ground. In truth, they were collections of rocks that had been piled up and covered with dirt, a common alternative to hauling them off to a remote location. They often became hazards because they were found at the most central of locations: the middle of the playing corridor (mainly because that was the only place early builders bothered to clear). Chocolate drops and dragon's teeth resembled small pyramidal mounds that abruptly rose from the existing grade. Once peaked, all sides of the hazard returned to the ground at whatever natural slope the covering dirt would allow. The process was repeated for the next pile of rocks, resulting in multiple adjacent mounds individually connected to existing grade.

Golden-age mounding became more of an aesthetic (and strategic) feature than just a function of covering up stones. Without the limiting factor of filling voids within a pile of rocks, these new builders were able to create more rounded features. They also implemented the Principle of Connection by joining each high point through a single base.

Chocolate drop mounds at Bedford Springs Golf Resort in Bedford, Pennsylvania, circa 1923. (Courtesy: Richard Mandell Golf Architecture)

For me, transition is extremely important when connecting the features of a green complex. One should avoid flat planes at all costs, which means the smallest of connections must have some element of roll to it, whether convex or concave. A connection between a putting surface and a bunker can be a rise or fall of no more than six inches. Just a semblance of a roll is enough. Nature is full of the smallest of transitions like those. Sand dunes never meet the ground plane at a right angle.

Hole #9, Bacon Park Golf Course in Savannah, Georgia. A concave roll connects the putting surface to greenside bunkers before transitioning into a convex connection between each bunker. (Courtesy: Richard Mandell Golf Architecture)

They gain mass through the displacement of adjacent material coming off the ground plane as the winds sweep material upward, creating a concave void. If one strives to replicate nature in their work, the detailing of a transition from a convex mound to a low point must have an element of concavity to it as well.

A sound golf course routing has many different interpretations, including how the holes are vertically connected to the ground. But the connection of each to the next is just as important to the overall experience. It's a simple task to route a solitary golf hole on a rolling piece of ground. The challenge is finding seventeen more to achieve a single, unified routing. In some ways, the smaller the property, the easier it becomes. Yet the challenge of a vertical connection on those sites increases. On the other hand, finding eighteen holes on a 1,000-acre tract should be simple enough but the horizontal connection between holes becomes the bigger challenge.

Over time, some golf architects have shown less and less initiative in connecting holes horizontally, choosing to allow "progress," - such as the ability to move large amounts of dirt and relying on the golf cart - to fill in the gaps. As a result, green-to-tee connections don't seem to be as important. Utilizing cart paths to justify a lack of effort on the architect's part is poor design, no matter how inspiring the ground may be for the golf holes themselves. The connection between holes is crucial to develop unity. The practicalities of pace of play must also be considered as well because the rhythm of a round of golf will suffer greatly with five-minute rides to multiple tees. The crippling effect it has on golfers that prefer to walk has fundamentally changed the game of golf for the worse.

The inherent comfort and intimacy created when the next tee is within steps of a previous green is all but lost in modern architecture. Such a connection was a hallmark of great routings that the architects of the past achieved so well. Although they were rarely challenged by factors such as residential development, environmental regulations, or the purview of attorneys ready to pounce on the effects of a stray shot, they embraced such a connection as crucial to their work. I'm not advocating that every tee should be within two club lengths of the previous hole, but a golf course routing is always better when the next tee is tucked on the other side of a large dune or just over the next ridge. It definitely beats passing a rusted swing set or a hot tub before crossing a street to get to the next hole.

One approach to routing golf courses on severely-sloped property is the use of par threes as connector holes. Many golf architects – Colt and Ross in particular – follow this method, allowing the site to dictate where par threes can fit in organically. A par-three connector can occupy a space that can't physically accommodate a par-four or five. The inherent form of a par three allows for flexibility in efficient routing by functionally connecting remote areas of the property as well.

A transition hole is different from a connector hole in that its primary function is to move a course from one landscape type to a different one. An example is the transition from a wooded area to an open area, which may require an adjustment in the scale of features as the holes move from closed (negative) space to open (positive) space. One may also need to balance the appearance of features so that they have some sense of unifying character.

A more challenging transition is from one habitat type to another. A great example of how to do this properly is the Bandon Trails course at Bandon Dunes Golf Club in Oregon. In fact, the team of Coore and Crenshaw transitions their layout from a Coastal Strand Dune habitat to a low-lying Coastal Headland, *and then* to a Temperate Coniferous Forest habitat before the finishing hole returns to the dunes. The first transition hole, number two, also happens to be a par-three connector hole, starting high within the dunes before dropping about twenty feet to the Coastal Headland. Bandon Trails' fourteenth hole is another connector hole. Although it begins and ends at relatively similar elevations, the designers ran it along a natural ridge to open up the routing for the next three holes. Those holes position the routing to allow the par-three seventeenth to act as the final connector back to the dunes, with the final hole returning to the highest point of the property.

Hole #2 at the Bandon Trails course at Bandon Dunes Golf Club in Oregon starts in a links-like Coastal Strand Dune habitat before transitioning to a more heathlands-like Coastal Headland.
(Courtesy: Richard Mandell Golf Architecture)

My Beiluo Bay Country Club project in Yangjiang, Guangdong Province, China, along the edge of the South China Sea, is set on two completely different landscapes: a tropical mountain bordered by a beach. The transition between the two required utilizing the Principle of Connection, not only aesthetically but also practically to avoid routing golf holes 138 meters straight up the mountain. The solution was to keep the front nine on the lower portions of the property with two holes skirting up the outer edge of the mountain roughly fifty or sixty meters. The back nine sidesteps the forested mountain.

The visual Connection between the beach holes and the mountain holes is achieved through similar fairway widths as well as a cape-and-bay bunker style. The large dunes and exposed natural sand on the beach holes is replaced by the forest land that borders the holes on the back. The Principle of Connection depended on each high point being anchored to a broader dune formation, some of which encompasses multiple holes.

Beiluo Bay Country Club in China visually connects beach holes to mountain holes through fairway shapes and sizes and cape-and-bay bunkering. (Courtesy: Richard Mandell Golf Architecture)

The Principle of Connection is crucial when dealing with small golf course properties. Lacking the mythological "land-stretcher," the architect and shaper must counter-intuitively bring adjacent features closer together than usual to maximize a site's needs, particularly on older sites where driving ranges and short game areas were added after the fact. For example, connecting the side slopes of a driving range teeing ground to adjacent features and cutting practice bunkers into those slopes helps visually connect a short-game area to the tee and saves space as well. Those connection points are opportunities to introduce more short-game challenges rather than wasting flat space previously relegated to a pre-conceived notion of visual separation.

I lean on the Principle of Connection to build multiple major feature complexes as a single unit when they are so close to each other (typically separated by forty paces or less). This not only connects each complex more naturally to the ground but to each other as well. From a shaping standpoint, building multiple complexes as a single unit eliminates abrupt tie-ins to existing grade. That's because even if each feature has tie-ins that are floated out far enough, once they reach

Practice Facility, Country Club of North Carolina in Pinehurst, North Carolina. Cutting a practice bunker into the left-side slope of the driving range tee and incorporating an "area of undulation" on the tee box expands practice options through the Principle of Connection. (Courtesy: Richard Mandell Golf Architecture)

existing grade without tying in to each other just a few yards away a disconnect is clear. Counter-intuitively, bringing adjacent features together eliminates a crowded appearance through the Principle of Connection.

One such scenario is our renovation work at Isla Del Sol Yacht & Country Club in St. Petersburg, Florida. The seventeenth green, tenth green, and eleventh tee complex are each separated by less than twenty-five yards. Originally built as three separate features (a typical 1970's construction practice), there was a clear lack of cohesiveness. In addition, the area between each feature were ditches that collected water. The reconstruction approached the entire area as one single feature. Not only did we create a natural connection to the ground and each feature, the seamless transition between holes improved drainage as well. We also balanced the earthwork, which further connected the holes to each other and the ground.

Isla Del Sol Yacht & Country Club in St. Petersburg, Florida. Standing on #17 green slope looking toward #10 green with #11 tee beyond. (Courtesy: Richard Mandell Golf Architecture)

Isla Del Sol Yacht & Country Club. Portions of holes 10, 11, and 17 all built as one connected unit. (Courtesy: Google Earth)

Despite its nomenclature, the minimalist movement doesn't mean that man's hand has little influence on the ground (although it should). Rather, the final results of minimalist shaping simply gives the impression that little earthwork was done. Another misconception of minimalism (as well as modern shaping in general) is the need to include virtually an entire site within the project's limits of disturbance. Many builders feel compelled to shape everything within those limits, even if those areas are out of play. One of the most egregious examples of over-shaping is when there is an effort to rearrange the land between a tee complex and a fairway even though it has no effect on either the tee complex or fairway. It's an area that should be left in its natural form as a connection between the golf course and the ground.

Transitioning golf holes to the margins of the property is another area rife with over-thinking and resultant over-shaping. One of the great attributes of Golden Age courses in America and heathlands courses across the Atlantic is the simplicity of a natural connection to property edges. Features are built, tied to the ground, and the ground chases itself naturally into the woods. The Principle of Transition occurs organically, allowing the existing grade to be the connection.

Most designers are uncomfortable with the nuance inherent in the Principles of Connection and Transition so the tendency is to over-design features rather than simplify connections. For me, the simplest transition - such as when a fairway rolls into a putting green with no more than a few inches of vertical change - is one of the most intimate and memorable features in golf architecture. Its simplicity in design, however, does not necessarily mean a simple shot choice. In fact, with such a connection, golfers must consider a chip or even a "Texas Wedge" (using a putter from a variety of lies adjacent to a green) rather than automatically playing a pitch shot.

If one looks closely, all landforms are naturally connected, sometimes abruptly but most often subtly through centuries of erosion. Yet it's the abrupt lack of connection that seems to garner all of the visual attention, a telltale explanation of why shock value has replaced sound design principles and is even passed off as *great* design. The Principle of Connection creates more unity which, unfortunately, seems to be less and less important among critics who value eye candy over substance.

33 The Principle of Subtlety

Subtlety - The quality of being complicated, delicate, or difficult to notice, often in a skillful or attractive way.

The quality of being *"delicate or difficult to notice"* speaks mostly to the aesthetics of a golf course. The *"complicated"* aspect of subtlety is more applicable to the strategic side of golf architecture. The Principle of Subtlety takes time to reveal itself in either case. Obvious features, developed through principles such as Emphasis or Contrast, catch one's attention right away. But elements born out of subtlety inherently require extra effort to be noticed due to their delicate nature. A ridge bleeding out from a mound or a counterintuitive approach to playing a golf hole may require multiple plays before a golfer notices them.

Utilizing the Principle of Subtlety is mostly a design choice. Minimalists at heart are more apt to replicate nature as a slow process of erosion. The opposite end of the spectrum are architects like Pete Dye, who viewed nature more dramatically, with no place for subtlety.

The Principle of Subtlety is applied to strategy in two ways: when an architect develops a specific challenge which, on the surface, seems counter to what one's intuition may reveal; and an overall strategic approach that's applied throughout a golf course. Either way, such alternative thinking requires a few rounds before the golfer picks up on such an approach.

The most fundamental example of the Principle of Subtlety is simply the discovery that the best solution may not be a play to the middle of the fairway, especially when one finds a hazard occupying that space. This wasn't such a shocking revelation in the early days of the game when wide fairways produced multiple options. But as penal design crept to the forefront and holes got narrower and narrower, golfers almost universally accepted the middle of the fairway as the place to be. But there is nothing subtle about a narrow golf hole with minefields lining both sides.

The possibility that the center of the fairway may not be the best choice confuses many. In reality, the best route is the one that gives each golfer their best shot at shooting their best score. That may mean the shorter route for some or a longer route for others, knowing that bogey from sand may be the more palatable solution than a double-bogey because one couldn't carry a water hazard. For many who think a play to the middle is the only option, the subtleness of another possibility can at first seem more complicated, but over time may emerge as the better solution.

Playing from the center of the first hole at Burnham & Berrow Golf Club in Burnham-on-Sea, England (far right above) is not the best place to be. The result will be a blind approach. A better play is an open angle to the green from the left edge of the fairway. (Courtesy: Richard Mandell Golf Architecture)

A similar use of the Principle of Subtlety is creating what I call a "juxtaposition strategy" which encourages golfers to counter-intuitively play as close to a hazard as possible to gain an advantage, such as a better angle to the target. It still reflects the ideal of a hazard to challenge the golfer rather than penalize, but the subtlety lies in how golfers may learn to bring a bunker on the outside of a dogleg into play to gain the advantage, for example, instead of taking the more obvious and direct route.

An example of juxtaposition strategy is the third hole at Creekside Golf & Country Club in Georgia. A creek runs along the left side of this dogleg-left par five from the tee, eventually crossing the fairway in front of the green. If one were to play down that side to take advantage of the shorter route, a series of tall oak trees will effectively block any direct second shot to the green from that side. Instead, the best angle for those who want to go for the green in two requires a tee shot played as close as possible to the fairway bunker flanking the outside of the dogleg. Such a strategy will require a few replays before one realizes the trees can't be carried but the green might be reachable from the outside.

A thematic approach toward subtle strategic design is experienced over a series of holes. Almost every hole at the Old Course at St. Andrews Links offers a shorter but riskier route down the right side. The longer route down the left offers all the room in the world but also poor approach angles and obscured views. Mounds and other features block the route from that side as well, whereas it seems the greens are more open and receptive to shots played from the more perilous right side. It's an overall blueprint that takes time for one to appreciate.

Hole #3, Creekside Golf & Country Club in Hiram, Georgia. The closer a tee shot is to this fairway bunker, the better angle into the green. (Courtesy: Richard Mandell Golf Architecture)

As consistently subtle as the strategy appears, it isn't intentional. The shepherd's crook shape of the layout, with out-of-bounds flanking the right side going out as well as returning, may have something to do with it. Nonetheless, the strategy is a subtle, repeating theme that makes the Old Course stand out among other courses.

Originally known as Pilmour Links, the Old Course's "shepherd's crook" shape is evident in this 1821 layout and still is today, two centuries later. (Courtesy: St. Andrews Links Trust)

Many golfers view Donald Ross's greens at Pinehurst No. 2 in North Carolina as notorious plateaus that deter them from fishing for flags. Those that have played the course often are quick to point out that the smart shot is to the middle of each green. Whereas this theme runs through all eighteen greens, it's far from subtle. The way Ross used the Principle of Subtlety was by making each green more receptive on the side where there was a bunker. If a shot hits that side and holds, then well done. If it doesn't and rolls into the bunker, it offers a fairly easy recovery from the sand. For those shots missing on the bunker-less side, however – the seemingly harmless one by all appearances – the recovery is much more difficult. Again, it's the counter-intuition revealed through the Principle of Subtlety that fools many golfers.

Minimalism is the concept of making a golf course appear as if little was changed to the original property. Yet, in fact, much of the feature work is more shock value rather than subtle shaping. One who advocates for the Principle of Subtlety tends to favor actual minimalism over shock value. There simply is no subtlety in moving prodigious amounts of dirt, whatever the final appearance. The primary difference between subtlety and shock value is the degree to which a feature presents itself. A ten-foot mound is clearly not subtle yet a one-foot mound certainly is. The subtlety of a one-foot mound and other low-profile features is best expressed when a golf course is set up fast and firm. Primarily, the low-cut grass will highlight features that get overlooked in three- or four-inch rough. On the other hand, it's hard to notice a twelve-inch feature if it's obscured by grass one-fourth of its height. In addition, with fast and firm conditions, one might expect the ground game to be a factor. Subtle landforms, such as a two-foot mound or a low ridge crossing the approach on a fairway will redirect a golf shot rolling along the ground. The friction created by the thickness of higher grass will stop balls sooner.

Subtlety is about breaking up the ground just enough so that it's no longer flat, nothing more. As long as there is movement on the ground, as subtle as it may be, I don't care if the golfer notices it anytime soon. To me, the delicate transitional rolls between a putting surface and an adjacent feature are the epitome of subtlety.

The Principle of Subtlety is crucial to my design of greens approaches as well. I use it by creating little rises here and there or a ridge running through it that may not be so obvious. Strategically, the initial lack of awareness of such subtle details may affect the way golfers plan their shots. Only after repeated play might they notice that each time their approach shot bounces in front of a green it gets re-directed by a subtle landform. Aesthetically, subtle movement is more visually stimulating than one that's as flat as a pool table. The Principle of Subtlety is a form of camouflage that forces golfers to focus on the details in order to succeed.

The Principle of Subtlety can also be very effective on the putting surface. Golfers who prefer fast greens rather than severe green contours can still have enough speed with minimal slopes. A variety of 1-3% slopes is subtle enough to make putting greens sometimes more challenging than those with big rolling slopes. In my opinion, a combination of subtle and bold contours makes for the best putting surfaces.

The Principle of Subtlety was essentially stifled for much of the latter half of the twentieth century. At the time, efficiencies of recently-introduced heavy machinery

Hole # 12, Bacon Park Golf Course in Savannah, Georgia. A subtle ridge bisects the approach and is concealed by a bunker face slope. (Courtesy: Richard Mandell Golf Architecture)

were valued more than aesthetic details better measured in inches rather than feet. The craftsmanship that helps define subtlety (*the quality of being complicated, delicate, or difficult to notice, often in a skillful or attractive way*) requires more handwork than that which large-scale machines can produce. Ten-foot-wide bulldozer blades and similarly-sized attachments for other machines produced large-scale features lacking any hint of craftsmanship. A reliance on such machinery didn't exactly translate to a lack of talent but it certainly didn't lend itself to the details that are associated with an innate sculpting ability, either. What resulted was a "dumbing down" of the art of golf architecture. Human-scale features could only be built by humans running machines that are human scale as well. Large machines just couldn't produce such complicated detail.

Subtle design doesn't necessarily mean *boring* design, though. Boring design is repetitive, such as every green flanked by bunker left/bunker right. Boring is routing six doglegs-left in a row. The same green complex with the same number of mounds directly behind the putting surface that's repeated over and over is boring. However, if the mounds behind the greens each have small visual variations, it may subtly capture the golfer's attention. Subtlety is a principle that may stand on its own in its quality but relies on other principles of design in order to pull it off. This is why the Elements and Principles of Design, such as Variety and Balance, are subtly critical to successful design (no pun intended). Without them, subtle can turn to boring in a heartbeat.

A topography-heavy golf course requires the Principle of Subtlety for the design of features to visually balance the contours. On the other side of the coin, when a bold statement is necessary to create some third dimension on a flat site, there should be a balance from hole to hole to avoid creating too much visual stimulation. Without subtlety to balance shock value, an architect's design can tumble into chaos and disorder, negatively affecting the golfer's experience without them fully realizing it, even those who crave the wow.

The Principle of Subtlety is not a roadblock to memorable design. A great subtle golf course can indeed be built on less than dramatic property instead of deferring to shock value. The first step is to route enough variety of dogleg and straight holes and the next step is ensuring variety in selection and placement of hazards. If every hole has a different strategy, then the pieces are in place for great golf even if the site is devoid of natural features. If those strategic options don't immediately reveal themselves, it gets even better. This second level of strategy, something that slowly reveals itself in such a subtle way, is just another mark of a great golf course.

Hole #7, Myers Park Country Club in Charlotte, North Carolina. This bunkerless green relies on its contours unfurling over the ground for its subtlety.
(Courtesy: Richard Mandell Golf Architecture)

In a world of instant gratification, it's hard to be exclusively subtle. Because modern golf architecture seems to center around instant gratification, most golfers lack the patience for subtlety. Most designers are uncomfortable with the Principle of Subtlety because of the inherent need to provide value, which is usually accomplished by making a visual statement. It takes a convicted designer to stand up for subtlety. Like much in life, such as a fine wine or a book that may outshine its movie version, the Principle of Subtlety in golf architecture is worth the savor.

Hole #4, Braemar Golf Course in Edina, Minnesota.
(Courtesy: Peter Wong)

34 The Principle of Simplicity

Simplicity - Freedom from artificial ornament.

The Principle of Simplicity is the effort to avoid overt decoration or embellishment in design. Irving Gill, a California modernist building architect who passed away in 1936, said the following that I believe sums up the "busyness" that spans many design professions, including golf architecture over the past half-century:

> *"Ornaments tend to cheapen rather than enrich, they acknowledge inefficiency and weakness. Complex ornament means that the designer was aware that his work lacked purity of line and perfection of proportion, so he endeavored to cover its imperfection by adding on detail, hoping thus to distract the attention of the observer from the fundamental weakness of his design."*

The ornamentation of the Victorian architectural style. (Courtesy: Alyssand | Dreamstime.com)

Gill's comments point to an inability to grasp the elements and principles of design and lead many designers to conceal flaws with details of ornament or decoration (defined as *"an addition that renders something more attractive or ornate"*). He apprenticed under the famous architecture team of Dankmar Adler and Louis Sullivan in Chicago, so it's no surprise his animosity toward ornamentation reflects Sullivan's "Form Follows Function" mantra.

In golf course design, Gill's reference to ornamentation can translate to poor golf course routings and excessive earthwork. In fact, excessive earthwork is what will *"distract the attention of the observer"* from poor course routings, because such work is needed to fit a hole into a site that cannot physically accommodate it. Designers can also distract the golfer with artificial movement of the ground and an excess of mounds, water, and/or bunkers (all in the name of aesthetics). This leads to inherent maintenance and operational problems as designers and operators each seek to provide a product that essentially distracts the golfer from the simple task of playing the game. Fun, enjoyment, and competition are eschewed for ornamentation.

The varied ornaments of golf are both literal and figurative. Literal ornaments are those golf course features that are part and parcel of the golf design process (mounds, hollows, bunkers, etc.). Yet what specifically qualifies as requisite ornamentation for some may be unnecessary ornamentation for others. For example, some critics would classify unnecessary ornamentation as any evidence that a landform is manufactured. Since beauty truly is in the eye of the beholder, the adequate number of mounds, bunkers, trees, etc., is up to the individual. Exposure to the Golden Age courses of the Met Area I grew up playing led to a predisposition toward the Principle of Simplicity. If, say, I had grown up in South Florida, I shudder to think of the plethora of mounding I may have produced.

Literal ornamentation of bunkers combined with the figurative ornamentation of a waterfall.
(Courtesy: Phartisan | Dreamstime.com)

I would classify figurative ornaments are those details which are adjunct to the actual golf experience. Some golf architects aim to create perfect conditions rather than simply present a fair test for all golfers. Flawless turfgrass from tee to green, *as well as* green to tee aided by wall-to-wall irrigation; stone walls and waterfalls, curbed wall-to-wall cart paths and routine edging of those cart paths, are some examples of figurative ornamentation.

The Principle of Simplicity is a system of checks and balances within the design process to reduce a design to its basic, most functional form. The designer must start by throwing every idea on the table. Once all the creative effort is out there, the process of stripping things down to that simplest form begins with a "less is more" mindset. The mark of a great designer is recognizing when that process begins and when it ends.

One element in the process is an analysis of excessive shaping to minimize earthwork. Another is the elimination of non-essential features. For example, if the removal of a mound doesn't change the aesthetic appearance of the hole, then that mound is unnecessary ornamentation. But if the removal of that mound creates visual imbalance issues with any mounds that remain, then that mound may be necessary for the overall composition.

One of my favorite golf course features is a bunkerless green. A first impression from golfers, I believe, is a dearth of sandy ornament replaced by interesting short game challenges and green contours. Hazards such as hollows, mounds, and other undulations require less technical ability but still present challenge and probably more enjoyment. Removing the ornamental crutch of sand makes the hole visually simple as well, emphasizing the target more than the trouble.

Hole #12, Skydoor Golf Club in Zhangjiajie, Hunan, China. The simplicity of the bunkerless green pairs well with the distant landscape. (Courtesy: Richard Mandell Golf Architecture)

Stripping things down strategically is an even easier task. When architects design for a hazard to challenge rather than penalize, they will find features to discard. For example, one cross-bunker provides four times the strategic value that four bunkers lining a fairway can provide. In many cases, a plethora of bunkers in the corner of a dogleg is unnecessary. As an architect begins to break down the necessity of all those bunkers, most likely the end result will be a single, specifically placed bunker to challenge the majority of golfers that's just as strategically effective as several.

Value engineering could eliminate multiple penal bunkers that don't change the strategic intent of the hole. (Courtesy: Richard Mandell Golf Architecture)

There may be times, though, when other design principles make a case for multiple bunkers. At that point, the architect's "eye" may be the deciding factor in moving ahead with such a scenario. Exceptions can also be made for multiple bunkers when the overall number of hazards is already at a minimum. However, if multiple bunkers are used again and again throughout a routing it may be time to take another look to simplify the situation.

Overall, the best way golf architects can utilize the Principle of Simplicity is by using the lay of the land to its utmost potential in the course routing process. The goal should always be to find a great golf hole and then to know when to leave well enough alone. If the hole naturally incorporates as many principles of design as possible, the best job that architects can do is to silently celebrate their ability to find it and then move on to the next task. The golf architect's success is found in the Principle of Restraint (*a measure or condition that keeps someone or something under control or within limits*), knowing that talent often comes in leaving the land alone, not necessarily through altering the land. Experience and understanding when not to fool with Mother Nature counts as much as anything.

Utilizing the land not only means routing holes in their simplest, most natural state, but using existing features, further eliminating any need for ornamentation. Incorporating natural undulation within a landing area or a putting surface renders ornament unnecessary and it's one of the best ways to challenge golfers. A site that's left in its natural state can also mean that less maintenance and manicured acreage is needed, minimizing the need for excessive chemicals and water. A golf course that plays hard and fast can provide an element of challenge that doesn't need ornament.

So where does the minimalist school of architecture fall within the realm of simplicity? If one were to move all the dirt in the world to create a simple and understated golf course, the result may seem minimalist but the execution is far from simple. But if the architect was truly challenged with numerous constraints, the result would be a more authentic representation of the Principle of Simplicity than any overworked attempt at minimalism. As one designs around constraints that can't be altered, what remains is a course in its simplest form, fitting within the complexities of nature.

Early golf designer and writer Max Behr said something that definitely relates to the Principle of Simplicity and how it's the dividing line between pretenders and professionals: *"The pseudo golf-architect will have faint glimmerings of an idea and will try to catch it with numerous bunkers; whereas the true artist will place just one bunker upon the sore spot and it is done."* He went on to say *"Such a bunker is the Road bunker in the face of the 17th green at St. Andrews. To have placed such a bunker required rare imagination and audacity."* Behr's observation, to me, points to the risk golf architects face at every juncture of simplicity. The reason so many golf architects fear such a principle, and rely so heavily on said ornamentation, is that true imagination is found in restraint rather than busy work - despite the risk that such a restrained effort may be lost on the majority.

The Principle of Restraint requires an element of creativity that doesn't rely on shock value for the easy sell. Rather, it's about keeping superfluous design ideas in check for the betterment of a project. Restraint brings a "less is more" mindset by sifting through the wants and desires architects consider before the Principle of Simplicity's stripping-down efforts even begin.

Road Hole bunker on the 17th hole at the Old Course.
(Courtesy: Callan Chesser | Dreamstime.com)

The success of restraint comes in the fact that golfers never know what "could have been," only "what is." For example, a green built within a wetland might possibly be the most spectacular hole on a site and the focal point of all marketing efforts. Yet showing restraint and instead building the green *adjacent* to the wetlands could move the permitting process through with minimal red tape *and* little design integrity lost. If the green in the wetland never existed in the first place, no one would be any wiser and it wouldn't be missed. Instead of building a green surrounded by wetlands as a signature hole, I'd rather weave eighteen strategic holes together as a great marketing story and possibly generate revenue sooner.

Even though it may seem to some that The Principle of Restraint merely eliminates tasks by leaving well enough alone, it's not a principle for the lazy. Restraint is working within the given site constraints and relying on the art of course routing rather than finding a way to work around a permit constraint. Recognizing a costly build or a controversial environmental decision is crucial because even the most extravagant design ideas may not ever be worth the return on investment.

The first hole at Keller Golf Course in Minnesota is a great example of restraint because we didn't touch one square foot of the fairway in our work. We were careful to disturb as little area as possible in cutting a pair of fairway bunkers into the right rough. We also re-built the green complex with a nod to the pre-Golden Age appearance of the original features. What nature previously provided, from the base of the tees to the green, required restraint and only a little work to preserve it.

Hole #1, Keller Golf Course in Maplewood, Minnesota, looking back from green.
(Courtesy: Richard Mandell Golf Architecture)

Amateurism in design is chock-full of efforts with nary a nod to the most basic design principles. Instead, a lust for ornamentation drives design decisions. Although she was primarily speaking about house architecture, early twentieth-century critic Eloise Roorbach, in discussing the work of Irving Gill, shared her impression of ornamentation within the principles of design:

"Ornamentation tends to cheapen rather than to enrich, and that art lies in elimination, in balance, proportion, in honesty, and fearlessness. Ornamentation as seen on most of the houses of today represents fear; a designer dare not leave it off, dare not depart from custom, dare not be simple." One can easily replace *"houses"* with *"golf courses"* and Roorbach's statement will ring just as true. It takes great discipline and bravery to embrace both Restraint and Simplicity. These principles are crucial to one's success, even if the designer is not fully aware the success was born out of such concepts.

35 The Principle of Character

CHARACTER - A DISTINCTIVE QUALITY OR TRAIT; THE ESSENTIAL NATURE OF SOMETHING.

"Each hole should have a character of its own. Its physiognomy should be quite distinct from that of its neighbors, and it should be one not easy to forget." – Robert Hunter, Author of The Links (1926)

The Principle of Character establishes a specific combination of qualities in a golf course that make it distinct from others. Character does not exist when distinctive qualities are shared by multiple courses because it's no longer the essential nature of something. Rather it becomes the essential nature of multiple things. In essence, golf courses which lack character simply look like other courses.

Incorporating the Principle of Character is one of my personal tenets of golf architecture. Allowing the land to dictate design, and not allowing one particular look to dominate decisions, is the only way to ensure character for each golf course. This happens through preserving what was already there, either through topography of the ground or determining which distinctive traits shall be preserved within an existing layout. Each step in the design process - from initial routing to the planning of each golf hole - is derived from the attributes of each individual landscape.

Hole #12, Braemar Golf Course in Edina, Minnesota.
(Courtesy: Richard Mandell Golf Architecture)

Derived from the Latin *Genius Loci*, the "Genius of the Place" is a location's distinctive atmosphere or "spirit" (as defined by the ancient Romans). That spirit is character in action, demanding that design shall be adapted to the context in which it's located before anything else. That's never more true than in the world of golf architecture. One allure of golf over other games is its playing fields. The Principle of Character brings out the spirit and identity of those playing fields.

Landscape designer Andre Lé Nôtre created his own "Genius of the Place" at Vaux-le-Vicomte in Maincy, France. (Courtesy: Richard Mandell Golf Architecture)

Genius of the Place was initially derived from a line of prose aimed at the ostentatious Italianate and French formal gardening style found at estates such as Villa d'Este and Versailles. Here landscape designers such as Andre Lé Nôtre built sprawling outdoor rooms utilizing the right angle as the dominant design element, requiring the re-distribution of large amounts of earth to create flat terraces within a rolling countryside. *"Consult the Genius of the Place in all"* were the specific words penned by 18th century English poet Alexander Pope. It was widely understood that he was thumbing his nose at the gentry of high society and their statement-making landscapes, yet he fell victim himself, building grottoes and other artifices for his own enjoyment. Nonetheless, his entire verse has become a staple of landscape design:

To build, to plant, whatever you intend,
To rear the Column, or the Arch to bend,
To swell the Terras, or to sink the Grot;
In all, let Nature never be forgot.
But treat the goddess like a modest fair,
Nor overdress, nor leave her wholly bare;
Let not each beauty ev'rywhere be spied,
Where half the skill is decently to hide.
He gains all points, who pleasingly confounds,
Surprises, varies, and conceals the bounds.

Consult the Genius of the Place in all;
That tells the waters or to rise, or fall;
Or helps th' ambitious hill the heav'ns to scale,
Or scoops in circling theatres the vale;
Calls in the country, catches opening glades,
Joins willing woods, and varies shades from shades,
Now breaks, or now directs, th'intending Lines;
Paints as you plant, and as you work, Designs.

Pope's call for a site's special qualities to establish character is born out in the world's best courses and is exactly what the great golf architects refer to when demanding character. George Thomas expressed it best when tying the site's topography to strategy: *"Length means nothing without character. Character means proper hazards and hazards should be on a natural and heroic scale for superlative golf; glorified mole hills are ruled out."* Thomas also bears notice that it isn't the inconsequential humps and bumps that bring out the character in a golf hole. It's the full embrace of the ground as it originally was in its natural state. Unique site features such as the two ridges that run through Seminole Golf Club in Florida, or the dunes within which Cypress Point in California is routed are such examples.

"Every hole should have different character." – Alister MacKenzie.

When an architect such as MacKenzie makes such a plea for character, he also calls upon nature to link strategy to the golf hole. What separates the best holes from all the other holes is that link. Golf courses which embrace the Genius of the Place stand out because they can't be replicated anywhere else. They are unique to their exact location and topography.

The 10th hole at MacKenzie's Pasatiempo Golf Club in Santa Cruz, California.
(Courtesy: Richard Mandell Golf Architecture)

Character to a golf course is what personality is to a human being and it's the golf architect's job to apply the Principles of Design to the Elements of Design to bring out that character and work to cultivate it as much as possible. A property's distinct features should be threaded throughout a golf course in a variety of ways, like the arroyos that weave through Pasatiempo outside San Francisco or how the Pacific Ocean forms the basis for nine of the holes at Pebble Beach. These features become the personality of the site, the distinction that makes it different from everywhere else.

Granted, multiple golf courses have arroyos, ravines, creeks, and other features that run through their property. The way MacKenzie specifically used such features at Pasatiempo is what makes it so memorable compared to other courses. The distinct utilization - on that particular site, one which exists nowhere else in the world - will be the differentiating quality when compared to other courses that possess similar landforms.

But if one creates something entirely new on a particular piece of property, effectively creating a new site, the Genius of the Place is erased. It's counter-productive to alter a piece of ground which is solely unique from any other on earth just to make it look like another location. Although a new "character" is developed, odds are it already exists somewhere else. This approach alters forever the distinctive quality of that particular piece of land.

When faced with a site devoid of any topographical features, one must utilize the Principle of Character to create an overall theme for the golf course. The challenge to create such character, however, comes in execution. Overuse of the Elements and Principles of Design can generate a hodge-podge of features, especially on a property without much character or none at all. Whereas courses often have multiple elements that contribute character, more than two or three distinctive traits will cancel out everything else. So instead of successfully incorporating the Principle of Character, the result turns to chaos.

Hole # 4, Bacon Park Golf Course Legends Nine in Savannah, Georgia. On completely flat ground, the putting surfaces were the "portraits" of the Legends nine, which intentionally lacked sand as well. (Courtesy: Richard Mandell Golf Architecture)

One approach to a piece of ground lacking natural interest is to adopt Charles Blair Macdonald's viewpoint that *"A putting green to a golf course is what a face is to a portrait."* In my estimation, he is implying that putting surfaces with enough detail and strategic interest can compensate for a lack of topographical interest. Coupled with a variety of hole distances and direction, the golf course the architect creates along these lines will have sufficient character. The smallest of green details become especially important in order to distinguish the layout from all the other flat layouts that dot the planet.

The best way to create a theme, though, is to create one or two dominant landforms that serve as the anchors of the golf course, weaving through multiple holes. Building eighteen different holes on a flat piece of ground without such unifying landforms minimizes the Genius of the Place and runs the risk of repetition.

One of my earliest designs was a nine-hole expansion of what is now called Hooper's Landing Golf Course in Seaford, Delaware. The original nine holes were designed on dead-flat property by Alfred Tull. Each of the greens complexes were plateaus with deep grass-faced bunkers surrounding multiple sides. The compact design of each green complex was the only distinctive trait for a relatively simple design. The impetus for the expansion was the need to dispose of 210,000 cubic yards of fly ash from the adjacent DuPont textile fibers plant. Rather than spend $7 million to truck the ash miles away, $2 million was spent as a joint venture between the club and DuPont to create nine additional holes.

One design solution could have been to simply create mounds everywhere which would have been a poor use of the Elements and Principles of Design. That approach has been taken so often that even if it was a good idea, it would never be distinct enough to gain its own character. Instead, I built a single ridge that ran through the property and routed the new holes up, along, and down it. Although this feature contrasted with the original nine, the greens complex design for the new nine ensured the layout was unified.

Hole # 11, Hooper's Landing Golf Course in Seaford, Delaware. The eleventh hole plays along the ridge that gives the nine its character. (Courtesy: Richard Mandell Golf Architecture)

The distinctive traits that reveal a course's character are as varied as the ground on which it sits. Five of my favorite golf courses illustrate how the Principle of Character can be established by a designer in a variety of ways:

White Bear Yacht Club in Dellwood, Minnesota (Willie Watson)

It should be no surprise that my favorite golf course sits on one of the best pieces of ground I have seen for such a purpose. The rolling moraine landscape is absolutely the contributing element to the character of the course. Each fairway tumbles to and fro like a drunk stumbling around an Irish headland.

There is almost a shock-scale quality to many of the fairways at White Bear Yacht Club.
(Courtesy: Richard Mandell Golf Architecture)

Yeamans Hall Club in Hanahan, South Carolina (Seth Raynor)

Great putting green portraits. They are the differentiating factor for me at Yeamans Hall. Although the architectural pedigree of Seth Raynor and the template holes are memorable, the putting surfaces stand out on this piece of ground.

In addition to the greens, walking the grounds of Yeamans Hall Club is a step back in time.
(Courtesy: Yeamans Hall Club)

The Old Course in St. Andrews, Scotland (Allan Robertson and Old Tom Morris)

Although the ground has a lot of natural movement, the double greens and the surrounding town are what gives the Old Course its character more than anything else. A close third is the strategic theme of choosing to play the holes along the riskier right side or the more conservative but still challenging left side once Tom Morris reversed the layout in the 1870's.

The town looms large in golfer's minds as one more challenge after playing the Road Hole.
(Courtesy: Sasalan999 | Dreamstime.com)

Seminole Golf Club in Juno Beach Florida (Donald Ross)

Seminole's character comes in the way Donald Ross routed the holes to take full advantage of the two ridges that weave through the property. It's rare to have such topography on a south Florida golf course and one must take advantage.

The 17th at Seminole is one of multiple holes that utilize the eastern ridge of the property.
(Courtesy: Richard Mandell Golf Architecture)

Pebble Beach Golf Course in Pebble Beach, California (Jack Neville and Douglas Grant)

The Pacific Ocean's presence on nine of Pebble's holes is the clear differentiator, making the Principle of Character an easy one to incorporate. That said, the small greens are also quite memorable.

Standing on the 7th tee at Pebble Beach Golf Links is a heart-pumping experience, with or without a golf club in one's hands (Courtesy: Richard Mandell Golf Architecture)

Here is how I incorporated the Principle of Character with five of my own designs:

Creekside Golf & Country Club in Hiram, Georgia (1999)

I named it Creekside because of the creek that comes in to play, both visually and strategically, on seven holes. It was a simple task to establish the Principle of Character around this landform.

Hole #10, Creekside Golf & Country Club in Hiram, Georgia. The par-three 10th plays over the course's namesake creek (foreground). (Courtesy: Richard Mandell Golf Architecture)

Braemar Golf Course in Edina, Minnesota (2019)

The topography at Braemar provides the character of the golf course. To me, it strongly recalls Long Island, New York, in its topography and expansiveness. The use of the ground to determine the strategy of the holes, especially the par fives, reminds me of one of my Long Island favorites, Bethpage Black. Some people may attribute the character of Braemar to the single drumlin found in the middle of the property that provides views of multiple holes. Granted that view allows one to take in the vastness of the property and how the holes are strategically presented. But it alone does not define Braemar's character.

Hole #11, Braemar Golf Course in Edina, Minnesota. The expansive topography created many dramatic high-point-to-high-point golf holes.
(Courtesy: Richard Mandell Golf Architecture)

The Easton Club in Easton, Maryland (with former design partner, Robert Rauch, 1995)

The Easton Club property is as flat as a tabletop. To compensate for a lack of topography and to connect the club to the community, we designed each hole to be reflective of the flora, fauna, or history of the Talbot County area. Although the features varied in design, the theme connected the holes and provided some colorful names like "No Corner for the Devil" and "Squall."

Hole #12, "Tack," The Easton Club in Easton, Maryland. Piggy-backing on the nautical heritage of the Eastern Shore, the tee shot at #12 - like the first of a series of straight runs that make up a zig-zag route of a sailboat attacking the wind - requires a straight shot to begin this double-dogleg hole. (Courtesy: Richard Mandell Golf Architecture)

Skydoor Golf Club in Zhangjiajie, Hunan, China (2012)

Skydoor is set in a valley surrounded by numerous mountain ranges, particularly Tianmen Mountain, which features an arched opening seen from multiple holes. They are the impetus for the Principle of Character at Skydoor. Many holes dramatically rise and drop off cliffs reminiscent of the harsh lines of Tianmen and its neighbors. In addition, the bunkering takes its cues from those same lines coming off the mountains.

Hole #3, Skydoor Golf Club in Zhangjiajie, Hunan, China. The par-five third hole drops past the first landing area before climbing to the green. (Courtesy: Richard Mandell Golf Architecture)

Army Navy Country Club in Arlington and Fairfax, Virginia (2012)

I undertook a major renovation of the twenty-seven holes at the club's Arlington campus and the twenty-seven holes at its sister campus in Fairfax at the same time. It was crucial to make each facility distinct in its own way, and the character of each comes in their contrasting bunker styles. The original eighteen at Fairfax was designed by Robert Trent Jones, Sr. so my approach was to re-create large-scale RTJ bunkers with long, flowing arcs to establish its character.

In contrast, the Arlington course derives its character from a more artistic cape-and-bay style of bunkering, with rough edges reminiscent of Golden Age architects such as Thomas and MacKenzie. This approach was also era-appropriate, as the original Arlington holes were designed in 1924.

Hole #6 Red, Army Navy Country Club in Fairfax, Virginia: A nod to RTJ, Sr.'s original 1948 layout is the bunker style characterized by broad, curving shapes. (Courtesy: Richard Mandell Golf Architecture)

Genius of the Place goes beyond the land within a course's property and surrounding views, and the adjacent architectural elements contribute greatly to the Principle of Character. Look no further than the town of St. Andrews while playing across the Swilcan Burn. As aesthetically inspiring as the Pacific Ocean is to Pebble Beach, the views of the old city and the Royal & Ancient clubhouse capture most of the attention from the golfers.

Simple on-site structures and site furnishings are vital to the Principle of Character as well. From the bell behind Yale Golf Club's third green used to signal "all clear" to the next group, to the stone rain shelters that dot Keller Golf Course in Minnesota, the visuals linger long after one leaves. The seventh hole at Keller is one of my favorites because the focal point of the hole, the shelter immediately behind the green, balances the low-profile putting surface hugging the ground. The green is challenging enough for such a long hole, receptive enough for a lesser-skilled golfer's approach, and unobtrusive enough to allow the shelter to supply great character.

The view from behind the third green at Yale Golf Course in New Haven, Connecticut (Courtesy: RMGA)

The Principle of Character is strong when a memorable clubhouse and a memorable golf hole are intertwined, especially when that relationship has evolved organically over time. One example is the terrace at Merion Golf Club in suburban Philadelphia. It's so close to the first tee that a diner could almost grab someone's club in mid-swing. Another is the clubhouse at Baltusrol Golf Club in Springfield, New Jersey. Stately as it may be, it interacts with the golf course because multiple holes run parallel to the building, allowing interaction between people for long periods of time rather than just serving as a central hub with golf holes coming and going.

A clubhouse is not the only structure on a golf course that contributes to the Principle of Character, especially if the pro shop is in a separate building. I spent two summers working at the Devereux Emmet-designed Bedford Golf & Tennis Club in Bedford, New York. Its pro shop and caddie area were separate from the clubhouse. The same was true of the pro shop at my home course, Rye Golf Club. In each case, the pro shop was the center of activity.

Keller Golf Course had utilized a separate pro shop building since its inception in 1929. When it came time to undergo renovations, I was adamant about keeping it that way rather than incorporating it into the new clubhouse. The old pro shop had been the epicenter of activity for decades and I felt it provided a lot of character. Although it wasn't really my fight, I made a case against the plan of centralizing everything. We then moved the practice green to the front of the pro shop and it created great synergy between the golfers and the professional. The nearby eleventh hole offers additional opportunity for interaction.

> *"How deadly dull are two or three holes of the same character when they follow each other! A drive and pitch followed by another drive and pitch is a good deal like serving a watery pudding after a watery soup!"* – Robert Hunter

The lack of variety that early course designer and writer Robert Hunter lamented reinforces the importance of the Principle of Character and its reliance on other principles to avoid the "deadly dull" he warned of. Rhythm, Balance, Movement, Contrast, and Unity all help to bring out that character. The architect who has mastered those principles knows how far to bend the rules to establish character without going overboard. Additional Principles such as Mystery, Quirk, Randomness and Chance elevate a course even more. All these Principles of Design ensure that the character of a site leads to great golf course architecture.

AF

Afterword

Trend – A development or change toward something new or different.

A trend is a prevailing tendency that evolves organically, gaining momentum until it becomes a style or simply retreats from the general consciousness as a fad. It sparks a new direction, creating a twist on something that already exists. The Principle of Innovation (*the process of creating value by applying novel solutions to meaningful problems*) is what spurs on trends.

Trends are audacious ideas that pivot away from the tried, true and the expected. Once they are acknowledged by the masses, they bring about a certain level of comfort and security. But once the point of ubiquity arrives, another risk is taken to combat that same comfort and security. Occasionally a trend breaks this cycle to become a legitimate style. Style is defined as *"A particular manner or technique by which something is done, created, or performed that is typical of a person, group of people, place, or period."* A style is dependent upon a trend solving specific problems for completely unconnected people for unrelated reasons. As generations of designers see the value in a trend, a style is born.

Those trends that are exposed as fads have little basis in design and often have no real form connected to a function that may not have ever really existed. A fad is defined as *"An intense and widely shared enthusiasm for something, especially one that is short-lived and without basis in the object's qualities."*

The time that it takes for a trend to become a fad or style varies. The most durable trends last thirty to fifty years and are known as mega-trends, yet they may never reach style status. Fads won't ever last that long but usually stick around longer than they should.

The various eras of golf architecture started out as trends; something that began in a certain place and time based on specific events and the Principle of Innovation was prevalent behind each of these trends. As the profession advanced and golf equipment technology developed, course architecture took on different reactionary turns. For example, when one new course came online to precipitate a concept and others followed, consensus among the masses took hold and the trend took hold.

Many of the mega-trends in golf architecture came as a result of socio-cultural factors. For instance, as private clubs became more widespread, after a while they sought to replicate the exclusivity of more well-known clubs such as Augusta National in Georgia. Over time, as the Masters tournament grew in stature and the club's impeccable conditioning took hold in the collective golfing consciousness, the "Augusta look" influenced countless golf courses that sought to duplicate such an atmosphere.

Another mega-trend came about as many clubs reacted to the idea of hosting national events by trending toward a more difficult presentation. That is true even for clubs that had no possibility of hosting such a tournament. This mega-trend evolved into a design style that favored conditioning to promote difficulty rather than architectural strategy. Narrow fairways, heavily bunkered holes, and lightning-quick putting surfaces became mega-trends in their own right.

Whereas there are many influential and memorable courses throughout the history of golf, there are very few touchstone courses that spark a trend and even fewer that transform into a style like Augusta National. National Golf Links of America introduced a different level of strategy to American golf and it triggered the dawn of the "Golden Age of Golf Architecture." Sand Hills Golf Club in Mullen, Nebraska, spurred on the minimalist era, a trend that's as universal as any other in the twenty-first century. Bill Coore and Ben Crenshaw took a page from the Golden Age by bringing back the art of the golf course routing with very little earthwork. Golden Age golf architecture and minimalist design were mega-trends that slowly evolved into genuine design styles.

Whereas National Golf Links and Sand Hills may be mega-trend golf courses, other courses became trend-setters in their own right. The Old Course at St. Andrews, whose double greens have never become a full fledged trend, nonetheless set the trend for the standard number of holes at eighteen.

#18, Sand Hills Golf Club, Mullen, Nebraska (Courtesy: Dick Youngscap)

Robert Trent Jones, Sr. and Pete Dye are two golf architects who qualify for trendsetter status. In fact, Harbour Town Golf Links on Hilton Head Island, South Carolina was a reaction to the ubiquity of the large-scale era. This particular reaction, ironically, was brought about by RTJ's own reaction to the pervasiveness of Golden Age classics built before and during the time he started his career in the 1930's.

Dye's TPC Sawgrass was the first of the "stadium" golf courses. Built in 1980, this hazard-filled, moonscape-like layout became a veritable trend for the following two decades. However, it never approached style status because the minimalist approach brought an abrupt end to that era in yet another reactionary movement.

The Ocean Course on Kiawah Island in South Carolina defined a second trend that was started by Pete Dye. A few years before Coore's and Crenshaw's landmark Sand Hills work was completed, Dye introduced the low-key natural appearance many minimalist golf courses define themselves by today. The complete transformation of the Ocean Course from barren seashore to rolling duneland set the stage for nondescript properties moving prodigious amount of dirt to create a minimalist appearance.

Charles Blair Macdonald and Seth Raynor were among the first designers to implement template golf holes (replicas of highly-regarded holes in England, Ireland and Scotland), a trend that for decades was a part of their design philosophy. By the twenty-first century, replicating template holes became a full-fledged trend bordering on fad. So many designers were determined to label golf holes as templates that it seemed like they actively sought out such situations rather than let the routing process unfold naturally. Nonetheless, some of Macdonald's concepts have become deeply ingrained in the golf architecture lexicon. His Cape hole, for example, wasn't just a mega-trend or style; It actually fostered its own school of design. The idea of taking on more risk to gain more reward is such an ingrained notion for anyone who ever picked up a golf club that it transcends almost anything else. Likely for a number of reasons, the Heroic School of Design satisfies a very basic need in all golfers.

Despite its Pete Dye shock-scale quality, the Ocean Course in Kiawah Island, South Carolina, has many minimalist qualities. The tenth hole (above) illustrates Dye's transformation from a flat site to an undulating links course. (Courtesy: Richard Mandell Golf Architecture)

Golf course restoration may be considered a mega-trend in and of itself. Over the life of a golf course, many hazards are created, removed, and then restored in the name of re-capturing original design intent. This cyclical nature is why restoration is such a challenging and contentious endeavor. Course restoration will either remain an inherent subset of golf architecture based on preserving a classic look and/or playability type, or it will become a need for change based simply on the whims of an owner, greens committee or the latest "hot" architect, revealing it as a fad. In some cases, the arguments against golf course restoration are that it inhibits growth of a club and members should not be beholden to a museum piece. Courses that strictly adhered to exact plans or could be restored through the use of old aerial and ground photos may fall victim in those cases.

Restorations with the foresight to consider technological advances, though, won't fall prey to re-design because it's simply a return to the basic principles of golf architecture. As equipment advances continue, there will always be a place and a moment for restoration. Over time, as all golf courses undergo one round of restoration or another, designers may develop a new style called "Golf Course Preservation."

Hole #13, Orangeburg Country Club in Orangeburg, South Carolina. Golf course preservation can include mid-twentieth century courses in addition to Golden Age layouts. (Courtesy: Richard Mandell Golf Architecture)

In my opinion, trends in golf course design evolve from a socioeconomic standpoint more than for any other reasons. Possibly the biggest roadblocks to the success of the game in the twenty-first century are money and time, and the return of the short course has become a trend to combat the time challenge. Previous generations thought the short course (also called an executive course and par-three course), was not worthy of anyone's time. Many operators who originally felt it wasn't a money-maker now think of it as a great profit center. The short-course trend, however, will only last if there continues to be innovation tied to each course, and the details of design produce compelling interest, challenge, and enjoyment. Many of the early links courses in the British Isles and elsewhere originally had companion short courses to promote the growth of the game. Many of them still exist in an environment that's more inclusive on the links than anywhere else in the world. If worldwide golf continues its trend of being all-inclusive, there won't be any reason to find alternative uses for these courses in the future.

At the point in which trends become ubiquitous, a pushback inevitably occurs. Trends which fade over time were probably forced ideas without legitimate origins. Their integrity begins to crumble as their imitations move farther and farther from the original. They not only become repetitive, they just look bad. Trends that fall into this category are those replica holes and drivable par fours that have become part and parcel of twenty-first century golf architecture. Drivable par fours were once ridiculed as too short when golf was all about difficulty and most trends leaned toward penalty rather than strategic design. The island green, deep rough, and pot bunkers were fashionable examples of that thinking. Nowhere in the annals of course design, however, is group-think better displayed than the trend to design for two nines of par - 36 for a course par of 72. Varying just a bit from that norm often turns owners and greens committees batty, which is why there are so many 450-yard par fives in this world.

A parcel of land that lends itself to great strategic design, whether it be used as a drivable par four or a split fairway, should be utilized to its utmost potential, regardless of trends. If such concepts simply evolve out of the routing process, design innovation contributes a meaningful solution to a design problem. Yet if it's forced, there is no other explanation beyond following the Principle of Fads.

Fads seem to come out of an inherent urge to label or simply follow the lead of someone else. One of the most common fads in golf design is the attempt to re-create links golf and calling it as such. Links principles such as hard and fast conditions, rippling fairways, and open, windswept sites are perfectly acceptable as long as form indeed follows function. But to fabricate such elements by completely clear-cutting a wooded site, or piecing flat ground planes together with manufactured ripples dotted with out-of-scale pot bunkers is not genuine. Many consider it a legitimate trend and even a design style. But links design on anything other than links ground is a misguided marketing effort rather than sound design.

Some of the biggest contributors to the distortion of sound design principles are random sand bunker styles, especially when used on the same golf course. The use of pot bunkers as a design theme on land far from anything that matches a links setting may be the most egregious. Whereas the Principle of Unity is most successful when a certain bunker style ties a golf course together, authenticity is destroyed when pot bunkers are utilized out of context. The evolution of the pot bunker is rooted in the need to maintain sand below the surface of the fairway to keep it from blowing away in high winds. The placement of numerous pot bunkers on a heavily-wooded site, for example – or one with little wind – is out of context and looks odd as well.

One trend associated with minimalist golf is the ragged bunker, also known as a blow-out, scalloped or lacework bunker. This trend is a direct response to the well-defined bunker edges that were so prevalent in the latter half of the twentieth century and the beginning of the twenty-first. Yet the ragged-bunker concept

The form of pot bunkers on a windswept site such as #8 at St. Enodoc Golf Links in Rock, England, follow the function of keeping sand in its place. (Courtesy: Richard Mandell Golf Architecture)

shouldn't become so trendy that it clashes with other design considerations. For example, a ragged bunker look would very much clash with a Willie Park restoration, especially when he once stated that *"The hazard should be sharply defined, so that there can be no doubt as to whether or not a ball lies in it."*

The Principle of Trends is often misused when it comes to bunker maintenance. From leaving bunker faces smooth and only raking the bottoms, to the two-inch vertical lip from grass to sand that seems to be everywhere (even places like Augusta National and Oakmont), trends surrounding the presentation of sand bunkers make little sense and are so short-lived they quickly go by way of the fad.

"Everything old is new again" is a perfect mantra for the cyclical nature of the Principle of Trends, especially in course architecture, with many cycles rooted in maintenance. Superintendents who tire of raking flashed-sand bunker undertake a renovation toward grass-faced bunkers. A decade later someone decides that it isn't the preferred look and reverse gears. Greens get smaller and fairways get narrower almost every day. They are eventually restored to their original size and width but soon after the cycle begins anew.

Vertical bunker lips at Oakmont Country Club can only be explained as a trend. (Courtesy: Wirestock | Dreamstime.com)

So what trends in golf architecture will become fads and which will be long-lasting styles? One hopeful trend is the continued re-introduction of wide fairways. One hundred years ago, wide fairways were not only the prevailing trend, they were crucial elements of the design palette. That is, until the advent of irrigated rough and difficulty became the primary requisite for golf. The resultant mega-trend of deep rough lining fairways lasted for five to six decades, becoming, in fact, the mainstream.

The trendy implementation of no-mow areas can balance expanded fairways. No-mow zones planted with native, low-maintenance grasses are a newer innovation. In an earlier time those areas were left alone, either because of a lack of manpower or less irrigation (which was a good thing, and hopefully a trend poised for a comeback as well). Nonetheless, I hope that the coupling of wide fairways and no-mow areas become an everlasting style.

The trend of bunker placement is rooted in one of the biggest cycles in the industry: Fun and enjoyment versus difficulty. Bunkers on so many course throughout the world have been filled in and restored multiple times. Those that were put in place based on the principles of design usually outlasted the cycle, while those placed strictly for penalty often went the way of the fad and never returned. The same is true of covering and uncovering creeks throughout a golf course. The practical needs for drainage coupled with the strategic challenges for the golfer create the cyclical nature of such a yin-yang existence. But as the world deals with increasing stormwater challenges, the advantages of an open system will hopefully outlast the trend of piping most watercourses.

Hole #3 Blue, Army Navy Country Club in Arlington, Virginia. Note to reader: If at anytime you see this creek covered up in the next century, go ahead and open it back up for me. Thanks. (Courtesy: Richard Mandell Golf Architecture)

The line between a trend and simply good design can be vague. Often times, trends are just logical design decisions based on the Elements and Principles of Design. For example, at some point in the history of golf architecture, scale was not a consideration. But at the onset of the Golden Age, as designers recognized the Element of Scale and brought consideration toward it, the critics of the day may have considered it a trend. Today, it's considered a crucial element of the design process for most architects.

Even the most basic philosophical approaches to design are occasionally misinterpreted as trendy. Fun and enjoyment somehow became the hottest trend in golf a decade into the twenty-first century. Suddenly the golf industry, which for decades buried fun and enjoyment underneath the Principle of Difficulty, woke up with a great idea.

Yet one thing is certain: Those trends that become lasting styles are deeply rooted in the Elements and Principles of golf course architecture. An *understanding* of the game of golf is just one trait needed to produce great design. The ability to call upon the principles of course architecture and apply them to the elements of a course to create a functional landscape is even more vital. Outside-the-box thinking entrenched in the Principles of Design leads to everlasting success.

So does anyone actually sit down and open up their recipe book to utilize the Principles of Design in golf course architecture? Why is there so much variation in what actually constitutes the basic Principles of Design? The reason there is so much confusion and vagueness is that most designers utilize the Principles of Design on such a subconscious level that few of them really stop to define it. The specific understanding of the Principles of Design is only a portion of the process. For many golf course architects, designers, painters, sculptors, etc. the utilization of all these principles comes naturally and it's through the artist's "eye" that those principles are brought to great success.

Hole #12, Skydoor Golf Club in Zhangjiajie, Hunan, China.
(Courtesy: Richard Mandell Golf Architecture)

ACKNOWLEDGMENTS

As always with these efforts of mine, I must thank my family, Mary, Thomas, and Joshua, for letting me sneak away to work on what has been a true labor of love decades in the making.

Specifically to this book, what you hold in your hands would be nothing without my Design Associate, Patrick Gainer. Patrick is solely responsible for all sketches and other drawings which supplement the text. But his drawing ability is far secondary to the input he has provided as a sounding board for both the text and graphics. In addition to Patrick, I must also thank my two editors, who with much tough love and effort have helped me clarify very complex subject matter. So, thanks so much to Danny Freels and Rick Shefchik.

This book is far from a recap of a career in the business of golf architecture because, frankly, I haven't even hit my prime yet and eagerly await that great piece of property. That said I do want to thank my past partner in Whole In One Design Group, Bob Rauch, as well as my design associates over the years, Jason Justice, Sam Bassett, Walter Young, Philip Picerno, Brian Ross, and Jim Ryan. Two particular associates I want to give special thanks to are Ben Hood and Heath Pray. Heath goes way back to LAR 343 drafting class at UGA where my technical journey toward golf architecture began.

The primary construction shapers in my career are another reason for this book: David Gray, Marc Burger, and, again, Brian Ross. From my days with Dan Maples Design and Denis Griffiths & Associates, I would like to thank Mike Gleason, Dan Maples, Don Maples, David Maples, Billy Craven, Molly Williamson, Rick McDermott, Tracy Parks, Denis Griffiths, and Tom Johnson.

Much of my approach to golf architecture, and this book, is tied to my own personal golf origins playing many rounds at Rye Golf Club and Bedford Golf & Tennis Club as well as the University of Georgia Golf Course (in addition to the many great courses I was exposed to in my youth). So I must thank those I associate with those great times such as Bobby Latkany, Tommy Codispoti, Ben Coleman, Mark Sasse, Chris Fornara, Peter Bevacqua, Rick Paonessa, the Santuccis, Dick Gonyea, Walt Ronan, Tony Chateauvert, Don Peterson, Frank Sergiovanni, and many others.

Of course, all the clients who have put their faith in me with what they value most - their golf courses - some for multiple decades. Most of all, they have become great friends over the years. In particular, I want to thank Greg Scott, Chuck French, Michael Shoun, Michael Teague, the Skydoor Crew, O.C. Welch, Greg Todd, Chuck and Jeff Clancy, Jimmy Casella, Kevin Sunderman, Josh Sawyer, Kevin McCracken, Ryan Groomes, and Mark Dahill, Kevin Finley, Paul Digneau, Tom

Bolon, Gary Bauman, Matthew Bunch, Scott Kennon, Tom Green, David Lackey and the Tourville Family, Tom Sung, Ron Willard, Sr., Ron Willard II., Jeff Snyder, Bob Wilbur, Carmen Giannini, Brandon Ingle, Sue Martin, Joe Abood, and Jeff Wyman.

Finally, I would like to thank some of the friends from the golf architecture community and golf industry I have made over the years who have had an influence on my work in some capacity (starting with the three I have known the longest): Klaus Ahlers, Don Roberts, and Dennis Wagner, as well as Rich Abbott, Tripp Cobb, Bob Crosby, John Derr, Jamie Diaz, Craig Disher, Steve Dockery, Janeen Driscoll, Derek Duncan, Ann & Perry Dye, Les Fleisher, Ron Forse, George Frye, Stuart Hackwell, Stuart Hall, Richard Humphreys, Sean Hyduk, Toby Ingleton, Rand Jerris, Pat Jones, Rees Jones, Pat Karnick, Dan Kelly, Mitch Laurence, Adam Lawrence, John Lawrence, Matt Lohmann, Ben McGinnis, Pat McGowan, Paul McMahon, Patty Moran, Audrey Moriarty, Ran Morrissett, Tony Munger, Doug Myslinski, Jim Nagle, Simon Pain, Joe Passov, Tom Paul, Pierre Peltier, Drew Rogers, Achmed, Chad Ritterbusch, Jim Schumacher, Nick Scigliano, Doug Show, Kris Shreiner, Aileen Smith, Steve Smith, Chris Stanley, Mark Stewart, Tom Stewart, Doug Thompson, Michael Whitaker, Marc Whitney, Ron Whitten, Richard Wolffe, Stu Wolffe, and Parson Yao.

(Courtesy: W. H. Smith & Son)

IN

INDEX

H

I

J

K

L

M

N

O

P

R

Bunkers.

You have far too many bunkers. The majority of them serve but one purpose, to make the shots easier for the good player. Your bunkers belong to what is termed the Penal School of design, well illustrated in Fig.1, your present first hole. Bunkers of this kind serve merely to punish the weaker player and to assist the good player, by charting his course, defining his channel and acting as points to range on. That is not as it should be.

Here is how Mr.Bernard Darwin described the bunkers on a course that we have reconstructed recently:-

"There are also, of course, bunkers, but not many of them. At some holes one bunker, insignificant in size, but compelling in character, dominates the entire play in a way that shows the master hand. "

Most of your bunkers are in a very bad state of repair. Indeed, it could not be otherwise unless the staff were augmented.

From the point of view of design, form and contour, there is hardly a bunker on the course that is not an actual disfigurement, taking one's mind back to the years 1890 - 1900, the dark age of golf course design.

When it is so simple to make bunkers and artificial hill work look natural, thus ↓

Why construct monstrosities thus ↓

A rant to a club about bunkers from golf architect Tom Simpson.
(Courtesy: Tom Simpson)

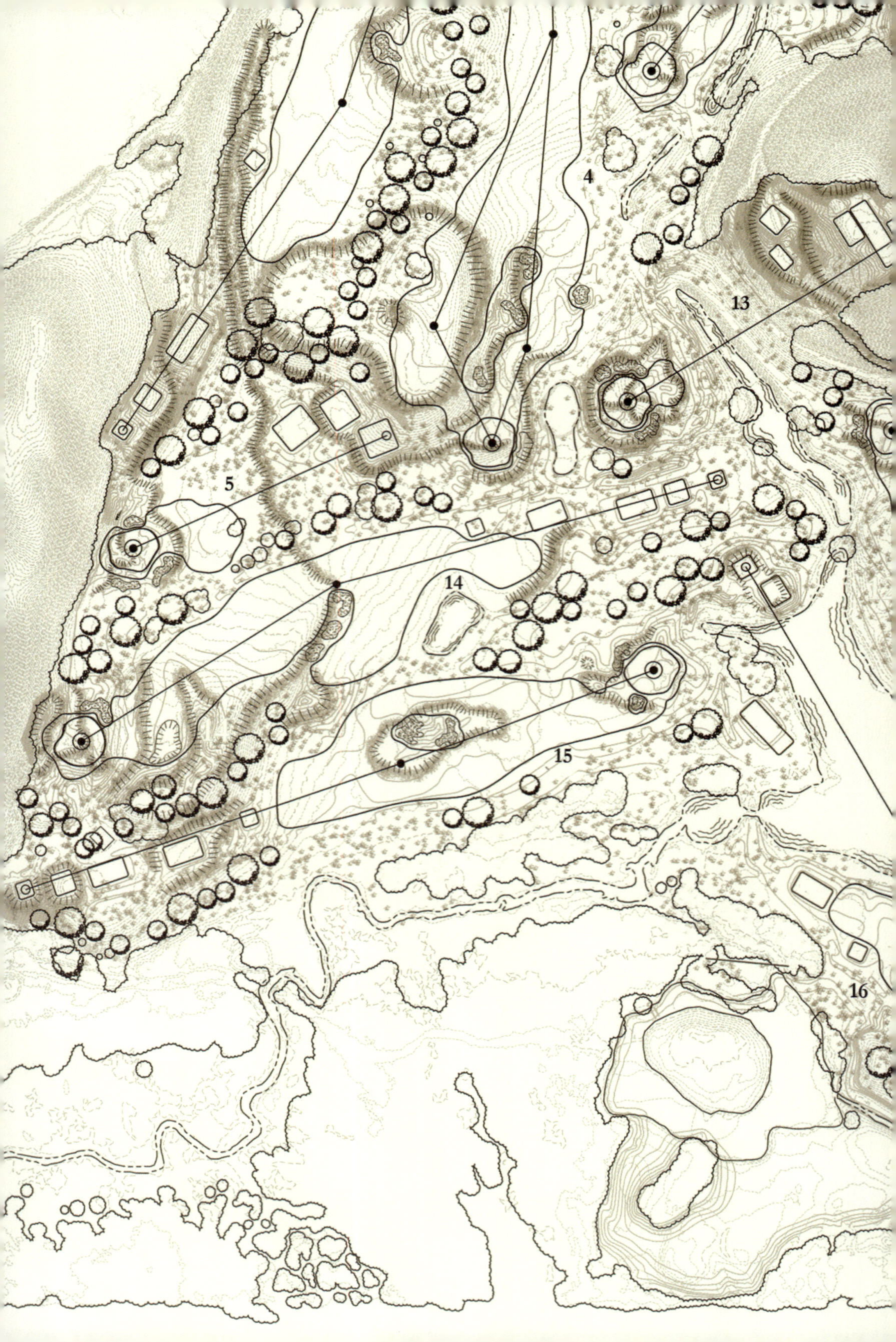
4
13
5
14
15
16